ABC
Foundations
for Young Children

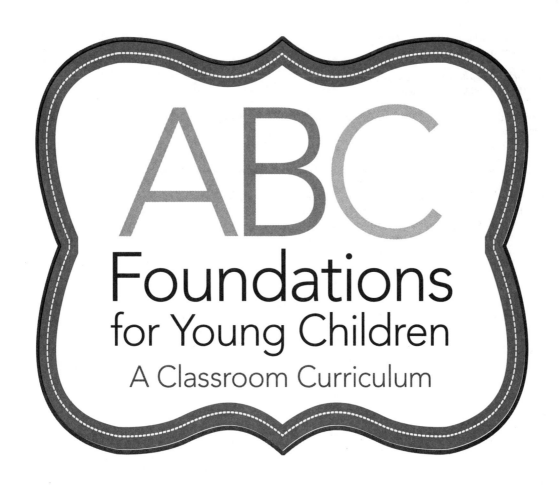

ABC
Foundations
for Young Children
A Classroom Curriculum

by

Marilyn Jager Adams, Ph.D.

·P·A·U·L·H·
BROOKES
PUBLISHING Cº ®

Baltimore • London • Sydney

Paul H. Brookes Publishing Co.
Post Office Box 10624
Baltimore, Maryland 21285-0624

www.brookespublishing.com

Typeset by Auburn Associates, Inc., Baltimore, Maryland.
Manufactured in the United States of America by
Victor Graphics, Inc., Baltimore, Maryland.

Library of Congress Cataloging-in-Publication Data

Adams, Marilyn Jager.
   ABC foundations for young children : a classroom curriculum / by Marilyn Jager Adams.
     p.   cm.
   Includes bibliographical references and index.
   ISBN 978-1-59857-275-9 (spiral bound pbk.)—ISBN 1-59857-275-X (spiral bound pbk.)
   1. English language—Alphabet—Study and teaching (Early childhood) 2. English language—Alphabet—
Study and teaching (Early childhood)—Activity programs. 3. English language—Composition and exercises—
Study and teaching (Early childhood) 4. English language—Phonetics—Study and teaching (Early childhood)
I. Title.
   LB1525.65.A35 2012
   372.46'5—dc23   2012024566

British Library Cataloguing in Publication data are available from the British Library.

2016   2015   2014   2013   2012

10   9   8   7   6   5   4   3   2   1

Contents

About the Author

. . . .

Marilyn Jager Adams, Ph.D., is a cognitive and developmental psychologist who has devoted her career to research and applied work in the area of cognition and education. Dr. Adams's scholarly contributions include the book *Beginning to Read: Thinking and Learning About Print* (MIT Press, 1994). Among honors, she has received the American Educational Research Association's Sylvia Scribner Award and The International Dyslexia Association's Samuel Torrey Orton Award.

Dr. Adams chaired the planning committee for the National Academy of Sciences (1998) report *Preventing Reading Difficulties in Young Children* and has served since 1992 on the planning or steering committees for the National Assessment of Educational Progress (NAEP) in reading. She also developed a vocabulary assessment for the 2014 National Assessment of Adult Literacy (NAAL) and was on the development team for the Common Core State Standards for English Language Arts and Literacy.

Dr. Adams has authored a number of empirically validated classroom resources, including *Odyssey: A Curriculum for Thinking* (Charlesbridge Publishing, 1986), which was originally developed for barrio students in Venezuela; *Phonemic Awareness in Young Children: A Classroom Curriculum* (Paul H. Brookes Publishing Co., 1998) on language and literacy basics for emergent readers and students with special needs; Open Court's 1995 edition of *Collection for Young Scholars*, a program for reading, writing, and literacy development for elementary school students; and Scholastic's *System 44* (2009) and *iRead* (2013), technology-based programs for building literacy foundations. She has also served on the advisory board for several of the Public Broadcasting System's educational programs including *Sesame Street* and *Between the Lions*, for which she was Senior Literacy Advisor.

Dr. Adams spent most of her career with the think tank Bolt Beranek & Newman (BBN Technologies—"Where Wizards Stay up Late") in Cambridge, Massachusetts. From 2000 to 2007, she was Chief Scientist at Soliloquy Learning, which she cofounded with the goal of harnessing automatic speech recognition for helping students learn to read and read to learn. She is currently a visiting scholar in the Cognitive, Linguistic, and Psychological Sciences Department at Brown University. She has two children: John, who is working toward a Ph.D. in social psychology, and Jocie, who is striving to be a musician. Her husband, Milton, is a rocket scientist at Massachusetts Institute of Technology's Charles Stark Draper Labs.

About the Online Materials

Across lessons, many of the games and activities require the use of letter cards, pictures, or other display materials. These resources are referenced in the materials lists for the appropriate lessons and are available for downloading and printing at http://www .brookespublishing.com/abc.

Online materials include an Alphabet Frieze, Long and Short Vowel Picture Cards, and Helicopter Game Picture Cards in color. Also included are additional examples of Name Poems, links to provide musical support for songs, and an application to create personalized Write Your Own Name activity sheets. In addition, the materials in Appendix B are available online, organized by unit.

Acknowledgments

· ·

I wish to thank the team at Paul H. Brookes Publishing Co. for their patience and support throughout this project—great people, great work, and greatly appreciated.

*To the many wonderful teachers
who have shared their minds, their
classrooms, and their needs with me*

Introduction

Ever since 1500 B.C., people all over the world—wherever an alphabetic system of writing was used—learned to read and write by the simple process of memorizing the sound of each letter in their alphabet.

Rudolf Flesch (1955/1985, p. 4)

Alas, the difference between theory and practice is that, in theory, there is none. Helping children to gain useful, usable knowledge of letters and letter–sound correspondences has proven far easier said than done.

Over and over, time and again, frustrated factions of educators have decried the very worth of the effort. Alongside, a number of substitutes for or arguments against teaching letters and sounds have been put forth: Skillful readers do not use letter–sound correspondences; children should learn to recognize words from their overall shapes; reading, like speech, will emerge naturally given meaningful engagement with print; alphabetic instruction is developmentally inappropriate for young children; asking children to attend to letters and sounds harmfully diverts their attention from the meaningful dimensions of literacy.

The list goes on, but none of the objections or alternatives has held up under the careful lens of research. Instead, through ever more sophisticated methodologies and technologies, and with ever more force and detail, research has affirmed that 1) given an alphabetic writing system, the ability to read productively and with comprehension depends on deep, ready, working knowledge of letters and their individual and combined mappings to the sounds of speech; and 2) learning those correspondences early and well is the best predictor of a child's educational success. (For reviews, see Adams, 1990; Chall, 1967/1983; Dehaene, 2009; National Research Council, 1998; Stanovich, 1986; and Torgesen, 1998.)

The question is thus raised: What is it about the alphabet basics that poses difficulty for so many children? And, more important, what can educators do to help them?

Part of the problem is the difficulty of gaining awareness of the *phonemes*, which are the "sounds" that the letters represent. In normal speech, the phonemes flow so rapidly—they are so thoroughly interweaved and blended together—that they cannot be individually heard, one by one. And worse, how any given phoneme actually sounds in running speech depends not only on the phonemes that come before and after it but also on such factors as the speaker's articulation speed and habits and the size and shape of his or her mouth.

That is not to say that phonemes do not exist. Nor does it mean that they are not "sounds." However, phonemes are sounds that are *produced* rather than sounds that are heard. Indeed, the way people "hear" phonemes is by internally imitating and reconstructing what others are saying (Liberman, Cooper, Shankweiler, & Studdert-Kennedy, 1967). Phonemes are the elementary speech gestures that make one word different from another; for example, the word *bat* differs by just one phoneme from the word *sat*. The phonemes of a language are defined by their proper place and manner of articulation—by the shape of the mouth, the position of the tongue, and by whether and how they are vocalized. That is, there is a proper or "ideal" way to articulate /b/, /s/, and /t/ as well as any other phoneme.

In keeping with this, games and activities that lead children to attend to the phonemes—to voice them, blend them, break them apart, and contrast them and the words that they make—are shown to significantly accelerate children's grasp of the alphabetic principle. As documented through the National Reading Panel's (2000) meta-analysis, such training significantly facilitates phonemic awareness and, in its wake, decoding, spelling, word recognition, reading, and reading comprehension as well. Conversely, without phonemic awareness, decoding and spelling remain out of reach, for the "sounds" of the letters make no sense.

But what if teachers could ensure that all children gained phonemic awareness? Would beginning reading failure then disappear? To make phonemic awareness useful, what else do children need?

Children need to know the alphabet. To use phonemic awareness for reading, children need to know which letter represents which phoneme. In turn, learning letter–sound correspondences requires that children not only be able to discern each letter but also to identify each letter by shape, confidently and securely. To use their phonemic awareness to write, children must be able to form the letters with legible accuracy and reasonable ease. For much of their classroom instruction on reading and spelling, they must be able not only to recognize each letter, but also to seek, recall, or even image the letter given only its name or sound.

Even so, the issue is deeper than that, for children's letter knowledge is a good predictor of their responsiveness to phonemic awareness training (Bowey, 1994; Byrne, 1992; Johnston, Anderson, & Holligan, 1996; Stahl & Murray, 1994). This may be related, directly or indirectly, to the fact that activities designed to develop phonemic awareness are far more effective when tied to letters rather than to, say, bingo markers, blocks, or sounds alone (Adams, Treiman, & Pressley, 1997; National Reading Panel, 2000); after all, this contrast would be moot to the extent that children did not know their letters. Yet, children's letter knowledge is a good predictor of their phonemic awareness *regardless* of training (e.g., Burgess, 2002; Evans, Bell, Shaw, Moretti, & Page, 2006; Wagner, Torgesen, & Rashotte, 1994). It may well be, as several have argued, that gaining phonemic awareness *depends* on prior letter knowledge (for discussion, see Blaiklock, 2004; Carroll, 2004; and Foulin, 2005).

In all, children's knowledge of letter names and sounds at school entry is the single best predictor of their reading and spelling growth, not just at the outset but throughout the elementary school years (Badian, 1995; Bond & Dykstra, 1967; Chall, 1967/1983; Hammill, 2004; Hecht & Close, 2002; Muehl & Di Nello, 1976; Schatschneider, Fletcher, Francis, Carlson, & Foorman, 2004; Wagner et al., 1997). Moreover, this is so even when other weighty predictors such as phonological awareness, language development, and intelligence measures are factored out of the equation (Burgess & Lonigan, 1998; Leppänen, Aunola, Niemi, & Nurmi, 2008; McBride-Chang, 1999; Scarborough, 2001; Wagner, Torgesen, & Rashotte, 1994). Children who enter school with poor knowledge of letter names and sounds face a far higher risk of reading delay and disability (Gallagher, Frith, & Snowling, 2000; O'Connor & Jenkins, 1999; Torppa, Lyytinen, Erskine, Eklund, & Lyytinen, 2010).

In recognition of such findings, alphabetic instruction has been given high priority in guidance and policy for early childhood educators. In their joint position statement, the International Reading Association and the National Association of Educators for Young Children (NAEYC; 1998) urge that children become proficient with letter discrimination, letter naming, and letter sounds in kindergarten. Similarly, developing children's alphabet knowledge in tandem with their phonological awareness, oral language, and print awareness is given highest priority within Early Reading First guidance (U.S. Department of Education, 2003). Within the Reading First program

2), the emphasis shifts to assessment of children's ... assumption that, for most children, alphabetic ... by first-grade entry.

... n's alphabetic knowledge is shown to range widely, ... but even through second grade (Diamond, Gerde, ...; Graham, Weintraub, & Berninger, 2001; Ritchey, ... w that only a minority of children are able to name ... d of first grade and that the number who know the ... ing contrast with these results, the much-publicized ... Longitudinal Study (ECLS) suggest that upwards of ... with letter names by the end of first grade (Denton & ... 8). However, ECLS's definition of *proficient* was too ... ogy too loose to permit approximation of how many ... Whatever the actual numbers, the ECLS data do make ... rty, alphabetic knowledge is well below the norm at ... at least through Grade 1.

... ffairs, Piasta and Wagner (2010) undertook a meta- ... phabetic instruction and outcomes. Through a broad ... d a total of 63 studies that were appropriate to the ... nd measures adequate for analysis. Collectively, the ... children, with some extending to children in the early ... conducted in preschool or kindergarten classrooms. ... dren deemed "at risk"—that is, children judged to be ... betic instruction.

... ches to alphabetic instruction produced significantly greater gains in letter-name and letter-sound knowledge than did their control conditions. However, the gains were quite modest—far smaller, Piasta and Wagner (2010) pointed out, than those reported for phonological or decoding interventions— and they wondered why.

The most positive possible explanation would be that the children in the control groups were learning about the alphabet at home to an extent that competed with the gains of the instructional programs in study. Unfortunately, this explanation seems implausible. If it were correct, Piasta and Wagner (2010) argued, then effect sizes should have been larger for those groups of children who entered the programs with little evidence of alphabet support at home. Instead, the gains for children at risk were just as small as for those who were not.

The most sobering explanation for their data, cautioned Piasta and Wagner, is that "the small-to-moderate effect size estimates may be an authentic representation of our current ability to foster alphabetic knowledge development during early literacy instruction" (2010, p. 22). This may well be so. The effect sizes calculated by Piasta and Wagner are substantially larger than those reported in field studies of the impact of Head Start (Diamond et al., 2008; U.S. Department of Health & Human Services, 2010). They are also substantially larger than most of the effect sizes reported for preschoolers and kindergartners in the U.S. Department of Education's evaluation of reading readiness curricula (Preschool Curriculum Evaluation Research Consortium, 2008).

How can this be? Alphabetic knowledge is so fundamental and so pervasively important to literacy development. Without a comfortable familiarity with the alphabet, the student is effectively locked out of virtually everything that formal education has to offer. Our schools *must* do far better in helping children to learn their ABCs. What could be the problem?

One issue raised by Piasta and Wagner (2010) is a failure to appreciate how much time is required for effective alphabetic learning. In terms of total instructional minutes, the interventions they collected ranged from about 2 to nearly 100 hours, with the shorter programs yielding especially weak results. A second issue raised by Piasta and Wagner is a failure to lend sufficient attention to the challenge. In many of the studies, they noted, "Letter name or sound instruction was often included only as a small or incidental portion of a larger literacy program (e.g., teaching letters to serve as 'placeholders' for facilitating phonological awareness development)" (2010, p. 22). In all, Piasta and Wagner concluded that if schools are to close the gap in young children's alphabetic knowledge—and they must—then they will need to accord more time and attention to intensive, explicit alphabet instruction.

Using a very different methodology, Connor, Morrison, and Slominski (2006) reached much the same conclusion. Observing 120 minutes per day in 34 preschool classrooms, Connor et al. reported that, on average, teachers gave code-centered instruction far less time than meaning-centered language and literacy activities such as read-alouds and discussion. Across classrooms, about 15 minutes per day were observed on all language and literacy activities. Of that time, alphabetic activities averaged only 2 minutes per day, including about 100 seconds of teacher-managed instruction on letters, letter-sounds, and spelling and about 22 seconds of independent work by the students on such activities as letter-writing practice. As it happened, however, the actual amount of time spent on alphabetic activities ranged widely both within and between classrooms, affording Connor et al. an opportunity to analyze how much it mattered. It mattered greatly. Connor et al. estimated that, regardless of the children's fall alphabetic scores, their spring alphabet scores increased by almost three letters for every additional 10 minutes per day of explicit, interactive alphabetic instruction that was conducted by their teachers.

Again, think about it. The alphabet was not designed with an eye toward learnability. The names of the letters are arbitrary and designated by cultural convention: There is no way to determine that the letter *b* is called "b" short of being told. The names of the letters are also highly confusable: They are short, meaningless, and generally rhyme with each other. Similarly, the shapes of the letters, abstract and graphically simple, are highly confusable. Indeed, the letters of the alphabet look more like each other than like anything else the child has yet had to learn (except perhaps numbers, which the child is likely being asked to learn alongside). Also, by convention, the child is required to learn not one, but two versions (uppercase and lowercase) of each letter. And worse, the lowercase forms bear little physical resemblance to their uppercase twins, even as they defy our normal visual recognition heuristics: A cup is a cup turned any which-way, but *d*, *b*, *p*, and *q* are categorically different from each other. On top of all that, the letters must be learned in such a way that they will be recognizable across a variety of hands, typefaces, and contexts. Of all of the literacy challenges that the child will ultimately confront, learning the letters of the alphabet is the *only* one that depends exactly and only on sheer rote memorization, and it must be over-memorization, at that.

The children who walk into school knowing all of their letters and sounds have typically been singing the "Alphabet Song" since they were 2 or 3. Many of them had ABCs on their baby quilts. By school entry, these children have already spent years "studying" the shapes, names, and sounds of the letters through educational television and alphabet books; with magnetic letters on the refrigerator; with puzzles, toys, and their iPads; with pencils, paper, and workbooks; and through countless other games and activities in preschool, in the car, and at home.

By contrast, consider the children who walk into school not knowing their letters adequately. If the support they need is offered neither at home nor at school, then how will they learn? And without solid alphabetic knowledge, how much else will remain unlearnable?

Letters can *only* be useful and useable as mediators for phonemic awareness development to the extent that they are familiar already. In turn, phonemic awareness and letter knowledge together—but *only* together—become useful and usable in making phonics, decoding, and spelling interesting and attainable.

Again, productive, reflective reading and writing depend on deep and ready, working knowledge of spellings and spelling–sound correspondences. Through productive reading and writing, children gain the language, knowledge, and modes of thought that enable literacy.

RATIONALE BEHIND THIS BOOK

Alphabetic knowledge refers to children's familiarity with the names, forms, and sounds of the letters of the alphabet as measured by recognition, production, and writing tasks (Piasta & Wagner, 2010). The goal of this book is to provide teachers with lesson plans, materials, and assessments that will help them give their students the instruction, practice, and support needed to master each of these dimensions of alphabetic knowledge.

In line with the Common Core State Standard Initiative (http://www.corestandards. org), the lessons are designed with the goal that by the time they enter first grade, all children will be able to do the following:

- Recognize and name all uppercase and lowercase letters.
- Print both the uppercase and lowercase letters.
- Produce the primary or most frequent sound for each consonant.
- Identify which letters represent the five major vowels (*Aa*, *Ee*, *Ii*, *Oo*, and *Uu*) and know the long and short sound of each.

The lesson materials are developmentally sequenced as guided by research and are divided into four units, each with two to four chapters:

- Unit I: Getting to Know the Alphabet
- Unit II: Writing Uppercase Letters
- Unit III: Writing Lowercase Letters
- Unit IV: Introducing Letters and Sounds

In Unit I, the children are introduced to the nature and purpose of the alphabet as a whole and, through the "Alphabet Song," to the names of the 26 letters. They are then engaged in a variety of activities designed to help them learn to recognize the shape of each of the letters and connect the shape to its name. Chapter 1 focuses on uppercase letters, and Chapter 2 focuses on lowercase letters, respecting the normal developmental sequence in which the uppercase and lowercase letters are learned. Chapter 3 introduces the children to those five "special" letters, the vowels, while providing more challenging letter recognition practice with both uppercase and lowercase letters.

Units II and III are devoted to helping the children learn how to print the letters. In Unit II, the focus is on uppercase letters, and in Unit III, it is on lowercase letters. Each of these units is divided into four chapters, with each chapter centered on letters involving one of the four basic writing strokes (vertical and horizontal; slanted; loops, humps, and troughs; and 2 o'clock strokes). Over the course of Units II and III, the children practice the proper sequence of strokes for each of the individual letters both in the air and on paper, thus gaining experience with each of the core strokes and their starting positions. There are two underlying motivations for this design. The first, of course, is to help the children learn to print each letter efficiently and legibly. The second is that learning to write the letters significantly hastens children's ability to recognize them as, deep in the brain, the motor habits involved in writing each letter become tightly tied to the letter's visual representation (Dehaene, 2009; Longcamp, Zerbato-Poudou, & Vely, 2005).

In Unit IV, the children are introduced to letter sounds. Chapter 12 marches them through the alphabet, introducing them to the most common sound of each consonant and the long sound of each vowel. Each sound is exercised both in isolation and in many words. Within words, the consonant phonemes are exercised in initial position, as the children play listening and thinking games designed to help them learn to hear and say each consonant phoneme, with ever more independence, as it begins different words. Vowels, by contrast, are more common in the middles and ends of syllables, so they are exercised by having the children listen, for example, for /ē/, when it occurs in the medial (*meet* versus *moat*) or final (*see* versus *sow*) position in words. In Chapter 13, the children are introduced to the fact that every English vowel has two sounds, "long" and "short," as they sing songs and play games requiring them to contrast the two sounds of each vowel, over and over, in many words. The primary goal is to prevent them from being bewildered when they encounter long and short vowels in decoding and spelling.

More detailed information about the structure, rationale, and goals of each unit is provided in each unit introduction. In general, however, the lessons in every unit have three basic parts.

1. *Warm-up and review:* The warm-up and review segments are intended to be brief and lively. They are designed to be conducted with the class as a whole, and their purpose is to remind, review, and strengthen prior lessons.

2. *New instruction:* The body of each lesson is devoted to new instruction and is also designed for use with the class as a whole. As is recommended practice for anchoring and clarifying new skills, every lesson requires the children's active, multisensory participation—where *multisensory* variously includes singing, marching, speaking, writing, and thinking, as well as physical movement.

3. *Small-group or individual activities:* The last section of the lessons is devoted to small-group and individual activities. These sessions have three general purposes: 1) to give students hands-on, minds-on opportunities to clarify, practice, and extend what they have learned; 2) to give teachers an organized flow of work samples with which to monitor the children's growth and needs; and 3) to give teachers time, while the class as a whole is productively busy, to administer individual assessments or to work with individuals or small groups who need extra instruction, practice, or encouragement.

In complement to the lessons, assessment forms and instructions are provided to document the children's entry, progress, and exit levels on each of the core skills:

- Uppercase Letter Recognition (Appendix A.1)
- Lowercase Letter Recognition (Appendix A.1)
- Uppercase Letter Writing (Appendix A.2)
- Lowercase Letter Writing (Appendix A.3)
- Initial Consonant Sounds (Appendix A.4)
- Vowel Identification and Sounds (Appendix A.5)

The purpose of the assessments is to help teachers adjust pacing and support as appropriate to the class as a whole and to each student.

When using this book with kindergartners, the goal is to complete all of the lessons by mid-year so that the children have the rest of the school year for phonemic awareness and early reading and writing activities. There are a total of 57 lessons in the book such that all can be comfortably completed by mid-year. In schools where nearly all children come to kindergarten with considerable alphabetic knowledge, that may be enough.

For most children, however, more is better. Even though the lessons can be completed in a single semester, students who are less familiar with the alphabet on entry cannot be expected to learn the lessons adequately in a single semester. The best way to make the lessons stick is to revisit and cumulate them across the preschool and kindergarten years as shown in the table below.

Year	Students	School quarter			
		First	Second	Third	Fourth
Year 1	Preschool (3.5–4.5 years old)			Units I and II	
Year 2	Prekindergarten (4.5–5.5 years old)	Unit I	Unit II	Unit III	Unit IV
Year 3	Kindergarten (5.5–6.5 years old)	Units I and II	Units III and IV	Phonemic awareness and early reading and writing	
Year 4+	Elementary students (6.5 years and older)	As indicated by assessed needs			

Regardless of how much of this schedule is adopted, effective instruction must be sensitive to the needs, progress, and grade level of the students. For students who need extra practice, the games can be played and replayed. If you have other alphabet activities or software that you feel would serve the children well in complement, use them alongside this curriculum. The goal is to ensure that all students gain the alphabetic knowledge they need to move comfortably, confidently, and productively into phonemic awareness, reading, and writing.

REFERENCES

Adams, M.J. (1990). *Beginning to read: Thinking and learning about print.* Cambridge, MA: The MIT Press.

Adams, M.J., Treiman, R.A., & Pressley, M.P. (1997). In I. Sigel & A. Renninger (Eds.), *Handbook of child psychology: Vol. 4. Child psychology in practice* (pp. 275–356). New York, NY: Wiley.

Badian, N.A. (1995). Predicting reading ability over the long term: The changing roles of letter naming, phonological awareness and orthographic processing. *Annals of Dyslexia, 45,* 79–96.

Blaiklock, K.E. (2004). The importance of letter knowledge in the relationship between phonological awareness and reading. *Journal of Research in Reading, 27*(1), 36–57.

Bond, G.L., & Dykstra, R. (1967). The cooperative research program in first grade reading instruction. *Reading Research Quarterly, 2*(1), 5–142.

Bowey, J.A. (1994). Phonological sensitivity in novice readers and nonreaders. *Journal of Experimental Child Psychology, 58*(1), 134–159.

Burgess, S.R. (2002). The influence of speech perception, oral language ability, the home literacy environment, and pre-reading knowledge on the growth of phonological sensitivity: A one-year longitudinal investigation. *Reading and Writing, 15*(7–8), 709–737.

Burgess, S.R., & Lonigan, C.J. (1998). Bidirectional relations of phonological sensitivity and prereading abilities: Evidence from a preschool sample. *Journal of Experimental Child Psychology, 70*(2), 117–141.

Byrne, B. (1992). Studies in the acquisition procedure for reading: Rationale, hypotheses, and data. In P.B. Gough, L.C. Ehri, & R. Treiman (Eds.), *Reading acquisition* (pp. 1–34). Hillsdale, NJ: Lawrence Erlbaum Associates.

Carroll, J.M. (2004). Letter knowledge precipitates phoneme segmentation, but not phoneme invariance. *Journal of Research in Reading, 227*(3), 212–225.

Chall, J.S. (1967/1983). *Learning to read: The great debate.* New York, NY: McGraw-Hill.

Connor, C.M., Morrison, F.J., & Slominski, L. (2006). Preschool instruction and children's emergent literacy growth. *Journal of Educational Psychology, 98*(4), 665–689.

Dehaene, S. (2009). *Reading in the brain: The science and evolution of a human invention.* New York, NY: Viking.

Denton, K., & West, J. (2002). *Children's reading and mathematics achievement in kindergarten and first grade* (NCES 2002125). Washington, DC: National Center for Education Statistics. Retrieved from http://nces.ed.gov/pubsearch/pubsinfo.asp?pubid=2002125

Diamond, K.E., Gerde, H.K., & Powell, D.R. (2008). Development in early literacy skills during the pre-kindergarten year in Head Start: Relations between growth in children's writing and understanding of letters. *Early Childhood Research Quarterly, 23*(4), 467–478.

Douglas, K., & Montiel, E. (2008). *Learning to read in American elementary school classrooms: Poverty and the acquisition of reading skills.* Newark, DE: International Reading Association. Retrieved from http://www.reading.org/downloads/resources/ECLS-K%20SES%20Report.pdf

Duncan, L.G., Seymour, P.H.K., & Hill, S. (1997). How important are rhyme and analogy in beginning reading? *Cognition, 63*(2), 171–208.

Evans, M.E., Bell, M., Shaw, D., Moretti, S., & Page, J. (2006). Letter names, letter sounds and phonological awareness: An examination of kindergarten children across letters and of letters across children. *Reading and Writing, 19*(9), 959–989.

Flesch, R. (1955/1985). *Why Johnny can't read.* New York, NY: Harper and Row.

Foulin, J.N. (2005). Why is letter-name knowledge such a good predictor of learning to read? *Reading and Writing, 18*(2), 129–155.

Gallagher, A., Frith, U., & Snowling, M.J. (2000). Precursors of literacy delay among children at genetic risk of dyslexia. *Journal of Child Psychology and Psychiatry, 41*(2), 203–213.

Graham, S., Weintraub, N., & Berninger, V. (2001). Which manuscript letters do primary grade children write legibly? *Journal of Educational Psychology, 93*(3), 488–497.

Hammill, D.D. (2004). What we know about correlates of reading. *Exceptional Children, 70*(4), 453–469.

Hecht, S.A., & Close, L. (2002). Emergent literacy skills and training time uniquely predict variability in responses to phonemic awareness training in disadvantaged kindergartners. *Journal of Experimental Child Psychology, 82*(2), 93–115.

Johnston, R.S., Anderson, M., & Holligan, C. (1996). Knowledge of the alphabet and explicit awareness of phonemes in pre-readers: The nature of the relationship. *Reading and Writing, 8*(3), 217–234.

Leppänen, U., Aunola, K., Niemi, P., & Nurmi, J.-E. (2008). Letter knowledge predicts grade 4 reading fluency and reading comprehension. *Learning and Instruction, 18*(6), 548–564.

Liberman, A.M., Cooper, F., Shankweiler, D., & Studdert-Kennedy, M. (1967). Perception of the speech code. *Psychological Review, 74,* 431–461.

Longcamp, M., Zerbato-Poudou, M.-T., & Vely, J. L. (2005). The influence of writing practice on letter recognition in preschool children: A comparison between handwriting and typing. *Acta Psychologica, 119*(1), 67–79.

McBride-Chang, C. (1999). The ABCs of the ABCs: The development of letter-name and letter-sound knowledge. *Merrill-Palmer Quarterly, 45,* 285–308.

Muehl, S., & Di Nello, M.C. (1976). Early first-grade skills related to subsequent reading performance: A seven year follow up study. *Journal of Reading Behavior, 8*(1), 67–81.

National Association for the Education of Young Children. (1998). Learning to read and write: Developmentally appropriate practices for young children. A joint position statement of the International Reading Association and the National Association for the Education of Young Children. *Young Children, 53*(4), 30–46.

National Reading Panel. (2000). *Teaching children to read: An evidence-based assessment of the scientific research literature on reading and its implications for reading instruction: Reports of the subgroups* (NIH Publication No. 00-4754). Washington, DC: U.S. Government Printing Office.

National Research Council, Committee on Preventing Reading Difficulties in Young Children. (1998). *Preventing reading difficulties in young children.* Washington, DC: National Academies Press.

O'Connor, R.E., & Jenkins, J.R. (1999). Prediction of reading disabilities in kindergarten and first grade. *Scientific Studies of Reading, 3*(2), 159–197.

Piasta, S.B., & Wagner, R.K. (2010). Developing early literacy skills: A meta-analysis of alphabet learning and instruction. *Reading Research Quarterly, 45*(1), 8–38.

Preschool Curriculum Evaluation Research Consortium. (2008). *Effects of preschool curriculum programs on school readiness* (NCER 2008–2009). Washington, DC: U.S. Department of Education, National Center for Education Research, Institute of Education Sciences.

Ritchey, K.D. (2008). The building blocks of writing: Learning to write letters and spell words. *Reading and Writing, 21*(1), 27–47.

Scarborough, H.S. (2001). Connecting early language and literacy to later reading (dis)abilities: Evidence, theory, and practice. In S.B. Neuman & D.K. Dickinson (Eds.), *Handbook of early literacy research* (pp. 97–110). New York, NY: The Guilford Press.

Schatschneider, C., Fletcher, K.M., Francis, D.J., Carlson, C.D., & Foorman, B.R. (2004). Kindergarten prediction of reading skills: A longitudinal comparative analysis. *Journal of Educational Psychology, 96*(2), 265–282.

Stahl, S.A., & Murray, B.A. (1994). Defining phonological awareness and its relationship to early reading. *Journal of Educational Psychology, 86*(2), 221–234.

Stanovich, K.E. (1986). Matthew effects in reading: Some consequences of individual differences in the acquisition of literacy. *Reading Research Quarterly, 21*(4), 360–407.

Torgesen, J.K. (1998). Catch them before they fall: Identification and assessment to prevent reading failure in young children. *American Educator, 22*(Spring/Summer), 32–39.

Torppa, M., Lyytinen, P., Erskine, J., Eklund, K., & Lyytinen, H. (2010). Language development, literacy skills, and predictive connections to reading in Finnish children with and without familial risk for dyslexia. *Journal of Learning Disabilities, 43*(4), 308–321.

U.S. Department of Education. (2002). *Guidance for the Reading First program.* Washington, DC: Author. Retrieved from http://www2.ed.gov/programs/readingfirst/guidance.pdf

U.S. Department of Education. (2003). *Guidance for the Early Reading First program.* Washington, DC: Author. Retrieved from http://www2.ed.gov/programs/earlyreading/erfguidance.doc

U.S. Department of Health and Human Services, Administration for Children and Families. (2010). *Head Start Impact Study: Final report.* Washington, DC: Author. Retrieved from http://www.acf.hhs.gov/programs/opre/hs/impact_study/reports/impact_study/hs_impact_study_final.pdf

Wagner, R.K., Torgesen, J.K., & Rashotte, C.A. (1994). Development of reading-related phonological processing abilities: New evidence of bidirectional causality from a latent variable longitudinal study. *Developmental Psychology, 30*(1), 73–87.

Wagner, R.K., Torgesen, J.K., Rashotte, C.A., Hecht, S.A., Barker, T.A., Burgess, S.R., …Garon, T. (1997). Changing relations between phonological processing abilities and word-level reading as children develop from beginning to skilled readers: A 5-year longitudinal study. *Developmental Psychology, 33*(3), 468–479.

Getting to Know the Alphabet

ASSESSMENT ALERT: The Entry-Level Uppercase Letter Recognition and Entry-Level Lowercase Letter Recognition assessments (see Appendix A.1) should be completed for every child before beginning this unit.

By the end of this unit, children should be able to

- Recite the alphabet
- Recognize and name many of the letters, both uppercase and lowercase
- Match the letters with reasonable ease and accuracy
- Name the five vowels
- Spell their first names aloud

These goals sound like a lot, but it will take far more time and experience before the children are able to recognize the letters as quickly and surely as reading requires. What the children will learn in this unit is only the beginning. It is the first layer, the foundation. Its purpose is to establish the mental Velcro to which everything else must stick. As such, it is very important that every child leave this unit feeling bright eyed and comfortable with the lessons it offers.

The unit is divided into three chapters. The first introduces the alphabet and the uppercase letters. In the second, focus is turned to the lowercase letters. The third chapter introduces the vowels and offers additional independent practice with both uppercase and lowercase letters.

CHAPTER 1: THE ALPHABET AND THE UPPERCASE LETTERS

An initial goal of Chapter 1 is to give children a sense of value and perspective about the journey on which they are embarking. The chapter begins with a brief exploration of print, drawing attention to its ubiquity and exploring the kinds of stories and information that it offers. As a more personal entrée into literacy, the children also receive necklaces and poems to learn how to spell their own names—a useful way to seed the children's letter knowledge and a reliable parent pleaser.

The traditional "Alphabet Song" is used to introduce the alphabet itself. Although a number of other songs and poems featuring the alphabet are shared over the course of the program, this song is put first because of its wide familiarity. Encourage the children to sing it at home with their parents.

In turn, the "Alphabet Song" is used as the primary mnemonic to lead the children in learning the names and shapes of the uppercase letters. Each lesson culminates in hands-on letter recognition and naming games played cooperatively by the children in small groups.

One reason for beginning with the uppercase letters is simply that if they are not taught first, then they tend to be neglected. A second is that, as documented historically, developmentally, and now, neurologically (see Adams, 1990; Dehaene, 2009), the uppercase letters are visually much easier to learn. A third is that because the uppercase letters are easier, they provide a good anchor for learning the names and shapes of the lowercase letters.

CHAPTER 2: INTRODUCING THE LOWERCASE LETTERS

Although the focus of Chapter 2 is shifted to the lowercase letters, its structure is very similar to that of Chapter 1. Each lesson is again capped with small-group games for hands-on practice with the names and shapes of the lowercase letters. The "Alphabet Song" continues as a main platform for classroom letter play. In addition, a second song, "Alphabet Bounce," is introduced near the end of the chapter. This is done partly for variety and partly to help the children learn to "hear" the separate letters as they sing them.

Bear in mind that the shapes of lowercase letters are difficult to master. It is extremely important that all of the children leave this chapter with a comfortable ability to play the lowercase matching games because this is a critical first step. At the same time, be warned that occasional lapses and confusion in recognizing the lowercase letters may still be expected for some time, even among children who entered with a relatively strong command of the uppercase letters.

CHAPTER 3: INTRODUCING THE VOWELS

This chapter also has two major objectives. The first is to provide more practice with the names and shapes of the letters, both uppercase and lowercase, and with the relations between them. The second is to alert the children to the fact that vowels are very special letters, making up a special class unto themselves. One reason for lending extra attention to the vowels from the outset is that phonemic awareness is significantly more difficult for vowel phonemes than for consonant phonemes. Soon enough, too, the children will also find the spelling and sound behaviors of the vowels, as a group, are very different and far more complicated than those of the consonants. It is wise to make sure the children already understand that the vowels make up a special category of letters and phonemes before such complications arise.

The last activity in the last lesson of this chapter is a group-administered Entry-Level Uppercase Letter Writing assessment (see Appendix A.2).

ASSESSMENT

Two assessments, Entry-Level Uppercase Letter Recognition and Entry-Level Lowercase Letter Recognition (see Appendix A.1), should be completed *before* beginning this unit. The assessment for Entry-Level Uppercase Letter Writing (see Appendix A.2) is administered at the very end of this unit, just before moving on to Unit II: Writing Uppercase Letters.

When	Assessment	How	Resource
Prior to beginning Chapter 1	Entry-Level Uppercase Letter Recognition	Individual	Appendix A.1
Prior to beginning Chapter 1	Entry-Level Lowercase Letter Recognition	Individual	Appendix A.1
At the end of Chapter 3	Entry-Level Uppercase Letter Writing	Whole group	Appendix A.2

HANDS-ON GAMES AND INDIVIDUAL DIFFERENCES

Across the lessons in the unit, the students engage in a variety of hands-on letter recognition games during the small-group activity sessions. These games involve matching separate Letter Cards to their alphabetically ordered twins on an Alphabet Strip. Sometimes the games involve only half of the letters (A–M/a–m, or N–Z/n–z), and sometimes they require the full alphabet (A–Z or a–z). Sometimes they require only one Letter Card for each letter, and sometimes they require more than one.

The purpose of these games is to give the children the self-monitored, hands-on, minds-on experience needed for independent letter recognition. Asking the children to replay these games from time to time throughout the year is an excellent way of promoting their letter recognition growth. As a rule of thumb, as long as the game is entertaining, it remains challenging, and as long as the game is challenging, it continues to offer learning opportunities.

Similarly, students' individual progress and needs can be observed through these games. In this, be advised that *the first games in both Chapter 1 and Chapter 2 are key and critical.* In these games, the Letter Cards are arranged face up so that they can be openly examined and compared. The challenge is to match the cards to their twins on the Alphabet Strips in alphabetical order so that on each turn, the letter to be matched stands out, providing a clear model of the letter in quest. This game becomes easy as the children develop an internal model of each letter that is relatively complete and well integrated. Until that point, children see the letters in terms of their parts and pieces, so the games are very hard. The games require careful attention and analysis, but they also offer direct feedback for each choice, right or wrong.

Watch the children carefully as they play these first games because until the children become comfortable with this basic level of letter matching, there is no gain in moving on. *Take the time to ensure that every child has the amount of replay and support that he or she needs.*

Children Who Need Extra Help

If some students are having special difficulty with the letters, ease into these games more gently by having them begin play with fewer letters at once.

- Break the alphabet into sets of 6–7 letters: A–F (a–f), G–M (g–m), N–S (n–s), and T–Z (t–z). Once the children are comfortable with each set, move on to the next.
- When the children have conquered all of these sets, they should be ready to play with half of the alphabet at a time: A–M (a–m) and N–Z (n–z).

Children Who Are Already Facile with the Alphabet

If some groups of children are playing far more quickly and successfully than others, variations in replay may keep these children productively engaged and learning while the others are working.

- Replay the matching game in backwards alphabetical order (e.g., from *M* to *A* instead of *A* to *M*). This helps to refine the children's letter recognition skills because they cannot use their knowledge of the letters' sequence as an aid.
- Replay the game by having the person "in charge" choose the next card from any of those that remain unmatched (rather than progressing in order).

LESSON MATERIALS AND RESOURCES

The following table summarizes the materials and resources needed for both whole-group and small-group activities. *Note:* This book contains online materials (refer to About the Online Materials at the beginning of this book for more information). In the Notes column, *online* indicates that the materials are only provided online. The Notes column also indicates whether materials require additional assembly, or *special preparation*. Instructions for special preparation are provided following the table.

Chapters	Materials	Use	Notes
1, 2, and 3	Board, easel, or projection system	Displaying activity-specific materials	None
1	Various books and print samples	Whole group	See Chapter 1, Lesson 1, Materials
1, 2, and 3	Alphabet Frieze	Whole group	Online or special preparation
1 and 2	Name Necklaces and Name Poems	Whole group	Special preparation
1, 2, and 3	Links to music for the "Alphabet Song," "Alphabet Bounce," and "Vowel Name Song"	Whole group	Online
1 and 3	Uppercase Letter Cards	Small group	Appendix B.2 and special preparation
1 and 3	Uppercase Half-Alphabet Strips	Small group	Appendix B.1 and special preparation
1 and 3	Uppercase Full-Alphabet Strips	Small group	Appendix B.1 and special preparation
1, 2, and 3	Blank Half-Alphabet Strips	Small group	Appendix B.1 and special preparation
1, 2, and 3	Blank Full-Alphabet Strips	Small group	Appendix B.1 and special preparation
2 and 3	Lowercase Letter Cards	Small group	Appendix B.2 and special preparation
2 and 3	Lowercase Half-Alphabet Strips	Small group	Appendix B.1 and special preparation
2 and 3	Lowercase Full-Alphabet Strips	Small group	Appendix B.1 and special preparation

Note: Appendix B materials are also available online, organized by unit.

INSTRUCTIONS: SPECIAL MATERIALS AND PREPARATION

Alphabet Frieze

Most of the activities in the units depend on a good classroom display of the alphabet, which this book terms an *Alphabet Frieze*. The online materials include color 8 ½" × 11" Alphabet Frieze cards that you may print for your convenience, but you may choose to create your own Alphabet Frieze. If you choose to create your own, use the following guidelines:

- The Alphabet Frieze should include both uppercase and lowercase letters.
- The five vowels should stand out visually from the other letters so that they are easy to see and to refer to as a group. The vowels for the online Alphabet Frieze are red.
- If the vowels are not already specially marked in your Alphabet Frieze, then you might, for example, make a bright frame or border around each vowel pair, outline each with glitter ink, or overlay each with a sheet of removable highlighter.
- It is helpful if the Alphabet Frieze includes alliterative pictures for each letter (e.g., a picture of a cat on the *Cc* card).
- In addition to supporting the phonemic significance of the letters, such pictures are useful for directing the children's attention to a given Letter Card when their letter recognition is not yet secure.
- The display should be located or arranged where it will be clearly visible to all students when you work with it and you can easily touch every letter with your hand while you are working with the class.

Name Necklaces and Name Poems

To create an uppercase Name Necklace for each child in the class, print each child's first name in *uppercase* letters on *both* sides of stiff stock (e.g., half of a 3" × 5" index card), and add string to make a necklace.

Have a Name Poem ready for the first name of each child in the class (see the online materials). Try to assign a different poem framework to each child, but it is okay to reuse one or more of the frameworks—the children will have fun noticing.

Compile a List of Name Poems, with space next to each poem to check off once you have taught the poem to the child.

Alphabet Strips and Cards for Small-Group Letter Games

Before beginning each chapter, make the game pieces the students will need for the small-group letter recognition games. In Chapter 1, the games involve only uppercase letters. In Chapter 2, they involve only lowercase letters. In Chapter 3, the games require both uppercase and lowercase letters, all of which have already been made for Chapters 1 and 2.

To prepare these materials, use the following:

- Templates for each set of pieces (Appendixes B.1–B.2)
- Baggies to organize the Letter Cards
- Glue or tape to finish construction of the Alphabet Strips
- (*Optional*) Laminating the templates can protect and stiffen the materials. It is best to laminate the templates *before* cutting them into game pieces.

Step-by-step instructions for preparing each set of game pieces are provided next.

Uppercase Letter Cards

Uppercase Letter Cards (see Appendix B.2) are the manipulatives that the children will use to play the hands-on match and draw games involving uppercase letters in Chapters 1 and 3. Make one set of cards for each student in the class.

Each set of cards should be divided into two groups, corresponding to the first and second half of the alphabet (*A–M* and *N–Z*) and put in separate baggies. If, for example, there are 24 children in the class, 24 baggies will contain the letters *A–M* and 24 more baggies will contain the letters *N–Z*.

Uppercase Half-Alphabet Strips: A–M and N–Z

Each Uppercase Half-Alphabet Strip is a strip of paper that displays the letters of either the first (*A–M*) or second (*N–Z*) half of the alphabet in order. Each group will need one Half-Alphabet Strip. In addition, make a few extra Half-Alphabet Strips as backup and for teacher use in individual or small-group support sessions.

Both the *A–M* and *N–Z* Half-Alphabet Strips are on the same template (see Appendix B.1), so the total number of copies of the template needed is as follows:

- *For small-group sessions:* Divide the total number of children in the class by 3. For example, if there are 24 children, make 24 ÷ 3 = 8 copies of the template for small-group sessions.

- *For individual work and backup:* Make four additional copies of the template.

- *Total:* Divide the total number of children in the class by 3 and then add 4. For example, (24 children ÷ 3) + 4 = 12 copies of the template.

After making (and, if wished, laminating) the right number of copies of the Alphabet Strip template, cut out each row of the template.

To construct the Half-Alphabet Strips for the first half of the alphabet (*A–M*), use the first two rows (*A–G, H–M*), taping or pasting the end tab following the letter *G* to the backside of the letter *H*.

Similarly, to construct the Half-Alphabet Strips for the second half of the alphabet (*N–Z*), join the third and fourth row of the template by taping or pasting the end tab following the letter *T* to the backside of the letter *U*.

If, as in this example, there are 24 children in the class, use the following:

- 12 Half-Alphabet Strips displaying the letters *A–M* in order
- 12 Half-Alphabet Strips displaying the letters *N–Z* in order

Uppercase Full-Alphabet Strip

To construct the Uppercase Full-Alphabet Strips, make the same number of copies of the Alphabet Strip template (see Appendix B.1) as you did for the Uppercase Half-Alphabet Strips (i.e., if there are 24 children in the class, make 12 copies of the template).

Cut the template into rows, and affix each row to the next to construct full, ordered Alphabet Strips, *A–Z*.

Note: In place of making a separate set of Full-Alphabet Strips, ask the children to use both of their group's Uppercase Half-Alphabet Strips, piecing them together into a full *A–Z* line-up.

Blank Half-Alphabet Strip

Blank Half-Alphabet Strips have 13 blank squares for the students to place the Letter Cards when matching them to the letters on the Half-Alphabet Strips. These Blank Half-Alphabet Strips will be used in small-group games in Chapters 1, 2, and 3.

Make one copy of the Blank Half-Alphabet Strip template (see Appendix B.1) for each group plus extras for back-up and individual work. (For example, if there are 24 children in the class, make 12 copies of the template [(24 ÷ 3) + 4 = 12].)

Blank Full-Alphabet Strips

Blank Full-Alphabet Strips have 26 blank squares for the students to place the Letter Cards when matching them to the letters on the Full-Alphabet Strips. The Blank Full-Alphabet Strips will be used in small-group games in Chapters 1, 2, and 3.

Make one copy of the Blank Alphabet Strip template (see Appendix B.1) for each group plus extras for back-up and individual work. (For example, if there are 24 children in the class, make 12 copies of the template [(24 ÷ 3) + 4 = 12].)

Note: Piecing together the Blank Half-Alphabet Strips will not substitute for Blank Full-Alphabet Strips because there will not be enough strips for each small group.

Lowercase Letter Cards

Children will use the Lowercase Letter Cards (see Appendix B.2) to play the hands-on match and draw games involving lowercase letters. Follow the instructions given for the Uppercase Letter Cards, but use the template for the Lowercase Letter Cards. Again, make as many full copies of these card sets as there are children in the class.

Lowercase Half-Alphabet Strips a–m and n–z

Each Lowercase Half-Alphabet Strip is a long strip of paper that displays the letters of either the first (*a–m*) or second (*n–z*) half of the alphabet in order. Follow the instructions for making the Uppercase Half-Alphabet Strips, but use the Lowercase Half-Alphabet Strip template (see Appendix B.1). Make the same number of sets as you did for the Uppercase Half-Alphabet Strips.

Lowercase Full-Alphabet Strip

Each Lowercase Full-Alphabet Strip is a long strip of paper that displays the letters of the full lowercase alphabet (*a–z*) in order. Follow the instructions for making the Uppercase Full-Alphabet Strips, but use the Lowercase Alphabet Strip template (see Appendix B.1).

Note: In place of making a separate set of Lowercase Full-Alphabet Strips, children can use both of their group's Lowercase Half-Alphabet Strips, piecing them together into a full *a–z* line-up.

The Alphabet and the Uppercase Letters

LESSON 1 | Introducing the Alphabet

Objective	To introduce the alphabet, its nature, and its value
Materials	**1. Introducing the Alphabet** Alphabet Frieze (*Make sure that you can reach it!*) **2. The Importance of the Alphabet** Variety of books and other items with print or writing in or on them: • Stack of illustrated children's books, both fiction and nonfiction • One or two big, thick, print-intensive books for mature readers • Two or more reference books, including a dictionary A few things that are *not books* but that have some print on them • For more specific suggestions, see the lesson body of Activity 2. **3. Read an Alphabet Book** Alphabet book of your choice

ACTIVITIES

1. Introducing the Alphabet: Overview and Basic Terms

    Because you, as well as the children's many teachers to come, will be using such terms as **alphabet, letter, uppercase,** and **lowercase** during instruction, it is a good idea to anchor their meanings from the outset. The children are not expected to master these terms during this session, but given proper introduction, they will do so over time.

    • Point to the Alphabet Frieze, and ask the children what they see.
      • Lead the children to understand that the whole thing, all together, is what is called the **alphabet.**
      • Make sure that the children repeat the word **alphabet** several times; call on several individuals as well as the group as a whole.
    • Help the children to understand that the separate symbols are called **letters.**
      • Point to several **letters,** and explain that each symbol is one of the **letters** in the **alphabet.**

- Make sure that the children repeat the word *letter* several times; call on several individuals as well as the group as a whole.
- Tell the children that there are 26 *letters* in the alphabet.
  - Point out that each of the 26 letters has two shapes. One shape is called the *uppercase,* and the other is called the *lowercase.*
  - Point to the letter *A* and explain that
    - The first shape is the *uppercase* A
    - The second is the *lowercase* a
- Ask who can name any of the *letters* of the alphabet.
  - Call on a few volunteers to name a letter. For each letter named,
    - Rephrase the answer to emphasize the words *letter* and *alphabet* (e.g., "Yes, A is one of the *letters* in the *alphabet*")
    - Locate the letter in the Alphabet Frieze (e.g., "Yes, here is the *letter* A")
    - Point out its *uppercase* and *lowercase* forms (e.g., "This one is the *uppercase* A… and this one is the *lowercase* a")
- Anchor the terms *uppercase* and *lowercase.*
  - Ask the children to tell again what the *first* shape of each letter is called. (uppercase)
    - Make sure that the children repeat the word *uppercase* several times. Point to several *uppercase* letters, and call on several individuals as well as the group as a whole.
  - Ask the children to tell again what the *second* shape of each letter is called. (lowercase)
    - Make sure that the children repeat the word *lowercase* several times. Point to several *lowercase* letters, and call on several individuals as well as the group as a whole.

2. The Importance of the Alphabet: Exploring Different Kinds of Print

Learning to recognize and name all of the letters takes a lot of time and practice. The purpose of this activity is to lead the children to think about the value and uses of the alphabet so that they will know the challenge is worth it.

- Ask the children to offer reasons why it would be useful to know the alphabet.
- Agree that the reason for learning the alphabet is so that people can read and write. That is what the alphabet is for.
- Ask the children what kinds of things they might like to be able to read, encouraging them to offer suggestions and discuss freely.
- Enrich this discussion by sharing the print materials you have chosen (see Materials at the beginning of this chapter).

2.1. Illustrated Storybooks for Children

- Show the children your stack of illustrated storybooks for children.
- Pick one of the books from the stack, and give a brief show and tell about the book.
  - Point out that the children need to learn the alphabet to read
    - The name, or *title,* of the book
    - The names of the people who wrote the book and drew the pictures (the *author* and *illustrator*)

- Give the children
  - A brief teaser on what the book is about
  - A peek at the print and pictures inside
- Ask the children to tell about their own favorite storybooks.
- Assure them that there are many, many wonderful storybooks for children. When they learn how to read, they can read whichever books they choose, whenever they choose, all by themselves.

2.2. Illustrated Nonfiction Books for Children

There are many, many books about the world and how it works. People who can read can learn about anything they want.

- Show the children your stack of illustrated nonfiction children's books.
- Explain to the children that books like these are about the real world. From books like these, they can learn about snakes, whales, spiders, volcanoes, or famous people—about just about anything they want.
- Do a brief show and tell with one of the illustrated nonfiction books for children that you have gathered, including
  - The name, or **title,** of the book
  - A brief teaser on what the book is about
  - A peek at the print and pictures inside
- Ask the children to share what they might like to learn more about.
- Assure the children that there are books about nearly anything that they might want to know. If they can read, they can learn about anything they want.

2.3. Books for Good Readers

- Show the children one or more big, thick, print-intensive books (e.g., one of the *Harry Potter* volumes, a favorite novel).
  - Lead the children to notice how such books are different from children's books.
    - They are very long—they usually have more than 100 pages.
    - The print is very small.
    - There are hundreds and hundreds of letters on each page.
    - There are hardly any pictures at all.
- Explain to the children that when they become really good at reading, it becomes so easy to read that it's like having somebody else read aloud to them. They don't need the pictures because they can imagine everything as they read. It's almost like watching a movie.

2.4. Reference Books

- Show the children the stack of reference books you have gathered.
- Explain that there are many books like these for finding out specific things.
- For almost anything they might want to know, there is a book like one of these where they can look it up.
- Briefly share several of the reference books you have gathered.
  - Explain the kind of information it holds.
  - Give the children a peek inside.

- Examples of references that might be good to share include the following:
  - Dictionary, Spanish dictionary
  - Almanac/book of records
  - Atlas
  - Field guide (e.g., birds, fish, rocks)
  - How-to books
  - Phone book
  - *TV Guide*

2.5. Besides Books: Print Scavenger Hunt

- Point out that there is print on a lot of things besides books. To know what the print says, they must learn to read.
- Raise a few examples, getting the children to say what the print is for and why it is important. Examples might include the following:
  - Newspapers
  - Game instructions
  - Street signs
  - Menus, lists of ice cream flavors
- Give the children 5 minutes to get up and search around the room for things that have print on them.
  - Ask them to look for print on things that are *not* books.
  - Examples might include the following:
    - Cubby labels
    - Labels on the outsides of boxes, packages, or containers
    - Labels on or in clothes or shoes
    - Wall displays such as posters, maps, and the calendar
    - Clerical items such as memos, lists, and envelopes
    - Labels on manufactured items such as pencils, crayons, scissors, erasers, computers, pencil sharpener, and mugs

3. Read an Alphabet Book

- Tell the children that there are also a lot of books that are about the alphabet.
- Read an alphabet book to the children.

The "Alphabet Song"

Objective	To introduce the "Alphabet Song"
Materials	**1. Introducing the "Alphabet Song"**
	Alphabet Frieze
	Board (easel, projection system)
	(*Optional*) Music for the "Alphabet Song" (see online materials for links)
	2. Uppercase Letter Face-Up Match: *A–M* (Small-Group Activity)
	Uppercase Half-Alphabet Strip (letters *A–M*) (one for each group)
	Blank Half-Alphabet Strip (13 squares long) (one for each group)
	Uppercase Letter Cards (letters *A–M*, shuffled) (one set for each group)

ACTIVITIES

The traditional "Alphabet Song," to the tune of "Twinkle, Twinkle Little Star," is a time-honored way of familiarizing children with the names of the letters of the alphabet. Best of all, the "Alphabet Song" is known by many of the children's parents, too, making it a wonderful vehicle for enlisting home support from the outset.

> TEACHER TIP
> Take time to send notes home encouraging parents to find ways to sing the song often with their child—in the car, in the tub, while looking at alphabet books, or in pace with their steps when they walk or climb stairs.

1. Introducing the "Alphabet Song"
   - Gather the children in a way that all can see the Alphabet Frieze.
     - Ask how many children already know the "Alphabet Song," and invite all of the children to sing it with you.
       - Congratulate the children on how well so many of them know the song already, and tell them that everyone is now going to learn the song **perfectly.**

   1.1. Teaching Line by Line
   - Please use the following version of the "Alphabet Song" because it reduces the crowding of the letters *L-M-N-O-P*. Like the more familiar version, it is to be sung to the tune of "Twinkle, Twinkle Little Star."

     The ABC Song

     A B C D   E F G,

     H I J K   L M N,

     O P Q,   R S T,

     U V W   X Y Z,

     Now I know my ABCs!

     Next time won't you sing with me?

- Alert the children that this version may be a little different from the one they have heard before. Everyone should pay close attention.
  - First line
    - Sing the first line of the song for the children, pointing to each letter pair on the Alphabet Frieze as its name is sung:

      Aa Bb Cc Dd Ee Ff Gg

    - Using *uppercase letters only*, write the first line of the song on the board for the children, leaving extra space as shown to mark phrasing:

      A B C D   E F G

    - Lead the children to sing the line at least once while you point in time to the uppercase letters written on the board.
    - Lead the children to sing the line at least once while you point in time to the letter pairs in the Alphabet Frieze.
  - Second line
    - Sing the second line of the song for the children, pointing to each letter pair in the Alphabet Frieze as its name is sung:

      Hh Ii Jj Kk Ll Mm Nn

    - Using *uppercase letters only*, write this second line of the song on the board beneath the first, leaving extra space midline, as shown, to mark phrasing:

      A B C D   E F G
      H I J K   L M N

    - Lead the children to sing the line at least once while you point in time to the uppercase letters written on the board.
    - Lead the children to sing the line at least once while you point in time to the letter pairs in the Alphabet Frieze.
  - Third line
    - Repeat the instructions for the second line with Line 3:

      A B C D   E F G
      H I J K   L M N
      O P Q   R S T

  - Fourth line
    - Repeat the instructions for the second line with Line 4:

      A B C D   E F G
      H I J K   L M N
      O P Q   R S T
      U V W   X Y Z

  - Final stanza
    - Sing the final stanza for the children, and have them sing it again with you:

      Now I know my ABCs!

      Next time won't you sing with me?

1.2. Singing the "Alphabet Song," Beginning to End

- Have the children sing the "Alphabet Song" several times with you, start to finish.
  - Sing the whole song at least once while pointing to the uppercase letters written on the board.
  - Sing the whole song at least once while pointing to the letter pairs in the Alphabet Frieze.
- Point out that only one of the shapes for each letter is written on the board.
  - Ask the children if they can name which one.
  - Make sure that the children repeat the answer (*uppercase letters*) several times; call on several individuals as well as the group as a whole.
- Tell the children to ask their parents to sing the "Alphabet Song" with them at home.

INSTRUCTIONAL TIP

For those who missed today's class and for any who need extra support in learning the alphabet, such line-by-line practice of the "Alphabet Song" is also useful in small-group support sessions, particularly when combined with letter pointing by the children (using, e.g., the Alphabet Strips and Letter Cards in Appendixes B.1 and B.2).

---

2. Uppercase Letter Face-Up Match: *A–M*

   2.1. Game Set-Up

   - Divide the children into groups of three or four; ask each group to sit in a semicircle.
     - Give each group an Uppercase Half-Alphabet Strip for the letters *A–M*, and tell the children to place the strip before them so that it is right-side up and can be easily seen by everyone in their group.
       - Explain that what they see on the strip is the first half of the Alphabet Strip, the letters *A* through *M*.
     - Give each group one Blank Half-Alphabet Strip (with 13 squares), and tell the children to place it just beneath and in alignment with the Uppercase Half-Alphabet Strip.
     - Give each group one shuffled set of 13 Uppercase Letter Cards, including *one card for each of the letters A–M*.
       - Ask the children to look at the cards to see that each card shows one **uppercase** letter.
   - Tell the children that to begin the game, they will need to lay all 13 of their Uppercase Letter Cards face up in the space between themselves and the two aligned strips.
     - The cards should be thoroughly mixed up so that the children have to look carefully to find the card they are seeking.
     - Every card should be visible to everyone in the group.
     - There is a star at the top of each card to make it easy to tell whether it is right-side up.

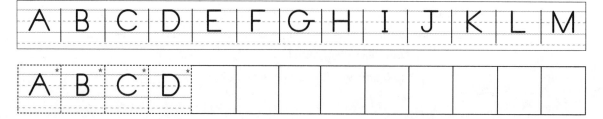

2.2. Game Play

The goal of the game is to place each Uppercase Letter Card onto the Blank Alphabet Strip directly beneath its match, thus building the first half of the uppercase alphabet with the Letter Cards. For each letter, or "round," one child is "in charge" and that child should engage the rest of the group in searching for the letter. Once the letter is found, the children place it on the blank strip, beneath its match on the Uppercase Alphabet Strip.

After the letter is placed, the next student is in charge. The game continues until all of the letters, from A to M, have been placed in their appropriate spots on the Blank Alphabet Strip. Lead the children through the first few rounds.

- Explain that the *object of the game* is to place every one of the uppercase letters on the Blank Alphabet Strip beneath its match.
- To do this, they will start with *A*, because it is the first letter of the alphabet, and continue through the last one on the strip, *M*.
- Explain that they will take turns being *in charge* of their group.
  - The first person in charge for each group will be the person on the *right end* of their semicircle.
    - Ask the groups to identify which child is on the *right* end and will be in charge first.
- Explain how to *play the game.*
  - The person in charge for each group *names* the letter that everybody must search for.
  - Pointing to the *A* on the Letter Strip, lead the children to agree that the first letter to be named and sought is *A*.
  - Have the person in charge of each group announce the *A*.
  - Everyone in the group (including the person "in charge") is then to start chanting *A*: "A-A-A-A-..." and to look among the cards laid out for the *A*.
- When any child sees the card with the *A*
  - He or she is *not* to touch it or to give away where it is. Instead, the child should do the following:
    - Announce, "I see the *A*!"
    - Raise his or her hand (and keep it raised)
    - Return to chanting, "A-A-A-A-...," while teammates continue looking for the letter

---

TEACHER NOTE

The letter naming and chanting during these games is intended to boost learning in two ways: 1) It adds a whole-group recall requirement, rather like playing "flashcard" games; and 2) it helps to keep all of the children engaged (and allows you to see who is not engaged more easily).

- Lead the students to play the first round, searching for the uppercase *A*, as explained.
- As soon as everybody in a group has spotted the *A* and all hands are raised,
  - The person in charge chooses somebody to point to the card and ask if everyone else in the group agrees
    - If there is any disagreement, then the group must work together to resolve which is the correct card.

- When there is full agreement, the person in charge places the Letter Card with the *A* on the Blank Alphabet Strip beneath its twin.
- Once the Letter Card has been placed, the next student is in charge, and the next round begins.
  - Ask who is now in charge of each group.
    - Ask what letter the person in charge will announce for this round.
    - Confirm that it is *B* because *B* is the next unmatched letter.
    - Lead the groups to play the *B* round.
- Have the groups play the *C* round; monitor to see if more clarification is needed.
- By the end of the *C* round, the children should know how to play without help.
  - Tell them to keep going until they have laid out the entire first half of the alphabet.
  - Wander among groups as the children play to praise the children's progress and to see if there are problems.

MANAGEMENT TIP

Wandering from group to group during these small-group activities is invaluable. Beyond allowing you to help with the games, it will give you a special opportunity to learn about the strengths, needs, and nature of your individual students.

- As soon as any group has completed the entire array, the group members should sing the "Alphabet Song," pointing to each of the placed letters as they do.
  - Tell the children that, when you hear them singing the "Alphabet Song," you will come over to check their work.
  - If the children have any misplaced cards on the strip, remove the misplaced cards and ask the group to try again.
  - When the line-up is perfect
    - Congratulate the group
    - Ask the children to scramble the cards, lay them out again, and replay

---

INSTRUCTIONAL ALERT

Take the time needed to ensure that every child gets as much support and practice as needed to play this game with confidence and accuracy.

    As the children play this game, observe them carefully to determine

- Which children need extra support or time to become accurate and comfortable
- Which children would benefit from additional challenge

For guidance, see Hands-On Games and Individual Differences in the Unit I Introduction.

Introducing Name Poems

Objectives
- To review the "Alphabet Song"
- To introduce the Name Poems
- To give the children practice in recognizing and naming the uppercase letters

Materials
1. **"Alphabet Song" Review**

   Alphabet Frieze

   Line-by-line display of the letter lines of the "Alphabet Song" written on the board in *uppercase* letters

   (*Optional*) Music for the "Alphabet Song" (see online materials for links)

2. **Name Necklaces and Name Poems**

   Name Necklaces (one for each child)

   List of Name Poems

3. **Uppercase Letter Face-Up Match: *N–Z* (Small-Group Activity)**

   Uppercase Half-Alphabet Strip (letters *N–Z*) (one for each group)

   Blank Half-Alphabet Strip (13 squares long) (one for each group)

   Uppercase Letter Cards (letters *N–Z*, shuffled) (one set for each group)

ACTIVITIES

1. "Alphabet Song" Review
   - Write the four letter lines of the song on the board in uppercase letters:

A B C D	E F G
H I J K	L M N
O P Q	R S T
U V W	X Y Z

   - Ask the children what is written on the board. Keep probing the children for each of the following answers:
     - The **alphabet**
     - The **uppercase** letters
   - Review the "Alphabet Song" line by line as in Lesson 2, Activity 1.1.
   - Sing the entire "Alphabet Song"
     - At least once while pointing to the uppercase letters written on the board
     - At least once while pointing to the letter pairs on the Alphabet Frieze

2. Name Necklaces and Name Poems
   - Ask the children if anybody knows how to spell his or her own name.
     - Call on a few volunteers to spell their names, and lead the class to agree that this is very impressive as well as very important.
     - Tell them that it is time for all of them to learn how to spell their names.

LESSON 3

2.1. Name Necklaces

- Distribute the Name Necklaces, giving each to its owner.
- Ask the children what they see, making sure that they all understand that it is their own name that is printed on the necklace.
- Ask the children to turn the Name Necklace over to see that their names are printed on both sides. Ask them why that might be.
- Ask the children to put their Name Necklaces on, and to check out each other's names.
- Ask the children to hold the Name Necklaces straight out away from their necks (not turning the cards over). Ask them what they see.
  - Explain that if they want to see their own names, they can hold out their Name Necklaces and look.

2.2. Introducing the Name Poems

Name Poems are a catchy way for children to remember how to spell their names. The following are examples of Name Poems, and more poem frameworks are provided online.

J' - O **C'** - E **L'** - **Y'** **N'** ! That's how You spell Jocelyn !	Can I spell my name? Oh Yes! It's **C'** - A **S'** - S **I'** - U **S'** !	**A'** - L **F'** - R **E'** - D **O'** ! I can spell it Fast or slow !

- Choose one student's Name Poem from your List of Name Poems.
  - Call on the child to whom it belongs, and borrow his or her Name Necklace.
    - Spell the child's name while pointing to each letter on the Name Necklace.
    - Tell the children that you have a special way for them to learn how to spell their own names: You have a Name Poem for each of them.
    - Recite the selected child's Name Poem while pointing to the letters on the child's Name Necklace.
  - To lead the child to do it with you,
    - Give the Name Necklace back
    - Ask the child to recite his or her Name Poem with you, pointing to each of the letters on the Name Necklace as they are said
    - Ask the child to put the Name Necklace on again and to hold it out so that he or she can see the name printed on its backside
    - Ask the child to repeat his or her Name Poem with you, this time pointing to each letter on the backside of the card while saying it
- To teach every child his or her Name Poem
  - With the whole group still gathered, teach Name Poems to two more children

- Explain that over the next several days, you will visit with each child to teach the child his or her own Name Poem (*Note*: Teach the Name Poems during the small-group activities.)

MANAGEMENT ALERT

- As the children play, call out individual children who still need to learn their Name Poems.
- Aim to teach at least one third of the children their Name Poems in one day.
- Keep track of which Name Poems have been reviewed and which ones still need to be taught using the List of Name Poems.
- Collect the Name Necklaces at the end of the day.

---

3. Uppercase Letter Face-Up Match: *N–Z*

   3.1. Game Set-Up

   - Divide the children into groups of three or four; ask each group to sit in a semicircle.
     - Give each group an Uppercase Half-Alphabet Strip for the letters *N–Z*, and tell the children to place it before them so that it is right-side up and can be easily seen by everyone in their group.
       - Explain that what they see on the strip is the second half of the Alphabet Strip, the letters *N* through *Z*.
     - Give each group one Blank Half-Alphabet Strip (with 13 squares), and tell the children to place it just beneath and in alignment with the Uppercase Half-Alphabet Strip.
     - Give each group one complete shuffled set of 13 Uppercase Letter Cards, including one card for each of the letters *N–Z*.
       - Ask the children to look at the cards to see that each card shows one **uppercase** letter.
       - Tell the children to lay all 13 of their Uppercase Letter Cards face up in the space between themselves and the two aligned strips.

   3.2. Game Play

   - Remind the children how to play (see Lesson 2, Activity 2.2).
     - Ask who is in charge first in each group. (In-charge students should raise their hands.)
     - Remind children to chant each letter name until everyone in the group has spotted the letter.

TEACHER NOTE

The letter naming and chanting during these games is intended to boost learning in two ways:
1) It adds a whole-group recall requirement, rather like playing "flashcard" games; and 2) it helps to keep all of the children engaged (and allows you to see who is not engaged more easily).

   - As soon as any group has completed the entire array, group members should sing the "Alphabet Song," pointing to each of the placed letters as they do.
     - Tell the children that when you hear them singing the "Alphabet Song," you will come over to check their work.

- If the children have any misplaced cards on the strip, remove the misplaced cards and ask the group to try again.

- When the line-up is perfect, ask the children to scramble the Letter Cards, lay them out again, and replay the game.

INSTRUCTIONAL ALERT

Take the time needed to ensure that every child gets as much support and practice as needed to play this game with confidence and accuracy.

As the children play this game, observe them carefully to determine

- Which children need extra support or time to become accurate and comfortable

- Which children would benefit from additional challenge

For guidance, see Unit I, Introduction, Hands-On Games and Individual Differences.

Uppercase Letter Draw with Duplicates: *A–M*

Objectives	• To review the "Alphabet Song" • To continue sharing individual Name Poems • To give the children more practice in recognizing and naming the uppercase letters
Materials	**1. Sing as I Point** Line-by-line display of the letter lines of the "Alphabet Song" written on the board in *uppercase* letters **2. Name Necklaces and Name Poems** Name Necklaces (one for each student) List of Name Poems **3. Uppercase Letter Draw with Duplicates: *A–M* (Small-Group Activity)** Uppercase Half-Alphabet Strip (letters *A–M*) (one for each group) Blank Half-Alphabet Strip (13 squares long) (one for each group) Uppercase Letter Cards (two or more copies of letters *A–M*, shuffled) (one set for each group)

ACTIVITIES

1. Sing as I Point

   1.1. Review the "Alphabet Song"

   • Sing the "Alphabet Song" together as a warm-up.

   1.2. Introduce the Sing as I Point Game

   The goal of this game is to lead the children to think about the alphabet as a set of separate letters rather than as one long, multisyllabic rant. To make the game work best, be playful, giving children time to anticipate and think about the name of the different letters before touching the letters.

   • Ask the children to sing the "Alphabet Song" again as you point to the letters, except that this time they will not sing any letter until you actually point to it.

      • Lift your finger away between letters, moving it very slowly from letter to letter, thus leading the children to leave real space between the letter names as they sing them.

         • Repeat the song again, keeping the basic pace nice and slow as before, but every now and then vary the pace unpredictably.

      • Remind the children that they will sing each letter *only when* you point to it.

2. Name Necklaces and Name Poems

   • Distribute the Name Necklaces to the children.

   • Ask the children to raise their hands if they have been taught their Name Poem.

      • Call on a few volunteers to recite their Name Poems.

- Tell the children who have not yet been taught their own Name Poem that more Name Poems will be taught today.

MANAGEMENT ALERT

- As the children play, call out individual children who still need to learn their Name Poems.
- Aim to teach at least one third of the children their Name Poems in one day.
- Keep track of which Name Poems have been reviewed and which ones still need to be taught using the List of Name Poems.
- Collect the Name Necklaces at the end of the day.

---

3. Uppercase Letter Draw with Duplicates: *A–M*

   3.1. Game Set-Up

- Divide the children into groups of three or four; ask each group to sit in a semicircle.
  - Give each group an Uppercase Half-Alphabet Strip for the letters *A–M*, and tell the children to place the strip before them so that it is right-side up and can be easily seen by everyone in their group.
    - Explain that what they see on the strip is the first half of the alphabet, the letters *A* through *M*.
  - Give each group a Blank Half-Alphabet Strip (with 13 squares), and tell the children to place it just beneath and in alignment with the Uppercase Half-Alphabet Strip.
  - Give each group one shuffled stack of Uppercase Letter Cards, including two or more cards for each of the letters *A–M*.
    - Ask the children to look at the cards to see that each card shows one uppercase letter.
  - Tell the children to place the stack face down in the middle of their group.

   3.2. Game Play

- Explain how to play the Letter Draw game.
  - The first child in charge should
    - Choose one of the face-down cards
    - Hold the card up for the others to name and chant
    - Place the card on the Blank Alphabet Strip beneath its match
  - Warn the children that there may be more than one card for each letter. When an extra card is found, the children should stack the new card on top of its twin.
  - The children who are not in charge for each round should provide help when needed by chanting the letter's name
    - More quickly and loudly as the person in charge moves the letter closer to its correct spot
    - More slowly and softly whenever the person in charge moves the letter farther from its correct spot

- After each card is placed, the next child is then in charge, similarly choosing a card, holding it up for the others to name and chant, and then placing it on the Blank Alphabet Strip beneath its match.

- Play continues until all of the cards have been placed in their proper position on the Blank Alphabet Strip.

- As soon as the children in any group finish placing all of the cards, they should sing the "Alphabet Song," pointing to each letter, until you come to inspect.

- If there is time, they should move all of the cards back in the draw pile, face down, and play the game again.

- Remind the children that, when they have completed their arrangement, they should sing the "Alphabet Song" while pointing to each letter so that you know they are ready for you.

TEACHER NOTE

The letter naming and chanting during these games is intended to boost learning in two ways: 1) It adds a whole-group recall requirement, rather like playing "flashcard" games; and 2) it helps to keep all of the children engaged (and allows you to see who is not engaged more easily).

LESSON 5 Uppercase Letter Draw with Duplicates: *N–Z*

Objectives	• To review the "Alphabet Song" and the names and shapes of the uppercase letters
	• To teach a Name Poem to any children still without one
	• To give the children more practice with the names and shapes of the uppercase letters

Materials

1. Sing It Soft, Sing It Loud Game

Alphabet Frieze

Line-by-line display of the letter lines of the "Alphabet Song" written on the board in uppercase letters

2. Name Necklaces and Name Poems

Name Necklaces (one for each student)

List of Name Poems

3. Uppercase Letter Draw with Duplicates: *N–Z* (Small-Group Activity)

Uppercase Half-Alphabet Strip (letters *N–Z*) (one for each group)

Blank Half-Alphabet Strip (13 squares long) (one for each group)

Uppercase Letter Cards (two or more copies of letters *N–Z*, shuffled) (one set for each group)

ACTIVITIES

1. Sing It Soft, Sing It Loud Game

   1.1. Review the "Alphabet Song"

   • Sing the "Alphabet Song" together as a warm-up.

   1.2. Review Sing as I Point

   • Play the Sing as I Point game.

     • Remind the children how to play: Sing the "Alphabet Song," taking care to sing each letter when you actually point to it.

       • Lift your finger between letters, moving it slowly to the next, leading the children to leave real space between the letter names as they sing them.

   1.3. Sing It Soft, Sing It Loud

   As with Sing as I Point, the goal of this game is to lead the children to think about the alphabet as a set of separate letters. This game is a bit livelier for the children, making it easier to discern which children are most and least confident with letter names. Again, to make the game work best, be playful, giving the children time to anticipate and think about the names of the different letters before touching the letters.

   • Sing It Soft

     • This game is conducted exactly like Sing as I Point, except for the following:

- Point to each letter with your *pinkie* finger.
- The children sing each letter in a soft, gentle voice when you point to it.
- Sing It Loud
    - This game is conducted exactly like Sing as I Point, except for the following:
        - Point to each letter with your *thumb.*
        - The children sing each letter in a loud, booming voice when you point to it.
- Sing It Soft, Sing It Loud
    - This game also is conducted like Sing as I Point, except for the following:
        - Pointing to any letter with your pinkie makes the children sing the letter in their soft, gentle voices.
        - Pointing to any letter with your thumb makes the children sing the letter in their loud, booming voices.
- First Play
    - Use your *pinkie* for most of the letters, switching to your *thumb* only occasionally.
- Second Play
    - Use your *thumb* for most of the letters, switching to your *pinkie* only occasionally.
- Subsequent Play
    - Once the children have basically learned how to play the game,
        - Surprise the children; keep the overall pace slow enough for them to look and think about each letter to come, but vary the timing to tease them
        - Make a mental note of any children who err audibly, as this set of children will include those who still need work on recognizing and naming the uppercase letters

2. Name Necklaces and Name Poems

- Distribute the Name Necklaces to the children.
- Ask the children to raise their hands if they have been taught their Name Poem.
    - Call on a few volunteers to recite their Name Poems.
    - Tell the children who have not yet been taught their Name Poem that the rest of the poems will be taught today.

MANAGEMENT ALERT

- As the children play, share Name Poems with any individuals who have not learned theirs yet.
- Aim to finish teaching all of the Name Poems today.
- Collect the Name Necklaces at the end of the day.

---

3. Uppercase Letter Draw with Duplicates: *N–Z*

3.1. Game Set-Up

- Divide the children into groups of three or four; ask each group to sit in a semicircle.

- Give each group an Uppercase Half-Alphabet Strip for the letters *N–Z*, and tell the children to place the strip before them so that it is right-side up and can be easily seen by everyone in their group.
  - Explain that what they see on the strip is the second half of the alphabet, the letters *N* through *Z*.
- Give each group a Blank Half-Alphabet Strip (with 13 squares), and tell the children to place it just beneath and in alignment with the Uppercase Half-Alphabet Strip.
- Give each group one shuffled stack of Uppercase Letter Cards, including two or more cards for each of the letters *N–Z*.
  - Ask the children to look at the cards to see that each card shows one **uppercase** letter.
  - Tell the children to place the stack face down in the middle of their group.

3.2. Game Play

- Explain how to play the Letter Draw game.
  - The first child in charge should
    - Choose one of the face-down cards
    - Hold the card up for the others to name and chant
    - Place the card on the Blank Alphabet Strip beneath its match
  - Warn the children that there may be more than one card for each letter. When an extra card is found, the children should stack the new card on top of its twin.
  - The children who are not in charge for each round should provide help when needed by chanting the letter's name
    - More quickly and loudly as the person in charge moves the letter closer to its correct spot
    - More slowly and softly as the person in charge moves the letter farther from its correct spot
  - After each card is placed, the next child is then in charge, similarly choosing a card, holding it up for the others to name and chant, and then placing it on the Blank Alphabet Strip beneath its match.
  - Play continues until all of the cards have been placed in their proper position on the Blank Alphabet Strip.
  - As soon as a group finishes placing all of the cards, the children should sing the "Alphabet Song," pointing to each letter, until you come to inspect.
  - If there is time, children should move all of the cards back in the draw pile, face down, and play again.
  - Remind the children to sing the "Alphabet Song" while pointing to each letter when they have completed the arrangement so you will know they are ready for you.

Uppercase Letter Face-Up Match: *A–Z*

Objectives
- To review the "Alphabet Song" and the names and shapes of the uppercase letters
- To give the children special practice with their Name Poems
- To give the children more practice with the names and shapes of the uppercase letters

Materials

1. **Sing It Soft, Sing It Loud**

   Alphabet Frieze

   Line-by-line display of the letter lines of the "Alphabet Song" written on the board in uppercase letters

2. **Name Necklaces and Name Poems**

   Name Necklaces (one for each student)

   List of Name Poems

3. **Uppercase Letter Face-Up Match: *A–Z* (Small-Group Activity)**

   Uppercase Full-Alphabet Strip (letters *A–Z*) (one for each group)

   Blank Full-Alphabet Strip (26 squares long) (one for each group)

   Uppercase Letter Cards (letters *A–Z*) (one set for each group)

4. **"Alphabet Bounce" Song**

   Alphabet Frieze

   Line-by-line display of the lines of the "Alphabet Bounce" song written on the board in uppercase letters.

   (*Optional*) Music for the "Alphabet Bounce" song (see online materials for links)

ACTIVITIES

1. Sing It Soft, Sing It Loud

   1.1. Review the "Alphabet Song"

   - Sing the "Alphabet Song" together as a warm-up.

   1.2. Review Sing as I Point

   - Play the Sing as I Point game.
     - Remind the children how to play: Sing the "Alphabet Song," taking care to sing each letter when you actually point to it.
       - Lift your finger between letters, moving it slowly to the next, leading the children to leave real space between the letter names as they sing them.

   1.3. Review Sing It Soft, Sing It Loud

   - Remind the children how to play the game.
     - As in Sing as I Point, they should sing the "Alphabet Song," taking care to sing each letter when you actually point to it.
       - Pointing to a letter with your pinkie means children are to sing it in a soft, gentle voice.

- Pointing to a letter with your thumb means the children are to sing out the letter's name in a loud, booming voice.
  - Play Sing It Soft, Sing It Loud several times, getting more playful as the children become more comfortable.

2. Name Necklaces and Name Poems
   - Distribute the Name Necklaces to the children.
     - Call on a few volunteers to recite their Name Poems.
     - Ask the children if they have shared their Name Poems with their parents and, if so, ask how their parents responded.

2.1. Sharing (Practicing) Name Poems
   - Tell the children that their challenge right now is to share their Name Poem with every one of their classmates.
     - Each child should turn to another student.
       - One child should recite his or her Name Poem for the other, pointing to each letter on his or her Name Necklace when naming it.
       - The second child should then do the same for the first.
       - Each child should then find somebody else to partner with and repeat the sharing.
     - If there is any child who has not yet learned his or her Name Poem, teach the child now. Then, ask the child to join the others in the Name Poem sharing activity.

3. Uppercase Letter Face-Up Match: *A–Z*

3.1. Game Set-Up
   - Divide the children into groups of three or four; ask each group to sit in a semicircle.
     - Give each group an Uppercase Full-Alphabet Strip (letters *A–Z*), and tell the children to place the strip before them so that it is right-side up and can be easily seen by everyone in their group.
     - Give each group a Blank Full-Alphabet Strip (with 26 squares), and tell the children to place it just beneath and in alignment with the Uppercase Full-Alphabet Strip.
     - Give each group a shuffled set of 26 Uppercase Letter Cards, including one card for each of the letters *A–Z*.
       - Ask the children to lay the cards out face-up in the middle of their group.

3.2. Game Play
   - Remind the children how to play the Match game.
     - The goal of the game is to place every one of the Letter Cards on the Blank Alphabet Strip beneath its match.
     - The person in charge for each group names the letter that everybody must search for.
       - Everyone in the group (including the person in charge) starts chanting, "A-A-A-A-...," and looks among the cards laid out for the *A*.
     - When any child sees the card with the *A*, he or she
       - Does *not* touch it or give away where it is

- Raises a hand (and keeps it raised)
- Continues chanting the letter's name while teammates continue looking for the letter
- When all hands are raised, the person in charge chooses somebody to point to the card and asks if everyone else in the group agrees.
  - If there is any disagreement, then the group must work together to resolve which is the correct card.
  - When there is full agreement, the person in charge places the Letter Card with the *A* on the Blank Alphabet Strip beneath its twin.
- Once the Letter Card has been placed, the next student is in charge, and the next round begins.
- As soon as any group has completed the entire array, the children should sing the "Alphabet Song," pointing to each of the placed letters as they do.
  - Tell the children that, when you hear them singing the "Alphabet Song," you will come over to check their work.
  - If the children have any misplaced cards on the strip, remove the misplaced cards and ask the group to try again.
  - When the line-up is perfect, the group should scramble the cards, lay them out, and play again.

4. "Alphabet Bounce" Song

- On the board (easel, projection screen) display the lines of "Alphabet Bounce" for the children.

Alphabet Bounce

(To the tune of "Jimmy Crack Corn")

A B C D	E F G
H I J K	L M N
O P Q R	S T U
V W	X Y Z

- The children should jump on every letter and beat.
- After Z, they should clap and sing again.
- Sing the song a bit faster each time through.

TEACHER TIP

"Alphabet Bounce" can be useful any time the children need to burn off a little energy.

Introducing the Lowercase Letters

LESSON 1 · Lowercase Letter Face-Up Match: *a–m*

Objectives
- To review the uppercase letters
- To introduce the lowercase letters
- To provide practice in naming and recognizing the lowercase letters

Materials

1. **Review the Uppercase Letters**

   Line-by-line display of the "Alphabet Song," written in uppercase letters on the board

   (*Optional*) Music for the "Alphabet Bounce" song (see online materials for links)

2. **Introduce the Lowercase Letters**

   Alphabet Frieze

   Line-by-line display of the "Alphabet Song" written in lowercase letters beside the uppercase letter display

   (*Optional*) Music for the "Alphabet Song" (see online materials for links)

3. **Lowercase Letter Face-Up Match: *a–m* (Small-Group Activity)**

   Lowercase Half-Alphabet Strip (letters *a–m*) (one for each group)

   Blank Half-Alphabet Strip (13 squares) (one for each group)

   Lowercase Letter Cards (letters *a–m*) (one set for each group)

ACTIVITIES

1. Review the Uppercase Letters
   - Open with a few rounds of "Alphabet Bounce."
   - Review the "Alphabet Song" with uppercase letters to set off the introduction of the lowercase letters.
     - Write the letter lines of the "Alphabet Song" on the board in uppercase letters.
     - Ask the children to sing the song with you as you point to the letters.

2. Introduce the Lowercase Letters

- Write the letter lines from the "Alphabet Song" on the board in lowercase letters, next to the letter lines in uppercase letters:

A B C D	E F G	a b c d	e f g
H I J K	L M N	h i j k	l m n
O P Q	R S T	o p q	r s t
U V W	X Y Z	u v w	x y z

- Ask the children to compare the new set of letter lines with the **uppercase** set already on the board and tell how the new one is different.

    - Make sure they understand that the letters in the first set are **uppercase** and those in the second set are **lowercase.**

    - Calling on several individuals as well as the group as a whole, point to each set and ask what kind of letters. Make sure that the children voice the answers—**lowercase** and **uppercase**—several times.

- Direct their attention back to the Alphabet Frieze, and remind the children that every letter has two different shapes.

    - They have been learning the **uppercase** letters.

    - Now it is time for them to learn the **lowercase** letters.

2.1. Sing the "Alphabet Song": Lowercase Letters

- Review the "Alphabet Song" line by line as in Lesson 2 but use the *lowercase* letters that are written on the board.

- Have the children sing the "Alphabet Song" with you

    - At least once while pointing to the *lowercase* letter lines written on board

    - At least once while pointing to the letter pairs on the Alphabet Frieze

3. Lowercase Letter Face-Up Match: *a–m*

3.1. Game Set-Up

- Have the children gather into groups of three or four.

- Give each group a Lowercase Half-Alphabet Strip for the letters *a–m*, and tell the children to place it before them so that it is right-side up and easily seen by everyone in their group.

- Give each group a Blank Half-Alphabet Strip (with 13 squares), and tell the children to place it just beneath and in alignment with the Lowercase Half-Alphabet Strip.

- Give each group a shuffled set of 13 Lowercase Letter Cards, including one card for each of the letters *a–m*.

    - Ask the children to look at the cards to see that each card shows one **lowercase** letter.

    - Tell the children to lay all 13 of their Lowercase Letter Cards face up in the space between themselves and the two aligned strips.

3.2. Game Play

- Tell the children that today's game is Lowercase Letter Face-Up Match. Explain that it is played the same way as Uppercase Letter Face-Up Match but with the lowercase letters.

- The person in charge for each group names the first letter of the alphabet that has not yet been matched.
- Everyone in the group chants the name of the letter (e.g., "a-a-a-a-...,") while searching among the cards for the *a*.
- When the children see the *a*, they do not touch it. They just say, "I see the *a*," raise their hand, and go back to chanting, "a-a-a-a-...."
- As soon as everybody in the group has spotted the target card,
  - The person in charge chooses somebody to point to the card and asks if everyone else in the group agrees
    - If there is any disagreement, then the group must work together to resolve which is the correct card.
    - When all agree, the person in charge places the Letter Card on the Blank Alphabet Strip beneath its twin.
- Once the Letter Card is placed, the next student is in charge, and the next round begins.
- The game continues until the group has laid out all of the letter cards, *a–m*.
- As soon as any group has completed the entire array, the group members should sing the "Alphabet Song," pointing to each of the placed letters as they do.
  - Tell the children that, when you hear them singing the "Alphabet Song," you will come over to check their work.
  - If the children have any misplaced cards on the strip, remove the misplaced cards and ask the group to try again.
  - When the line-up is perfect
    - Congratulate the group
    - Ask the children to scramble the cards, lay them out again, and replay

---

INSTRUCTIONAL TIP
Because the lowercase letters are more difficult, make time for every group to play the game at least twice.

INSTRUCTIONAL ALERT
Take the time needed to ensure that every child gets as much support and practice as needed to play this game with confidence and accuracy.
   As the children play this game, observe them carefully to determine
- Which children need extra support or time to become accurate and comfortable
- Which children would benefit from additional challenge
For guidance, see Hands-On Games and Individual Differences in the Unit I Introduction.

LESSON 2 ❯ Lowercase Letter Face-Up Match: *n–z*

Objectives	• To review the names and shapes of the lowercase letters
	• To give the children more hands-on practice with the lowercase letters

Materials
1. **Sing as I Point Game with Lowercase Letters**
   Alphabet Frieze
   Line-by-line display of the "Alphabet Song," written in lowercase letters on the board
   (*Optional*) Music for the "Alphabet Song" (see online materials for links)
2. **Lowercase Letter Face-Up Match: *n–z* (Small-Group Activity)**
   Lowercase Half-Alphabet Strip (letters *n–z*) (one for each group)
   Blank Half-Alphabet Strip (13 squares) (one for each group)
   Lowercase Letter Cards (letters *n–z*, shuffled) (one set for each group)

ACTIVITIES

1. Sing as I Point Game with Lowercase Letters
   - Direct the children's attention to the Alphabet Frieze and remind them that every letter has two different shapes.
     - Before, they were learning the *uppercase* letters.
     - Now, they are working on the *lowercase* letters.
   - Write the letter lines from the "Alphabet Song" on the board in lowercase letters.

a b c d	e f g
h i j k	l m n
o p q	r s t
u v w	x y z

   - Play Sing as I Point.
     - Remind the children how to play: They will sing the "Alphabet Song," taking care to sing each letter when you actually point to it.
       - Lift your finger between letters, moving it *slowly* to the next, leading the children to leave real space between the letter names as they sing them.

2. Lowercase Letter Face-Up Match: *n–z*
   2.1. Game Set-Up
     - Have the children gather into groups of three or four.
       - Give each group a Lowercase Half-Alphabet Strip for the letters *n–z*, and tell the children to place it before them so that is right-side up and easily seen by everyone in their group.
       - Give each group a Blank Half-Alphabet Strip (with 13 squares), and tell the children to place it just beneath and in alignment with the Lowercase Half-Alphabet Strip.

43

- Give each group a shuffled set of 13 Lowercase Letter Cards, including one card for each of the letters *n–z*.
  - Ask them to look at the cards to see that each card shows one lowercase letter.
  - Tell the children to lay all 13 of their Lowercase Letter Cards face-up in the space between themselves and the two aligned strips.

2.2. Game Play

- Remind the children how to play.
  - Ask who is in charge first in each group (raise hands).
  - Remind them that all will chant each letter name until everyone in the group has spotted the letter.
- Remind them that, when they have completed their arrangement, they should sing the "Alphabet Song" while pointing to each letter so that you will know they are ready for you to check their work.
- After you check their work, ask the children to scramble the Letter Cards, lay them out again, and replay the game.

INSTRUCTIONAL TIP
Because the lowercase letters are more difficult, make time for every group to play at least twice.

INSTRUCTIONAL ALERT
Take the time needed to ensure that every child gets as much support and practice as needed to play this game with confidence and accuracy.

As the children play this game, observe them carefully to determine

- Which children need extra support or time to become accurate and comfortable
- Which children would benefit from additional challenge

For guidance, see Hands-On Games and Individual Differences in the Unit I Introduction.

> **LESSON 3** Lowercase Letter
> Draw with Duplicates: *a–m*

Objectives	• To review the names and shapes of the lowercase letters
	• To give the children more hands-on practice with the lowercase letters

Materials
1. **Sing It Soft, Sing It Loud Game with Lowercase Letters**
   Alphabet Frieze
   Letter lines of the "Alphabet Song" written on the board in lowercase letters
2. **Lowercase Letter Draw with Duplicates: *a–m***
   Lowercase Half-Alphabet Strip (letters *a–m*) (one for each group)
   Blank Half-Alphabet Strip (one for each group)
   Lowercase Letter Cards (at least two cards for letters *a–m*, shuffled) (one set per group)

ACTIVITIES

1. Sing It Soft, Sing It Loud Game with Lowercase Letters
   - Write the letter lines from the "Alphabet Song" on the board in *lowercase* letters:

a b c d	e f g
h i j k	l m n
o p q	r s t
u v w	x y z

   - Ask the children what kinds of letters are written on the board. Have them repeat the answer: *lowercase* letters.
   - Remind the children how to play the Sing It Soft, Sing It Loud game.
     - Children sing the "Alphabet Song," taking care to sing each letter when you actually point to it.
     - Pointing to a letter with your pinkie means children sing it in a soft, gentle voice.
     - Pointing to a letter with your thumb means children sing in a loud, booming voice.
   - Play Sing It Soft, Sing It Loud several times, getting more playful as the children become more comfortable.

2. Lowercase Letter Draw with Duplicates: *a–m*
   2.1. Game Set-Up
   - Have the children gather into groups of three or four.
     - Give each group a Lowercase Half-Alphabet Strip for the letters *a–m*, and tell the children to place it before them so that it is right-side up and easily seen by everyone in their group.
     - Give each group a Blank Half-Alphabet Strip (with 13 squares), and tell the children to place it just beneath and in alignment with the Lowercase Half-Alphabet Strip.

- Give each group a shuffled stack of Lowercase Letter Cards that includes at least two cards for each of the letters *a–m*.
- The children may put the cards in a stack, like a draw pile, or they may spread them out, face down.

2.2. Game Play

- Remind the children how to play.
  - The child in charge
    - Chooses one of the face-down cards
    - Holds the card up for the others to name
    - Places the card on the Blank Half-Alphabet Strip beneath its match
  - The next child is then in charge and chooses a card, holds it up for the others to name, and then places it on the Blank Half-Alphabet Strip beneath its match.
- Tell the children the following:
  - Their card set only includes the letters *a–m*.
  - Their card set includes more than one copy of each letter. Duplicate Letter Cards should be stacked on the Blank Half-Alphabet Strip beneath their match and on top of their twin.
- Play continues until each of the cards in the draw pile has been placed in its proper position on the Blank Half-Alphabet Strip.
- If the children finish early, they can move all of the cards back into the draw pile, face down, and play again.

INTERVENTION NOTE

Once the children are busy playing the game, take the opportunity to work intensively with students who need more help in learning to name and recognize the letters.

 Lowercase Letter
Draw with Duplicates: *n–z*

Objectives • To review the names and shapes of the lowercase letters

• To give the children more hands-on practice with the lowercase letters

Materials **1. Sing It Soft, Sing It Loud Game with Lowercase Letters**

Alphabet Frieze

Letter lines of the "Alphabet Song" written on the board in lowercase letters

2. Lowercase Letter Draw with Duplicates: *n–z*

Lowercase Half-Alphabet Strip (letters *n–z*) (one for each group)

Blank Half-Alphabet Strip (one for each group)

Lowercase Letter Cards (at least two cards for letters *n–z*, shuffled) (one set for each group)

ACTIVITIES

1. Sing It Soft, Sing It Loud Game with Lowercase Letters

   • Write the letter lines from the "Alphabet Song" on the board in lowercase letters:

a b c d	e f g
h i j k	l m n
o p q	r s t
u v w	x y z

   • Lead the children in singing the "Alphabet Song"

     • At least once while pointing to the lowercase letters on the board

     • Again while pointing to the letter pairs on the Alphabet Frieze

   • Remind the children how to play Sing It Soft, Sing It Loud.

     • Pointing to a letter with your pinkie means children sing it in a soft, gentle voice.

     • Pointing to a letter with your thumb means children sing in a loud, booming voice.

   • Using the lowercase letter lines written on the board, lead the children in Sing It Soft, Sing It Loud.

2. Lowercase Letter Draw with Duplicates: *n–z*

   2.1. Game Set-Up

     • Have the children gather into groups of three or four.

       • Give each group a Lowercase Half-Alphabet Strip (letters *n–z*), and tell the children to place it before them so that it is right-side up and easily seen by everyone in their group.

       • Give each group a Blank Half-Alphabet Strip (with 13 squares), and tell the children to place it just beneath and in alignment with the Lowercase Half-Alphabet Strip.

       • Give each group a shuffled set of Lowercase Letter Cards including at least two cards for each of the letters *n–z*.

       • Tell the children to place the stack of cards face down in the center of their group.

2.2. Game Play

- Remind the children how to play Letter Draw with Duplicates.
    - The child in charge
        - Chooses one of the face-down cards
        - Holds the card up for the others to name
        - Places the card on the Blank Half-Alphabet Strip beneath its twin
    - The next child is then in charge and chooses a card, holds it up for the others to name, and then places it on the Blank Half-Alphabet Strip beneath its twin.
- Tell the children the following:
    - Their card set only includes the letters *n–z*.
    - Their card set includes more than one copy of each letter. Duplicate Letter Cards should be stacked on the Blank Half-Alphabet Strip beneath their match and on top of their twin.
- Play continues until each of the cards in their draw pile have been placed in the proper position on the Blank Half-Alphabet Strip.
- If the children finish early, they can move all of the cards back into the draw pile, face down, and play again.

INTERVENTION NOTE
Once the children are busy playing the game, take the opportunity to work intensively with students who need more help in learning to name and recognize the letters.

Lowercase Letter Face-Up Match: *a–z*

Objectives	• To review the names and shapes of the lowercase letters
	• To give the children hands-on practice with whole lowercase alphabet

Materials	**1. Say as I Point Game with Lowercase Letters**
	Alphabet Frieze
	Letter lines of "Alphabet Song" written on the board in lowercase letters
	2. Lowercase Letter Face-Up Match: *a–z*
	Lowercase Full-Alphabet Strip (letters *a–z*) (one for each group)
	Blank Full-Alphabet Strip (one for each group)
	Lowercase Letter Cards (letters *a–z*) (one set for each group)

ACTIVITIES

1. Say as I Point Game with Lowercase Letters
   - Write the letter lines from the "Alphabet Song" on the board in lowercase letters:

a b c d	e f g
h i j k	l m n
o p q	r s t
u v w	x y z

   - Play Sing as I Point.
     - Remind the children how to play: They will sing the "Alphabet Song," taking care to sing each letter when you actually point to it.
       - Lift your finger between letters, moving it *slowly* to the next, leading the children to leave real space between the letter names as they sing them.
   - Introduce Say as I Point.
     - Tell the children that you think it's time to play this game without singing: Same game but no singing.
       - Explain that instead of singing the name of each letter, they will *say* it when you point to it.
     - For first play,
       - Point to the letters in alphabetical order, just as you would if singing the song
       - Lift your finger between letters, moving it *slowly* to the next, leading the children to leave real space between the letter names as they say them
     - Play again, but this time make the game more challenging. For example, sometimes move your finger to
       - Repeat letter pairs or triples
       - Skip one or more letter
       - Name the letters in a line from last to first

2. Lowercase Letter Face-Up Match: *a–z*

   2.1. Game Set-Up

- Have the children gather into groups of three or four.
  - Give each group a Lowercase Full-Alphabet Strip (letters *a–z*), and tell the children to place it before them so that it is right-side up and easily seen by everyone in their group.
  - Give each group a Blank Full-Alphabet Strip (with 26 squares), and tell the children to place it just beneath and in alignment with the Lowercase Full-Alphabet Strip.
  - Give each group a shuffled set of 26 Lowercase Letter Cards, including one card for each of the letters *a–z*.
    - Ask the children to lay the cards out face-up in the middle of their group.

   2.2. Game Play

- Remind the children how to play the Match game.
  - The goal of the game is to place each Letter Card on the Blank Full-Alphabet Strip beneath its match.
  - The person in charge for each group names the letter that everybody must search for.
  - Everyone in the group chants the name of the letter (e.g., "a-a-a-a-...") while searching among the cards for the *a*.
    - When the children see the *a*, they do not touch it. They just say, "I see the *a*," raise their hand, and go back to chanting, "a-a-a-a-...."
  - As soon as everybody in the group has spotted the target card, the person in charge chooses somebody to point to the card and asks if everyone else in the group agrees.
    - If there is any disagreement, then the group must work together to resolve which is the correct card.
    - When there is full agreement, the person in charge places the Letter Card with the *a* on the Blank Full-Alphabet Strip beneath its twin.
  - Once the Letter Card has been placed, the next student is in charge, and the next round begins.
  - As soon as any group has completed the entire array, the children should sing the "Alphabet Song," pointing to each of the placed letters as they do.
    - Tell the children that, when you hear them singing the "Alphabet Song," you will come over to check their work.
    - If the children have any misplaced cards on the strip, remove the misplaced cards and ask the group to try again.
  - When the line-up is perfect, then the group should scramble the cards, lay them out, and play again.

Introducing the Vowels

LESSON 1 ## Lowercase Letter Draw with Vowels as Wild Cards: *a–z*

Objectives	• To provide more practice in recognizing and naming the lowercase letters
	• To introduce the vowels and the "Vowel Name Song"
Materials	**1. Say as I Point Game: Lowercase Letters**
	Letter lines of the "Alphabet Song" written on the board in lowercase letters
	2. Introducing the Vowels and the "Vowel Name Song"
	Alphabet Frieze
	Board (easel, projection system)
	(*Optional*) Music for the "Vowel Name Song" (see online materials for links)
	3. Lowercase Letter Draw with Vowels as Wild Cards: *a–z* (Small-Group Activity)
	Lowercase Full-Alphabet Strip (letters *a–z*) (one for each group)
	Blank Full-Alphabet Strip (26 squares) (one for each group)
	Lowercase Letter Cards (letters *a–z*) (one set for each group)

TEACHER NOTE

The vowel pairs in the Alphabet Frieze should be visually different from the other letters. As described in the Unit 1 Introduction, they can be visually different in a number of ways, but for ease of reference, this book refers to them as red.

ACTIVITIES

1. Say as I Point Game: Lowercase Letters

   • Write the 26 lowercase letters on the board:

   a b c d e f g h i j k l m n o p q r s t u v w x y z

   • Play the Say as I Point game.

      • Remind the children that, in this game, they say the name of each letter when you point to it.

- For first play,
  - Point to the letters in alphabetical order, while singing the "Alphabet Song"
  - Lift your finger between letters, moving it *slowly* to the next, leading the children to leave real space between the letter names as they say them
- For subsequent play, make the game successively more challenging by
  - Repeating letter pairs or triples
  - Skipping one or more letters
  - Pointing to letters in random order

2. Introducing the Vowels and the "Vowel Name Song"

2.1. Introducing the Vowels

- Direct the children's attention to the Alphabet Frieze. Compare the *Ee* pair to the *Cc, Dd,* and *Ff* pairs, and ask what is different, leading the children to notice that *Ee* is red while the other letter pairs are black.
- Challenge the children to find other letter pairs that are red.
  - As each red letter is named,
    - Point to it in the Alphabet Frieze
    - Write the letter pair on the board in position until the full list of major vowels is written on the board in correct order:

    Aa   Ee   Ii   Oo   Uu

- Ask the children to name all five letters with you, left to right.
- Tell the children that the reason that these letters are printed in red on the Alphabet Frieze is that they are very special letters.
  - Explain that these five letters belong to a special group called **vowels.**
  - Make sure that the children repeat the word **vowels** several times; call on several individuals as well as the group as a whole.
    - Tell the children that they will learn more about why the vowels are special as they learn how to read and spell.
    - Right now, what's important is that they know which letters are vowels.

2.2. Teach the "Vowel Name Song"

- Tell the children about a special song to help them to remember which of the letters are vowels.
- On the board (easel, projection screen) display the full text of the "Vowel Name Song" for the children.

The Vowel Name Song
(To the tune of "Bingo")
Five vowels in the alphabet,
I'll name them all for you!
A, E, I, O, U!
A, E, I, O, U!
A, E, I, O, U!
Now you can name them, too!

- Preview
  - Sing the entire song to the children, pointing to each word (or letter) as it is named.
- Teach Lines 1–2
  - While finger-pointing to the words, sing the first two lines again.
  - Ask the children to sing the first two lines again with you twice.
- Teach Lines 3–5
  - While finger-pointing to the letters, sing Lines 3–5 for the children.
  - Ask the children to sing Lines 3–5 again with you twice.
- Teach Line 6
  - While finger-pointing to the words, sing the final line of the song for the children.
  - Ask the children to sing the final line again with you.
- Singing the Whole Song
  - Ask the children to join you in singing the whole song, beginning to end.
    - Sing it at least once while pointing to the five vowels on the board as they are named.
    - Sing it at least once while pointing to the vowel pairs in the Alphabet Frieze as they are named.

3. **Lowercase Letter Draw with Vowels as Wild Cards:** *a–z*

   3.1. **Game Set-Up**
   - Have the children gather into groups of three or four.
     - Give a Lowercase Full-Alphabet Strip (*a–z*) and a Blank Full-Alphabet Strip (with 26 squares) to each group, and ask the children to set the strips one above the other, as they did for the other alphabet games.
     - Give each group a shuffled set of Lowercase Letter Cards, and ask the children to place them in the middle of the group, face down.

   3.2. **Game Play**
   - Remind the children how to play.
     - The child in charge
       - Chooses one of the face-down cards
       - Holds the card up for the others to name
       - Places the card on the Blank Full-Alphabet Strip beneath its match
     - The next child is then in charge and chooses a card, holds it up for the others to name, and then places it on the Blank Full-Alphabet Strip beneath its twin.
     - Tell the children that there is one more special thing about today's game: Whenever somebody draws a vowel, he or she gets another turn before giving a turn to the next person.
     - Play continues until each of the cards in the draw pile has been placed in its proper position on the Blank Full-Alphabet Strip.
   - If the children in any group finish early, they move all of the cards back to the draw pile, face down, and play again.

Uppercase Letter Draw
with Vowels as Wild Cards: *A–Z*

| Objectives | • To practice with the vowels and the "Vowel Name Song" |
| | • To provide practice in recognizing and naming the uppercase letters |

Materials

1. Practicing the Vowels

Alphabet Frieze

Board (easel, projection system)

(*Optional*) Music for the "Vowel Name Song" (see online materials for links)

2. Say as I Point Game: Uppercase Letters

Letter lines of the "Alphabet Song" written on the board in uppercase letters

3. Uppercase Letter Draw with Vowels as Wild Cards: *A–Z* (Small-Group Activity)

Uppercase Full-Alphabet Strip (letters *A–Z*) (one for each group)

Blank Full-Alphabet Strip (26 squares) (one for each group)

Uppercase Letter Cards (letters *A–Z*) (one set for each group)

ACTIVITIES

1. Practicing the Vowels

   1.1. Remembering the Vowels

      • Ask the children to name the five major **vowels,** writing each pair on the board as they do so:

         Aa   Ee   Ii   Oo   Uu

   1.2. Sing the "Vowel Name Song"

      • Sing the "Vowel Name Song" with the children:

         • At least once while pointing to the vowel pairs written on the board

         • At least once while pointing to the vowel pairs in the Alphabet Frieze

   1.3. Sing It Soft, Sing It Loud: Emphasizing Vowels

      • Remind the children how to play Sing It Soft, Sing It Loud.

         • They will sing the "Alphabet Song" as you point to the letters in the Alphabet Frieze.

            • Pointing to a letter with your *pinkie* means children sing it in a soft, gentle voice.

            • Pointing to a letter with your *thumb* means children sing in a loud, booming voice.

         • Play Sing It Soft, Sing It Loud at least twice:

            • Singing the vowels softly

               • Pointing to each of the *consonants* with your *thumb*

               • Pointing to each of the *vowels* with your *pinkie*

            • Booming the vowels

               • Pointing to each of the *consonants* with your *pinkie*

               • Pointing to each of the *vowels* with your *thumb*

2. Say as I Point Game: Uppercase Letters

- Write the uppercase letters on the board:

A B C D E F G H I J K L M N O P Q R S T U V W X Y Z

- Tell the children that you think it's time to play Say as I Point.

- Remind them that, in this game, they say the name of each letter when you point to it.

- For first play,

  - Point to the letters in alphabetical order, as if singing the "Alphabet Song"

  - Lift your finger between letters, moving it *slowly* to the next, leading the children to leave real space between the letter names as they say them

- For subsequent play, make the game successively more challenging by

  - Repeating letter pairs or triples

  - Skipping one or more letters

  - Pointing to letters in backwards order

  - Pointing to the letters in random order

3. Uppercase Letter Draw with Vowels as Wild Cards: *A–Z*

3.1. Game Set-Up

- Have the children gather into groups of three or four.

  - Give one Uppercase Full-Alphabet Strip (*A–Z*) and one Blank Full-Alphabet Strip (with 26 squares) to each group, and ask the children to set them one above the other, as they did for the other alphabet games.

  - Give each group a shuffled set of Uppercase Letter Cards, and ask the children to place them in the middle of the group, face down.

3.2. Game Play

- Remind the children how to play.

  - The child in charge

    - Chooses one of the face-down cards

    - Holds the card up for the others to name

    - Places the card on the Blank Full-Alphabet Strip beneath its match

  - The next child is then in charge and chooses a card, holds it up for the others to name, and places it on the Blank Full-Alphabet Strip beneath its twin.

  - Tell the children that there is one more special thing about today's game: Whenever somebody draws a vowel, he or she gets another turn before giving the next person a turn.

  - Play continues until each of the cards in the draw pile has been placed in its proper position on the Blank Full-Alphabet Strip.

- If the children in any group finish early, they move all the cards back into the draw pile, face down, and play again.

LESSON 3 · Alphabet March

> ASSESSMENT ALERT: **The Entry-Level Uppercase Letter Writing assessment is administered in Activity 4.**

Objectives
- To practice the vowels and the "Vowel Name Song"
- To teach the "Alphabet March"
- To challenge the children to match the uppercase and lowercase letters
- To administer the Uppercase Letter Writing assessment

Materials

1. **Practicing the Vowels and the "Vowel Name Song"**
   Alphabet Frieze
   Board (easel, projection system)
   (*Optional*) Music for the "Vowel Name Song" (see online materials for links)

2. **Introduce the "Alphabet March"**
   Board (easel, projection system)

3. **Uppercase-Lowercase Draw: *Aa–Zz***
   Uppercase Full-Alphabet Strip (letters *A–Z*) (one for each group)
   Blank Full-Alphabet Strip (26 squares) (one for each group)
   Lowercase Letter Cards (letters *a–z*) (one set for each group)

4. **Entry-Level Uppercase Letter Writing Assessment (Individual Activity)**
   Uppercase Letter Writing assessment (one for each child; see Appendix A.2)
   Pencils (one for each child)

ACTIVITIES

1. Practicing the Vowels and the "Vowel Name Song"

   1.1. Remembering the Vowels
   - Ask the children to name the five major *vowels*, writing each pair on the board as they do:

     Aa   Ee   Ii   Oo   Uu

   1.2. Sing the "Vowel Name Song"
   - Sing the "Vowel Name Song" with the children
     - At least once while pointing to the vowel pairs written on the board
     - At least once while pointing to the vowel pairs in the Alphabet Frieze

   1.3. Sing It Soft, Sing It Loud: Emphasizing the Vowels
   - Lead the children in playing Sing It Soft, Sing It Loud at least twice:
     - Singing the vowels softly
       - Pointing to each of the *consonants* with your *thumb*
       - Pointing to each of the *vowels* with your *pinkie*

- Booming the vowels
  - Pointing to each of the *consonants* with your *pinkie*
  - Pointing to each of the *vowels* with your *thumb*

2. Introduce the "Alphabet March"

- Tell the children that in the next lesson, they are going to move on to learning how to write the letters.
- To celebrate, teach them the "Alphabet March."

2.1. Teach the Children to March

- Ask the children if they know what marching is.
  - Agree that it is the way soldiers or marching bands walk. To march, everybody must
    - Lift their knees high
    - Take each step at the same time and with the same foot as everybody else
  - Have the children join you in marching in place while reciting
    "Left! Left! Left–right–left!"

2.2. Teach the "Alphabet March"

- Write or display the full text of the "Alphabet March" for the children.
- Recite the whole thing while pointing to the words and marching in place.

Alphabet March

Left! Left! Left, right left!

Left! Left! Left, right left!

A! B!   C D E!

Do the Alphabet March with me!

F G H!   I J K!

Alphabetically, on our way!

L! M!   N O P!

Keep it moving, A to Z!

Q R S!   T U V!

Just four left, and they would be:

W! X!   Y! Z!

Back to the start? Most definitely!

(return to beginning)

- Ask the children to join you in reciting the first couplet (Lines 3–4) as you point to the letters and words on the board:

A! B!   C D E!

Do the Alphabet March with me!

- Repeat at least once.
- Do the same for each of the other couplets.
- Ask the children to march in place, and have them recite the whole "Alphabet March" with you, beginning to end, at least twice.

> **INSTRUCTIONAL TIP**
> From now on, engage the children in the "Alphabet March" whenever they need to go to the library, the playground, the dismissal area, or anywhere. It is good practice educationally and can help with behavior management.

3. Uppercase-Lowercase Draw: *Aa–Zz*

    3.1. Game Set-Up

      - Have the children gather into groups of three or four.
        - Give each group an Uppercase Full-Alphabet Strip, and tell the children to place it before them so that it is right-side up and easily seen by everyone in their group.
        - Give each group a Blank Full-Alphabet Strip, and tell the children to place it just beneath and in alignment with the Uppercase Full-Alphabet Strip.
        - Give each group a full, shuffled set of Lowercase Letter Cards (*a–z*), and ask the children to place it face down in the middle of their group.

    3.2. Game Play

      - Remind the children how to play.
        - The child in charge
          - Chooses one of the face-down cards
          - Holds the card up for the others to name
          - Places the card on the Blank Full-Alphabet Strip beneath its match
        - The next child is then in charge and chooses a card, holds it up for the others to name, and places it on the Blank Full-Alphabet Strip beneath its match.

> **INSTRUCTIONAL NOTE**
> Students' ability to recognize and name the letters will not be perfect as they leave this unit. It is important, however, that children are reasonably comfortable and confident with letter recognition and naming.
>
> Students who lack sufficient confidence should spend more time on those games and activities in this chapter that best address their needs.
>
> If the students would benefit from a few more days with activities in this chapter before moving on, go for it. Alternatively—or in addition—the songs and games in this chapter can be carried forward—sung and played again and again throughout the year. Indeed, doing so is good practice even for the strongest students. Note that all of the games can be replayed as is or with such modifications as duplicate Letter Cards, shorter Alphabet Strips, tournaments, contests, and so forth. Just changing which children are in which group can create new opportunities for thinking and learning.
>
> For interim evaluation of students needing extra help with letter recognition, Extra-Check Uppercase and Lowercase Letter Recognition assessments are provided in Appendix A.1.

4. Entry-Level Uppercase Letter Writing Assessment

    This is an individual activity. The purpose of this activity is to benchmark students' entry ability to write the uppercase letters in order to gauge their needs and monitor their growth. The assessment is administered before beginning Unit II: Writing Uppercase Letters.

    Students complete the Entry-Level Uppercase Letter Writing assessment on their own—without cooperation and help from their friends. The form and instructions for its administration and scoring are provided in Appendix A.2.

UNIT

II

Writing
Uppercase Letters

ASSESSMENT ALERT: The Entry-Level Uppercase Letter Writing assessment should be completed for **every** child before beginning this unit (i.e., completed at the end of Unit I).

By the end of this unit, children should be able to

■ Recognize the uppercase letters with greater speed, accuracy, and confidence

■ Write most of the uppercase letters from memory or dictation

Score the Entry-Level Uppercase Letter Writing assessment before beginning this unit to gain a sense of the students' starting levels. Regardless of where each student begins, all of the children should be able to write most of the uppercase letters of the alphabet from memory or dictation by the end of this unit. Even so, the ability to write *all* of the uppercase letters accurately and reliably will take more time and practice for most of the children. The Progress-Check Uppercase Letter Writing assessment will be administered at the end of the unit (and as needed thereafter) to gauge how much more practice each student needs.

There are several strong reasons for anchoring letter writing as soon as possible. The most obvious, of course, is to engage children in writing as soon as possible—yet students will not be able to write much as long as the letters are insecure or onerous for them. A second reason is that spelling activities, both structured and independent, are shown to be a superlative means of advancing children's phonemic awareness, their grasp of the alphabetic principle, and their internalization of spelling patterns and conventions. However, spelling activities are thwarted to the extent that children are struggling with the letters.

Even so, learning to form the letters so that they *look* right is only part of the challenge. Mature readers and writers do not "draw" letters in the way they draw faces, bunnies, or trees. Instead, each letter is tied to a highly overlearned series of movements that are executed almost automatically as people write. Thus, most people can write more legibly with their eyes closed than they can with their nondominant hand. A more important consequence is that as letter formation becomes automatic, people can devote their active attention to their message, choice of wording, and spelling as they write.

Leading children to practice a consistent set of strokes for each letter serves to accelerate the development of letter-writing automaticity. Furthermore, as the hand movements involved in writing each letter become bound to the visual representation, they serve to hasten and secure the child's ability to recognize the letters.

This being so, the letter-writing lessons presented in Unit II are designed to help children write the letters so that they look and *feel* right. The goal is to help children acquire a distinct and serviceable sequence of strokes for each letter, one that will become habitual and will assist them in remembering and producing the letter correctly and efficiently. An added advantage of such multisensory practice, of course, is that it gives you an ongoing way of monitoring children's grasp of what they are learning: You can tell how well children are (or are not) understanding by watching them in action.

The unit is divided into four chapters, each focused on one of the four basic writing strokes:

■ Chapter 4: Uppercase Letters with Vertical and Horizontal Strokes
■ Chapter 5: Uppercase Letters with Slanted Strokes
■ Chapter 6: Uppercase Letters with Loops, Humps, and Troughs
■ Chapter 7: Uppercase Letters that Start at 2 o'Clock

Each chapter begins with practice on the focal stroke itself, then works through the set of real letters that involve that stroke. In the last chapter, students wrap up the unit by writing the whole alphabet and then printing their own names in uppercase letters for Name Displays. At the very end of the unit, the children complete the Uppercase Letter Writing assessment (Progress Check) again to gauge their growth and progress.

ASSESSMENT

The Uppercase Letter Writing assessment (Entry Level) is completed *before* this unit and then readministered (Progress Check) in the last lesson of the unit to gauge progress and continuing needs.

When	Assessment	How	Resource
Prior to beginning Chapter 4	Entry-Level Uppercase Letter Writing	Whole Group	Appendix A.2
At the end of Chapter 7	Progress-Check Uppercase Letter Writing	Whole Group	Appendix A.2

HANDS-ON GAMES AND INDIVIDUAL DIFFERENCES

During Small-Group Sessions

During small-group activities in this unit, the primary activity for the students is practice in writing the uppercase letters. Some of your time will be spent moving from group to group to offer encouragement and guidance on proper conduct. Otherwise, use this time to work with small groups or individuals who need extra support.

Give first priority to those students who are still having difficulty learning to recognize their letters. Although it is important not to short-change letter-writing practice with these children, make sure to include extra work on letter recognition.

As the lessons progress, children who need closer help specifically with writing the letters will become more obvious.

Between Small-Group Sessions

Between lessons, it is important to find time to go through the children's Personal Activity Folders (described later). While checking each child's activity sheet, add his or her name to prevent papers from wandering from folders.

Two different record forms can be created to keep track of the children's progress. The first of these forms (Whole-Class Record Form) is for the entire class, so only one copy is needed. The second form (Individual Record Form) is for individual students, so one copy is needed for each student in the class.

The Whole-Class Record Form should have a row for each student and four columns for each lesson, as follows:

1. *Unattempted:* Check this column if the child does not attempt the activity sheet on the day assigned; this may be because the child was absent or for another reason.

2. *Needs attention:* Check this column if the child fails to complete the sheet or makes errors that warrant attention.

3. *Satisfactory:* If the child's work is complete and looks acceptable, check this column.

4. *Date completed:* When children complete the sheet on a different day from the rest of the class, enter the date in this column.

Whole-Class Record Form

Unit: II: Writing Uppercase Letters

Student name	Chapter 4, Lesson 1 Date ____				Chapter 4, Lesson 2 Date ____				Chapter 4, Lesson 3 Date ____			
	Unattempted	Needs attention	Satisfactory	Date completed	Unattempted	Needs attention	Satisfactory	Date completed	Unattempted	Needs attention	Satisfactory	Date completed
Alvarez, Felicia												
Barnes, Joy												
Carney, James												
Cooper, David												
Cuthbert, Edward												

The purpose of the Individual Record Form is to organize your notes on children's progress and needs. There are a total of 14 lessons in this unit, which means that the Individual Record Form should have 14 rows to make notes about the child's work and any issues that warrant special attention or follow-up.

Individual Record Form

Student name: _____Sarah Jones_____

Unit: _____II: Writing Uppercase Letters_____

Entry assessment score: _____3/26_____

Chapter	Lesson	Letters	Notes
4	1	L, T,	Good job
4	2	I, H	Difficulty with T and L in dictation; okay on new letters
4	3	F, E	Difficulty with T and L in dictation
5	1	A, Z	Dictation improved; more workshop needed

Finally, feel free to use acclaim stickers (e.g., blue, red, or silver stars) on the children's activity sheets as an easy and pleasing way to let each child know that you have reviewed his or her work.

LESSON MATERIALS AND RESOURCES

The following table summarizes the materials and resources needed for both whole-group and small-group activities. *Note:* This book contains online materials (refer to About the Online Materials at the beginning of this book for more information). In the Notes column, *online* indicates that the materials are only provided online. The Notes column also indicates whether materials require additional assembly, or *special preparation*. Instructions for special preparation are provided following the table.

Chapters	Materials	Use	Notes
4, 5, 6, and 7	Board, easel, or projection system	Displaying activity-specific materials	Special preparation
4, 5, 6, and 7	Alphabet Frieze	Whole group	Online (see also Unit I instructions)
4, 5, 6, and 7	Display of uppercase letters on the board	Whole group	Special preparation
4, 5, 6, and 7	Large Letter Formation Guidelines (on board, for teacher's use)	Modeling/teaching letter formation	Special preparation
6 and 7	Smaller Letter Formation Guidelines (on board for students, one per team)	Team Grab Bag	Special preparation
4, 5, 6, and 7	Uppercase Flashcards	Whole group	Special preparation
5, 6, and 7	Grab Bag	Whole group	Special preparation
4	Popsicle stick mug	Optional	Special preparation
4, 5, 6, and 7	Links to music for the "Alphabet Song," "Alphabet Bounce," and "Vowel Name Song"	Whole group	Online
4, 5, 6, and 7	Personal Activity Folders (labeled, one per child)	Individual portfolios	Special preparation

Chapters	Materials	Use	Notes
4, 5, 6, and 7	Uppercase Alphabet Fill-In (one per child for entire unit)	Small group	Appendix B.3
4, 5, 6, and 7	Uppercase Letter Writing Practice Sheets (one per child per lesson)	Small group	Appendix B.3
4, 5, 6, and 7	Pencils for children	Small group	None
4, 5, 6, and 7	Crayons	Small group	None
7	Write Your Own Name (Uppercase) activity sheet	Individual	Special preparation
7	Name Poems	As needed	From Unit 1
7	Materials to create Name Displays	Whole group	Special preparation
4, 5, 6, and 7	Scissors for cutting out best letters	Optional	None
4, 5, 6, and 7	Baggies for storing best letters	Optional	None
4, 5, 6, and 7	Whole-Class Record Form and Individual Record Forms	For keeping track of progress and needs	Special preparation
4, 7	Uppercase Letter Writing assessment	Individual activity	Appendix A.2

Note: Appendix B materials are also available online.

INSTRUCTIONS: SPECIAL MATERIALS AND PREPARATION

Board, Easel, or Projection System

Each of the lessons in this unit requires teacher demonstration of the stroke sequence for the different letters that are taught or reviewed. The instructions are based on the assumption that a board or easel is used.

- When making the letters manually in the air and on the board, do not face the children or the letters will be backward.
- When making strokes and letters in the air, stand in various places in the classroom to make sure that all students have a good opportunity to see.
- At the board, model each stroke or letter at least twice—once standing to the right of the writing and once standing to the left—to give all students a good view.

A suitable projection system, such as an interactive tablet and whiteboard or an overhead projector, may be used instead of a board or easel. Such technologies have the advantage of projecting what is written from a distance without getting in the way. Just make sure that each stroke and letter appears large and in proper orientation on the projection surface.

Display of Uppercase Letters

The purpose of the display of uppercase letters is to keep track of which letters have been taught. Write the whole alphabet in uppercase letters only, on chart paper or on the board where it will not be erased. During each lesson, mark the letters taught (e.g., rewrite them in green) to give the children a sense of progress and to reinforce their growing sense of the alphabet as a whole. You may choose to use a different color to distinguish letters taught in the most recent lesson.

Large Letter Formation Guidelines (for the Teacher)

The lessons in this unit, as well as in Units III and IV, require writing or modeling the formation of the letters with Letter Formation Guidelines: a topline, a midline, and a baseline. Leave at least 12" between the midline and baseline and again between the midline and topline so that the letters will be big enough. In other words, the distance from the topline to the baseline should be at least 2 feet. In addition, take care to leave enough room beneath the baseline for letters that have tails.

Writing directly on a board requires the ability to write and erase letters without having to redraw the guidelines over and over. Two suggestions for making the guidelines follow:

■ *Permanent marker:* The easiest way to make the guidelines is with a nonerasable marker and a straight edge. *Warning:* Before doing this, make sure that you can erase the guidelines when you are done with them. Permanent marker will usually erase from a white board with solvent or lemon juice or by coloring over it with a dry erase marker; however, the operative word is *usually.* Some white board surfaces are more absorbent than others, and some become less erasable with time. Before using permanent marker on the white board, test its short-term (e.g., a few minutes) removability and, if that works, its long-term (e.g., a week) removability.

■ *Whiteboard tape:* A safer way to make the guidelines is by using tape. A number of manufacturers make removable tape for whiteboards (or blackboards). Use tape that is about ¼" wide. To make the set of three guidelines (topline, midline, and baseline) 2 feet long, use a roll of tape that is at least 6 feet (i.e., 2 yards) long.

Smaller Letter Formation Guidelines (for Students)

The Team Grab Bag games in Chapters 6 and 7 use Letter Formation Guidelines on the board for the students' use. These Smaller Letter Formation Guidelines will need to be smaller and closer to the bottom on the board so that they are within reach of all of the students. Leave about 6" between the midline and the baseline and another 6" between the midline and the topline so that the distance from the baseline to the topline is about 12". Be sure to leave enough room beneath the baseline for letters with tails.

Because the students need to be able to write and erase letters without having to redraw the guidelines, make the guidelines with whiteboard tape or a nonerasable marker (see instructions for Large Letter Formation Guidelines).

One option is to make a separate set of guidelines for each team. In this case, make as many Letter Formation Guidelines as you have teams; for example, if the students are in six teams, create six sets of guidelines. An alternative is to make a single set of guidelines—baseline, midline, and topline—that stretches all the way across the board.

If the board is wide enough, ask the children to add new letters to their team's list without erasing those already written by their team members. This allows good review of the whole set.

Uppercase Flashcards

Throughout the unit, Flashcards are used for reviewing letter recognition and letter formation. To make the Flashcards, print each of the uppercase letters on a card (e.g., an index card). Use a bold marker to make sure that the letters are easy to see from all corners of the classroom. The letters needed for each activity are specified in the lessons.

Grab Bag

Select a bag that is big enough to hold the Flashcards.

Popsicle Stick Mug (*Optional*)

The Popsicle stick mug is very handy for managing group activities, such as the Flashcard review of prior letters. It consists of a mug that contains labeled Popsicle sticks. There should be one Popsicle stick with the name of each child in the class. Depending on the activity, add one or more sticks labeled—for example, "all," "girls," and "boys."

Personal Activity Folders

The purpose of the folders is to collect the children's work each day. Closable, plastic portfolios work well, but there are many options. Be sure to label each child's Personal Activity Folder with his or her name.

Write Your Own Name (Uppercase) Activity Sheet

The Write Your Own Name (Uppercase) Activity Sheet is available as an online application and as a blank, photocopiable form in Appendix B.5. The application allows you to provide a printed letter model for each child's name. If you choose to use the blank form in Appendix B.5, photocopy enough copies for each child to have one. Hand-write the child's name in uppercase letters in the first row of his or her activity sheet. Leave the remaining four rows blank. Please create these individualized activity sheets prior to Lesson 4 in Chapter 7.

Other Small-Group Materials

Conducting the small-group activities also requires

- Pencil for each child (pencils with erasers are fine if you think they are appropriate)
- Crayons (at least one for each group)
- Name Poems (for your reference, in case anybody has forgotten)
- Craft materials for making Name Displays (e.g., colored mats, stickers, art supplies for decorating the mats, glue for affixing the names to the mats)

Whole-Class Record Form and Individual Record Forms

See Hands-On Games and Individual Differences for creating the Whole-Class Record Form and Individual Record Form.

Uppercase Letters with Vertical and Horizontal Strokes

ASSESSMENT ALERT: The Entry-Level Uppercase Letter Writing assessment should be completed for all children prior to beginning this chapter.

 **LESSON 1** ## Writing Letters with Vertical and Horizontal Strokes: *L, T*

Objectives
- To introduce starting spots and strokes
- To introduce vertical and horizontal strokes
- To introduce proper formation of uppercase *L* and *T*

Materials
1. **Flashcard Review: Uppercase Letters (*L, T, I, H, F, E*)**
   Flashcards for uppercase letters: *L, T, I, H, F, E*
   (*Optional*) Mug and labeled Popsicle sticks

2. **Introducing Vertical and Horizontal Strokes**
   Large Letter Formation Guidelines (on board for teacher)

3. **New Letters: *L, T***
   Alphabet Frieze
   Display of the uppercase letters on the board
   Large Letter Formation Guidelines (on board for teacher)

4. **Independent Thinking: Strokes and Letters: *L, T* (Small-Group Activity)**
   Uppercase Letter Writing Practice Sheet: *L, T* (one for each student)
   Uppercase Alphabet Fill-In activity sheet (one for each student)
   Pencils (one for each student)
   Crayons
   Personal Activity Folders

ACTIVITIES

1. Flashcard Review: Uppercase Letters (*L, T, I, H, F, E*)
    - The stack of Flashcards should include all of the straight-line uppercase letters: *L, T, I, H, F, E.*
    - Explain the game to the children.
        - There is one uppercase letter on each card.
        - When you hold up a card, the children think of the name of the letter shown.

- The children do not say anything until you give the signal.
- When their response sounds hesitant or confused, slip the letter back into the unused part in the stack, just a few cards down, so that it will quickly show up again.
- Review the entire stack of Flashcards at least once.

TEACHER TIP: POPSICLE STICK ROUTINE

Once the children are comfortable with the Flashcard game, it is wise to switch unpredictably between requesting the response from the whole group and calling on individuals (in surprise order).

A handy technique for managing whole-group response sessions is to use the Popsicle Stick Routine:

- Write each child's name on a Popsicle stick.
- Write "all" on several sticks (roughly one third as many as there are children in the class).
- Put all of the Popsicle sticks, name-side down, in a mug.
- Instead of choosing someone to call on, simply select a stick and read it.
- After reading a stick, replace it in the mug, allowing for it be chosen again at any time.

One benefit of the Popsicle Stick Routine is that it enforces the wait time. Better still, it encourages every child to prepare responses because any name can be drawn.

---

2. Introducing Vertical and Horizontal Strokes

- Tell the children that now that they have learned to name the letters, it is time to learn how to write them.
- Explain that all of the letters of the alphabet are made of just a few basic shapes or strokes. Writing the letters quickly and clearly depends on learning how to do these strokes correctly.
- Among the most common strokes are *straight lines.*
  - Some of the lines go up and down.
  - Some of the lines go side to side.
- Today they are going to begin by practicing how to make straight lines the way that writers do.
- Explain that the key to writing every stroke is to know where to start. Each letter has a *magic starting spot.*

UH-OH ALERT

Do not be tempted to face the children while modeling air writing or the actions will look backward to the children.

2.1. Vertical Strokes

- Draw or make Large Letter Formation Guidelines on the board, including a baseline, a midline, and a topline. (See Unit II Introduction, Instructions: Special Materials and Preparation.)

- Explain and demonstrate how to do vertical strokes on the board.
  - Tell the children that for up and down strokes the **magic starting spot** is *always at the top.*
  - Draw a *starting spot* on the topline for the start of the vertical stroke.
  - Show the children how to draw the *stroke,* beginning at its *magic starting spot* and extending down to the *baseline.*
  - Adding sound effects helps students' ability to follow and remember as well as your ability to monitor this activity.
    - "Pttt!" for the *magic starting spots*
    - "F-f-f-f-f-t!" for each vertical, top-down stroke

INSTRUCTIONAL ALERT
When making these strokes manually on the board, shift from one side to the other while writing so that all of the children get a good view.

- Repeat the vertical stroke several times with sound effects. (*Note:* Do not draw the arrows or numbers on the board. They are just for your reference.)

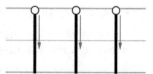

- Ask the children to join you in air-writing the top-to-bottom stroke with sound effects.
  - The children should hold their imaginary giant pencils with their writing hand.
  - To mark the **baseline,**
    - They should hold their other arm before them, palms down, fingers straight, elbows crooked, and forearm parallel to the ground
  - To begin the *stroke,* they should
    - Aim the tips of their imaginary giant pencils at the **magic starting spot** in the air, and at the same time
    - Make the sound effect for the *magic starting spot:* "Ptttt!"
  - To finish the stroke, they should
    - Draw a straight, vertical line from the **magic starting spot** down to the *baseline* marked by their other arm
    - Make the sound effect for a *top-down line:* "F-f-f-f-f-t!"

TEACHER TIP
Have the children make their strokes and letters nice and big so that you can clearly see their actions. The starting spot for top-down strokes should be just above their heads.

2.2. Horizontal Strokes

- Tell the children that for side-to-side strokes the *starting spot* is always at the *left*.
- Demonstrate how to do horizontal strokes on the Large Letter Formation Guidelines. (*Note:* Do not draw the arrows or numbers on the board. They are just for your reference.)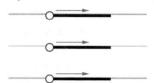
    - "Pttt!" for the *starting spots*
    - "T-ch-ch-cht!" for each horizontal stroke, from left to right
- Repeat several times, sometimes standing on the right of the display and sometimes on the left.
- Tell the children to grab their imaginary giant pencils with their writing hand.
    - Remind them to make the baseline with their other arm.
    - Lead them to add the sound effects as they air-write several horizontal strokes while you write them on the board.
        - "Pttt!" for the *starting spots*
        - "T-ch-ch-cht!" for each horizontal stroke
- Repeat several times.

3. New Letters: *L, T*

3.1. Uppercase *L*

- Ask the children to find the uppercase *L* in the display of uppercase letters on the board and the Alphabet Frieze.
- Demonstrate how to write the uppercase *L* on the board, as shown. The numbers indicate the order of the strokes. (*Note:* Do not draw the arrows or numbers on the board. They are just for your reference.)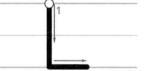
    - Tell the children that, for uppercase letters, when one of the strokes is a top-to-bottom line, it always comes *first*.
- Write the uppercase *L* again on the board, this time with sound effects.
    - "Pttt!" for the starting spot
    - "F-f-f-f-f-t!" for the vertical, top-down stroke
    - "T-ch-ch-cht!" for the left-to-right horizontal stroke at the baseline
- Lead the children to practice air-writing the uppercase *L* with sound effects.
- Repeat several times.

UH-OH ALERT

Do not be tempted to face the children while modeling air-writing or the actions will look backward to the children.

3.2. Uppercase *T*

- Ask the children to find the uppercase *T* in the display of uppercase letters on the board and the Alphabet Frieze.
- Demonstrate how to write the uppercase *T* on the board, as shown. The numbers indicate the order of the strokes. (*Note:* Do not draw the arrows or numbers on the board. They are just for your reference.)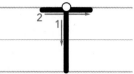
  - Remind the children that, for uppercase letters, the top-to-bottom line always comes *first*.
  - Point out that to make the second line, they lift the pencil and move it back up to the topline.
- Write the uppercase *T* again on the board, this time with sound effects.
  - "Ptttt!" for the starting spot
  - "F-f-f-f-f-t!" for the vertical, top-down stroke
  - "Tk!" as you lift your marker and move it back up to the top guideline
  - "T-ch-ch-cht!" for the left-to-right horizontal stroke that makes the top of the *T*
- Lead the children to practice making the uppercase *T* in the air with sound effects.
- Repeat several times.

3.3. Keeping Track of Letters

- Ask the children to find the *L* and the *T* on the display of uppercase letters on the board.
- Rewrite or otherwise mark each of the letters, *L* and *T*, to show that they have been taught.

4. Independent Thinking: Strokes and Letters: *L, T*

- Gather the children into groups of three or four.
- Make sure every child has his or her own Personal Activity Folder and a copy of the Uppercase Letter Writing Practice Sheet: *L, T* (see Appendix B.3).

TEACHER TIP: GROUPING

For this activity, it is best that the number of children in each group not be five. Otherwise, the same child will end up conducting only the tracing box for each letter.

4.1. Writing New Letters: *L, T*

- Provide an overview of the Uppercase Letter Writing Practice Sheet: *L, T*.
  - For each row, the children trace the strokes or letter shown in the first box.
  - They then rewrite the strokes or letter four times, once in each of the spaces provided on that line.

- Explain the activity.
  - A child in each group directs the tracing and accompanying sound effects for the first strokes or (dotted) letter.
  - The next child is then in charge of directing the sound effects and rewriting the same strokes or letter in the next box in the row. Continue until the row has been completely filled.
  - When the row is complete, the next child directs the tracing and sound effects for the first box on the next row, and so on.
- Remind the children that they must
  - Begin each line or letter at its **magic starting spot**
  - Trace or write the top-down stroke first, if there is one
- When they have completed the sheet, each of them should choose their very best job of writing the letter or strokes for each row.
  - To mark the *one best letter* in each row, they choose a crayon and draw a frame around the outside of the square in which it appears.

INSTRUCTIONAL NOTE
Asking the children to indicate their "very best letter" for each such activity motivates them to execute and examine their letters with the sort of intentional thoughtfulness that promotes learning. Watch them and see!

EXTENSION: UPPERCASE LETTER COLLAGE
After the last lesson of this unit, children may celebrate by creating an Uppercase Letter Collage with their best letters. It is helpful to ask the children to cut out their best letter from each line at the end of each day and to store the letters in a personally labeled baggie or envelope. *Note:* Asking the children to choose their best exemplars is a wholly worthwhile practice, even if they do not make a collage.

4.2. Uppercase Alphabet Fill-In
- Distribute a copy of the Uppercase Alphabet Fill-In activity sheet to each child.
- Guide the children in filling in the Uppercase Alphabet Fill-In activity sheet with the letters of the day.
  - Ask them what they see on this activity sheet.
    - Affirm that it shows the entire lowercase alphabet.
  - Point out that there is a writing box before each letter, and ask them what the box might be for.
    - Affirm that what's missing on this sheet are the *uppercase* letters.
  - Explain that, every day, they are to fill in their new uppercase letters on this sheet.
  - Remind the children that one of today's letters is the uppercase L.
    - Ask them where they think the uppercase L should be added to this page.
    - Affirm that it belongs in the space before the lowercase *l*.

- Ask the children to find and point to that spot on their own sheets and to make sure that everybody in their group agrees where the *L* goes.
- Ask the children to write the uppercase *L* in the spot where it belongs.
- Ask the children to work with their groups
  - To figure out where the uppercase *T* belongs
  - To write the uppercase *T* in that spot

4.3. Cleaning Up

- Ask the children to put *both* of the activity sheets into their Personal Activity Folders.

LESSON 2 | Writing Letters with Vertical
and Horizontal Strokes: *I, H*

Objectives	• To review starting spots and strokes
	• To review prior letters (*L, T*)
	• To introduce proper formation of uppercase *I* and *H*

Materials	**1. Flashcard Review: Uppercase Letters (*L, T, I, H, F, E*)**
	Flashcards for uppercase letters: *L, T, I, H, F, E*
	(*Optional*) Mug and labeled Popsicle sticks
	2. Review Prior Letters
	Display of the uppercase letters on the board
	Large Letter Formation Guidelines (on board for teacher)
	3. New Letters: *I, H*
	Alphabet Frieze
	Display of the uppercase letters on the board
	Large Letter Formation Guidelines (on board for teacher)
	4. Independent Thinking: Strokes and Letters: *I, H* (Small-Group Activity)
	Uppercase Letter Writing Practice Sheet: *I, H* (one for each student)
	Pencils (one for each student)
	Crayons
	Personal Activity Folder for each child (including Uppercase Alphabet Fill-In from prior lesson)

ACTIVITIES

1. Flashcard Review: Uppercase Letters (*L, T, I, H, F, E*)
   - The stack of Flashcards should include all of the straight-line uppercase letters: *L, T, I, H, F, E.*
   - Explain the game to the children.
     - There is one uppercase letter on each card.
     - When you hold up a card, the children think of the name of the letter shown.
     - The children do not say anything until you give the signal.
   - When their response sounds hesitant or confused, slip the letter back into the unused part of the stack, just a few cards down, so that it will quickly show up again.
   - Review the entire stack at least once.

> TEACHER TIP: POPSICLE STICK ROUTINE
> Once the kids are comfortable with the Flashcard game, use the Popsicle Stick Routine to switch **unpredictably** between requesting the response from the whole group and calling on individuals (in surprise order).

2. Review Prior Letters

- Direct the children's attention to the display of uppercase letters on the board.
  - Ask the children to find and name the letters that they learned how to write in the last lesson.
- Make sure that all of the children notice how these two letters are specially marked as having been taught in the display.

2.1. Review *L*

- Write the uppercase letter *L* on the board with sound effects.
  - "Pttt!" for the starting point
  - "F-f-f-f-f-t!" for the vertical, top-down stroke
  - "T-ch-ch-cht!" for the left-to-right stroke that makes the base of the *L*
- Ask the children to join you in air-writing the letter *L* several times.
  - Remind them to make the baseline for the letters with their idle arm.
  - Make sure they make the sound effects as they write—it will help them to remember the strokes.

UH-OH ALERT

Do not be tempted to face the children while modeling air-writing or your actions will look backward to the children.

2.2. Review *T*

- Write the uppercase letter *T* on the board with sound effects.
  - "Pttt!" for the starting point
  - "F-f-f-f-f-t!" for the vertical, top-down stroke
  - "Tk!" for lifting and moving their pencils
  - "T-ch-ch-cht!" for the left-to-right stroke that makes the top of the *T*
- Ask the children to join you in air-writing the letter *T* several times.

3. New Letters: *I, H*

3.1. Uppercase *I*

- Ask the children to find the uppercase *I*
  - In the display of uppercase letters on the board
  - In the Alphabet Frieze
- Demonstrate how to write the uppercase *I* on the board, as shown. The numbers indicate the order of the strokes. (*Note:* Do not draw the arrows or numbers on the board. They are just for your reference.)
  - Remind the children that, for uppercase letters, when one of the strokes is a top-to-bottom line, it always comes *first*.
  - Point out that they must lift the pencil before each of the horizontal strokes.

- Write the uppercase *I* again on the board, this time with sound effects.
  - "Pttt!" for the starting spot
  - "F-f-f-f-f-t!" for the vertical, top-down stroke
  - "Tk!" as you lift your marker and move it back up to the top guideline
  - "T-ch-ch-cht!" for the left-to-right horizontal stroke that makes the top of the *I*
  - "Tk!" as you lift your marker and move it back up to the top guideline
  - "T-ch-ch-cht!" for the left-to-right horizontal stroke that makes the top of the *I*
- Lead the children to practice making the uppercase *I* in the air with sound effects.

3.2. Uppercase *H*

- Ask the children to find the uppercase *H*
  - In the display of uppercase letters on the board
  - In the Alphabet Frieze
- Demonstrate how to write the uppercase *H* on the board, as shown. The numbers indicate the order of the strokes. (*Note:* Do not draw the arrows or numbers on the board. They are just for your reference.)

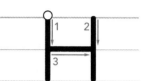

  - Remind the children that, for all uppercase letters, when one of the strokes is a top-to-bottom line, it always comes first.
  - Point out that the side-to-side stroke that holds the *H* together lies on the middle guideline.

INSTRUCTIONAL ALERT
When writing the letters on the board, shift from one side to the other while writing so that all of the children get a good view.

- Write the uppercase *H* again on the board, this time with sound effects.
  - "Pttt!" for the starting spot
  - "F-f-f-f-f-t!" for the first top-down stroke
  - "Tk!" when lifting your marker
  - "F-f-f-f-f-t!" for the second top-down stroke
  - "Tk!" as you lift your marker again
  - "T-ch-ch-cht!" for the left-to-right horizontal stroke that holds the *H* together
- Lead the children to practice making the uppercase *H* in the air with sound effects.

3.3. Keeping Track of Letters

- Ask the children to find the *I* and *H* on the display of uppercase letters on the board.
- Rewrite or otherwise tag each of the letters to show that they have been taught.

4. Independent Activity: Strokes and Letters: *I, H*

- Gather the children into groups of three or four.
- Make sure every child has
  - Personal Activity Folder
  - Uppercase Letter Writing Practice Sheet: *I, H*
  - Uppercase Alphabet Fill-In activity sheet

4.1. Dictation Plus Writing New Letters: *I, H*

- Uppercase Letter Dictation
  - Point out that today's writing sheet is almost the same as the last one except that the top row is blank lines only.
  - Explain that you are going to dictate letters for the top row.
    - *Dictate* means that you will name a letter, and they will write the letter you name.
  - Dictate the following, giving the children time to write each letter before saying the next:

    L   T   L   T   T

- New Letters: *I, H*
  - Remind the children how to complete the rest of Uppercase Letter Writing Practice Sheet: *I, H.*
    - A child in each group directs the tracing and accompanying sound effects for the first (dotted) letter.
    - The next child is then in charge of directing the rewriting of that letter in the second box in the row.
    - The turn-taking and writing continues until all boxes on the activity sheet are filled in.
  - Remind the children that they must
    - Begin each line or letter at its *magic starting spot*
    - Trace or write the top-down stroke first, if there is one
    - Write all vertical lines from top to bottom
    - Write all horizontal lines from left to right
- Remind the children that when they have completed the sheet, they will choose their very best job of writing the letter for each row.
  - To mark the *one best letter* in each row, they choose a crayon and draw a frame around the outside of the square in which it appears.

4.2. Uppercase Alphabet Fill-In

- Remind the children that their Uppercase Alphabet Fill-In activity sheets are in their Personal Activity Folders.
- Tell the children that when they have completed the Uppercase Letter Writing Practice Sheets, they should work together to add today's new letters, *I* and *H*, where they belong in their Uppercase Alphabet Fill-In activity sheets.

4.3. Cleaning Up

- Ask the children to put *both* of the activity sheets into their Personal Activity Folders.

Writing Letters with Vertical and Horizontal Strokes: *F, E*

Objectives
- To review starting spots and strokes
- To review prior letters (*L, T, I, H*)
- To introduce proper formation of uppercase *F* and *E*

Materials
1. **Flashcard Review: Uppercase Letters (*L, T, I, H, F, E*)**
   Flashcards for uppercase letters: *L, T, I, H, F, E*
   (*Optional*) Mug and labeled Popsicle sticks

2. **Review Prior Letters**
   Display of the uppercase letters on the board
   Large Letter Formation Guidelines (on board for teacher)

3. **New Letters: *F, E***
   Alphabet Frieze
   Display of the uppercase letters on the board
   Large Letter Formation Guidelines (on board for teacher)

4. **Independent Thinking: Strokes and Letters: *F, E* (Small-Group Activity)**
   Uppercase Letter Writing Practice Sheet: *F, E* (one for each student)
   Pencils (one for each student)
   Crayons
   Personal Activity Folder for each child (including Uppercase Alphabet Fill-In from prior lesson)

ACTIVITIES

1. Flashcard Review: Uppercase Letters (*L, T, I, H, F, E*)
   - The stack of Flashcards should include all of the straight-line uppercase letters: *L, T, I, H, F, E*.
   - Remind the children how to play the game.
     - There is one uppercase letter on each card.
     - When you hold up a card, the children think of the name of the letter shown.
     - The children do not say anything until you give the signal.
   - When their response sounds hesitant or confused, slip the letter back into the unused part of the stack, just a few cards down, so that it will quickly show up again.
   - Review the entire stack at least once.

TEACHER TIP: POPSICLE STICK ROUTINE
Once the children are comfortable with the Flashcard game, use the Popsicle Stick Routine to switch unpredictably between requesting the response from the whole group and calling on individuals (in surprise order).

2.   Review Prior Letters

• Direct the children's attention to the display of uppercase letters on the board.

  • Ask the children to find and name the letters that they have learned how to write already (*L, T, I, H*).

  • Make sure that all of the children notice how these letters are specially marked as having been taught on the display.

• For each of these previously taught letters (*L, T, I, H*)

  • Ask the children to join you in air-writing the letter with sound effects

  • Write the letter on the board with sound effects, reminding the children of anything special about the letter

  • Repeat and revisit air-writing as deemed useful

3.   New Letters: *F, E*

3.1.   Uppercase *F*

• Ask the children to find the uppercase *F* in the display of uppercase letters on the board and the Alphabet Frieze.

• Demonstrate how to write the uppercase *F* on the board, as shown. The numbers indicate the order of the strokes. (*Note:* Do not draw the arrows or numbers on the board. They are just for your reference.)

  • Remind the children that when one of the strokes is a *top-to-bottom line*, it always comes *first*.

  • Point out that the third stroke lies on the *midline*.

• Write the uppercase *F* again on the board, this time with sound effects.

  • "Pttt!" for the starting spot

  • "F-f-f-f-f-t!" for the top-down stroke

  • "Tk!" when lifting your marker

  • "T-ch-ch-cht!" for the top horizontal stroke

  • "Tk!" as you lift your marker again

  • "T-ch-ch-cht!" for the horizontal stroke that lies on the midline

• Lead the children to practice making the uppercase *F* in the air with sound effects.

3.2.   Uppercase *E*

• Ask the children to find the uppercase *E* on the display of uppercase letters on the board and the Alphabet Frieze.

• Demonstrate how to write the uppercase *E* on the board, as shown. The numbers indicate the order of the strokes. (*Note:* Do not draw the arrows or numbers on the board. They are just for your reference.)

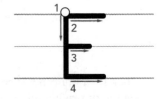

- Write the uppercase *E* again on the board, this time with sound effects.
  - "Pttt!" for the starting spot
  - "F-f-f-f-f-t!" for the top-down stroke
  - "Tk!" when lifting your marker
  - "T-ch-ch-cht!" for the top horizontal stroke
  - "Tk!" as you lift your marker again
  - "T-ch-ch-cht!" for the horizontal stroke that lies on the midline
  - "Tk!" as you lift your marker again
  - "T-ch-ch-cht!" for the horizontal stroke that lies on the baseline
- Lead the children in air-writing the uppercase *E* with accompanying sound effects.

3.3. Keeping Track of Letters

- Ask the children to find the *F* and the *E* on the display of uppercase letters on the board.
- Rewrite or otherwise mark each of the letters to show that they have been taught.

4. Independent Thinking: Strokes and Letters: *F, E*

- Gather the children into groups of three or four.
- Make sure every child has
  - Personal Activity Folder
  - Uppercase Letter Writing Practice Sheet: *F, E*
  - Uppercase Alphabet Fill-In activity sheet

4.1. Dictation Plus Writing New Letters: *F, E*

- Uppercase Letter Dictation
  - Remind the children that the top row of their Uppercase Letter Writing Practice Sheet is for dictation.
    - You will name a letter.
    - They will write the letter you name.
  - Dictate the following, giving the children time to write each letter before saying the next:

                    T   I   L   H   I

- New Letters: *F, E*
  - Remind the children how to complete the rest of Uppercase Letter Writing Practice Sheet: *F, E*.
    - A child in each group directs the tracing and accompanying sound effects for the first (dotted) letter.
    - The next child is then in charge of directing the rewriting of that letter in the second box in the row.
    - The turn-taking and writing continues until all boxes of the activity sheet are filled in.
  - Remind the children that when they have completed the sheet, they will choose their very best letter for each row.

- To mark the *one best letter* in each row, they choose a crayon and draw a frame around the outside of the square in which it appears.

4.2.   Uppercase Alphabet Fill-In

- Remind the children that their Uppercase Alphabet Fill-In activity sheets are in their Personal Activity Folders.

- Tell the children that when they have completed the Uppercase Letter Writing Practice Sheets, they should work together to add today's new letters, *F* and *E,* where they belong in their Uppercase Alphabet Fill-In activity sheets.

4.3.   Cleaning Up

- Ask the children to put *both* of the activity sheets into their Personal Activity Folders.

Uppercase Letters with Slanted Strokes

LESSON 1 Writing Uppercase Letters with Slanted Strokes: *A* and *Z*

Objectives
- To review starting spots and strokes
- To review prior letters (*L, T, I, H, F, E*)
- To introduce proper formation of uppercase *A* and *Z*

Materials

1. **Review Prior Letters**

   Display of the uppercase letters on the board

   Large Letter Formation Guidelines (on board for teacher)

   Grab Bag with Flashcards for uppercase letters: *L, T, I, H, F, E*

2. **Introduction to Slanted Strokes**

   Large Letter Formation Guidelines (on board for teacher)

3. **New Letters:** *A, Z*

   Alphabet Frieze

   Display of the uppercase letters on the board

   Large Letter Formation Guidelines (on board for teacher)

4. **Independent Thinking: Strokes and Letters: *A, Z* (Small-Group Activity)**

   Grab Bag with Flashcards for uppercase letters: *L, T, I, H, F, E*

   Uppercase Letter Writing Practice Sheet: *A, Z* (one for each student)

   Pencils (one for each student)

   Crayons

   Personal Activity Folder for each child (including Uppercase Alphabet Fill-In from the prior lesson)

ACTIVITIES

1. Review Prior Letters

   1.1. Review: *F, E*

   - Direct the children's attention to the display of uppercase letters on the board.

- Ask the children to name and find the letters taught in the last lesson (*F, E*).
- Quickly review the formation of each of these two new letters, writing them with sound effects on the Large Letter Formation Guidelines and, with the children, in the air.

1.2. Grab Bag Review

- The Grab Bag should contain a Flashcard for all of the prior letters: *L, T, I, H, F, E.*
- Call on a child to choose a letter from the Grab Bag and to
  - Signal for everyone to name the chosen letter (Don't forget wait time!)
  - Lead everyone in air-writing it together with sound effects

---

UH-OH ALERT

Make sure the child modeling the letter is facing forward (with his or her back to the rest of the students). If the child is allowed to face the rest of the students, the letter that is modeled will appear backward to them.

- If you see any hesitation or uncertainty,
  - Repeat the air-writing
  - Put the card back in the bag so that it may be drawn again during the session
- Call on another child to choose and lead the response for the next letter.
- Repeat until at least five letters have been reviewed.

INSTRUCTIONAL ALERT

This game provides an opportunity to watch all of the children carefully as they air-write the designated letters.

---

2. Introduction to Slanting Strokes

- Tell the children that many of the letters have strokes that slant.
- Tell them that sometimes the strokes slant in one direction.
- Demonstrate on the board. (*Note:* Do not draw the arrows or numbers on the board. They are just for your reference.)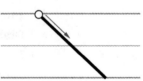
- Ask the children to air-write the stroke with you with sound effects.
  - "Pttt!" for the starting spot
  - "Sssssp!" for the slanted stroke
- Tell the children that sometimes the strokes slant in the other direction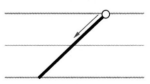
  - Demonstrate on the board.
  - Ask the children to air-write the stroke with you.
    - "Pttt!" for the starting spot
    - "Sssssp!" for the slanted stroke

3. New Letters: *A*, *Z*

3.1. Uppercase *A*

- Ask the children to find the uppercase A in the display of uppercase letters on the board and the Alphabet Frieze.
- Demonstrate how to write the uppercase A on the board, as shown. The numbers indicate the order of the strokes. (*Note:* Do not draw the arrows or numbers on the board. They are just for your reference.)
  - Point out that the sideways stroke should be halfway down, lying on the midline.

INSTRUCTIONAL ALERT

When writing on the board, shift from one side to the other while writing so that all of the children get a good view.

- Write the uppercase A again on the board, this time with sound effects.
  - "Pttt!" for the starting spot
  - "Sssssp!" for first slanted stroke
  - "Tk!" when lifting your marker
  - "Sssssp!" for second slanted stroke
  - "Tk!" when lifting your marker
  - "T-ch-ch-cht!" for the horizontal stroke that lies at the midline
- Lead the children to practice making the uppercase A in the air with accompanying sound effects.

3.2. Uppercase *Z*

- Ask the children to find the uppercase Z in the display of uppercase letters on the board and the Alphabet Frieze.
- Demonstrate how to write the uppercase Z on the board, as shown. The numbers indicate the order of the strokes. (*Note:* Do not draw the arrows or numbers on the board. They are just for your reference.)
  - Note that the whole Z can be made without lifting the pencil.
- Write the uppercase Z again on the board, this time with sound effects.
  - "Pttt!" for the starting spot
  - "T-ch-ch-cht!" for the first horizontal stroke
  - "Sssssp!" for the slanted stroke
  - "T-ch-ch-cht!" for the second horizontal stroke

- Lead the children to practice making the uppercase *Z* in the air with accompanying sound effects.

3.3. Keeping Track of Letters

- Ask the children to find the *A* and the *Z* on the display of uppercase letters on the board.
- Rewrite or otherwise mark each of the letters to show that they have been taught.

4. Independent Thinking: Strokes and Letters: *A*, *Z*

- Gather the children into groups of three or four.
- Make sure every child has
  - Personal Activity Folder
  - Uppercase Letter Writing Practice Sheet: *A*, *Z*
  - Uppercase Alphabet Fill-In activity sheet

4.1. Dictation Plus Writing New Letters: *A*, *Z*

- Uppercase Letter Dictation
  - Remind the children that the top row of their Uppercase Letter Writing Practice Sheet is for dictation.
    - You will name a letter.
    - They will write the letter you name.
  - Dictate five letters from among those taught in previous lessons.
    - Choose the letters one by one from the Grab Bag.
    - Give the children time to write each letter before dictating the next.
- New Letters: *A*, *Z*
  - Remind the children how to complete the rest of Uppercase Letter Writing Practice Sheet: *A*, *Z*.
    - A child in each group directs the tracing and accompanying sound effects for the first (dotted) letter.
    - The next child is then in charge of directing the rewriting of that letter in the second box in the row.
    - The turn-taking and writing continues until all boxes of the activity sheet are filled in.
  - Remind the children that when they have completed the sheet, each of them will choose their very best letter for each row.
    - To mark the *one best letter* in each row, they choose a crayon and draw a frame around the outside of the square in which it appears.

4.2. Uppercase Alphabet Fill-In

- Remind the children that their Uppercase Alphabet Fill-In activity sheets are in their Personal Activity Folders.
- Tell the children that when they have completed the Uppercase Letter Writing Practice Sheets, they should work together to add today's new letters, *A* and *Z*, where they belong in their Uppercase Alphabet Fill-In activity sheets.

4.3. Cleaning Up

- Ask the children to put *both* of the activity sheets into their Personal Activity Folders.

Uppercase Letters with
Slanted Strokes: *N* and *M*

Objectives
- To review starting spots and strokes
- To review prior letters (*L, T, I, H, F, E, A, Z*)
- To introduce proper formation of uppercase *N* and *M*

Materials

1. **Review Prior Letters**

   Display of the uppercase letters on the board

   Large Letter Formation Guidelines (on board for teacher)

   Grab Bag with Flashcards for uppercase letters: *L, T, I, H, F, E, A, Z*

2. **New Letters: *N, M***

   Alphabet Frieze

   Display of the uppercase letters on the board

   Large Letter Formation Guidelines (on board for teacher)

3. **Independent Thinking: Strokes and Letters: *N, M* (Small-Group Activity)**

   Grab Bag with Flashcards for uppercase letters: *L, T, I, H, F, E, A, Z*

   Uppercase Letter Writing Practice Sheet: *N, M* (one for each student)

   Pencils (one for each student)

   Crayons

   Personal Activity Folder for each child (including Uppercase Alphabet Fill-In
   from the prior lesson)

ACTIVITIES

1. Review Prior Letters

   1.1. Review: *A, Z*
   - Direct the children's attention to the display of uppercase letters on the board.
     - Ask the children to name and find the two letters taught in the last lesson (*A, Z*).
     - Quickly review the formation of each of these two new letters, writing them with sound effects on the Large Letter Formation Guidelines and, with the children, in the air.

   1.2. Grab Bag Review
   - The Grab Bag should contain a Flashcard for each letter that has already been taught: *L, T, I, H, F, E, A, Z.*
   - Call on a child to choose a letter from the Grab Bag, and to
     - Signal for everyone to name the chosen letter (Don't forget wait time!)
     - Lead everyone in air-writing it together with sound effects
   - If you see any hesitation or uncertainty,
     - Repeat the air-writing
     - Put the card back in the bag so that it may be drawn again during the session

- Call on another child to choose and lead the response for the next letter.
- Repeat until at least five letters have been reviewed.

UH-OH ALERT

Make sure the child modeling the letter is facing forward (with his or her back to the rest of the students). If the child is allowed to face the rest of the students, the letter that is modeled will appear backward to them.

---

2.   New Letters: *N, M*

2.1.   Uppercase *N*

- Ask the children to find the uppercase *N* in the display of uppercase letters on the board and the Alphabet Frieze.

- Demonstrate how to write the uppercase *N* on the board, as shown. The numbers indicate the order of the strokes. (*Note:* Do not draw the arrows or numbers on the board. They are just for your reference.)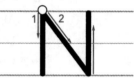

  - Point out that there is no need to lift the marker after the second stroke because the third stroke is made from bottom to top.

- Write the uppercase *N* again on the board, this time with sound effects.

  - "Pttt!" for the starting spot
  - "F-f-f-f-f-t!" for the first vertical stroke, from top to bottom
  - "Tk!" when lifting your marker
  - "Sssssp!" for the slanted stroke
  - "F-f-f-f-f-t!" for the second vertical stroke, from bottom to top

- Lead the children to practice making the uppercase *N* in the air with accompanying sound effects.

2.2.   Uppercase *M*

- Ask the children to find the uppercase *M* in the display of uppercase letters on the board and the Alphabet Frieze.

- Demonstrate how to write the uppercase *M* on the board, as shown. The numbers indicate the order of the strokes. (*Note:* Do not draw the arrows or numbers on the board. They are just for your reference.)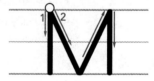

- Write the uppercase *M* again on the board, this time with sound effects.

  - "Pttt!" for the starting spot
  - "F-f-f-f-f-t!" for the first vertical stroke
  - "Tk!" when lifting your marker
  - "Sssssp!" for the first slanted stroke
  - "Sssssp!" for the second slanted stroke
  - "F-f-f-f-f-t!" for the second vertical stroke

- Lead the children to practice making the uppercase *M* in the air with accompanying sound effects.

2.3. Keeping Track of Letters

- Ask the children to find the *N* and the *M* on the display of uppercase letters on the board.
- Rewrite or otherwise mark each of the new letters to show that they have been taught.

3. Independent Thinking: Strokes and Letters: *N, M*

- Gather the children into groups of three or four.
- Make sure every child has
  - Personal Activity Folder
  - Uppercase Letter Writing Practice Sheet: *N, M*
  - Uppercase Alphabet Fill-In activity sheet

3.1. Dictation Plus Writing New Letters: *N, M*

- Uppercase Letter Dictation
  - Remind the children that the top row of their Uppercase Letter Writing Practice Sheet is for dictation.
    - You will name a letter.
    - They will write the letter you name.
  - Dictate five letters from among those taught in previous lessons.
    - Choose the letters one by one from the Grab Bag.
    - Give the children time to write each letter before dictating the next.
- New Letters: *N, M*
  - Remind the children how to complete the rest of Uppercase Letter Writing Practice Sheet: *N, M.*
    - A child in each group directs the tracing and accompanying sound effects for the first (dotted) letter.
    - The next child is then in charge of directing the rewriting of that letter in the second box in the row.
    - The turn-taking and writing continues until all boxes of the activity sheet are filled in.
  - Remind the children that when they have completed the sheet, they will choose their very best letter for each row.
    - To mark the *one best letter* in each row, they choose a crayon and draw a frame around the outside of the square in which it appears.

3.2. Uppercase Alphabet Fill-In

- Remind the children that their Uppercase Alphabet Fill-In activity sheets are in their Personal Activity Folders.
- Tell the children that when they have completed the Uppercase Letter Writing Practice Sheets, they should work together to add today's new letters, *N* and *M*, where they belong in their Uppercase Alphabet Fill-In activity sheets.

3.3. Cleaning Up

- Ask the children to put *both* of the activity sheets into their Personal Activity Folders.

LESSON 3 — Uppercase Letters with Slanted Strokes: *V, W,* and *X*

Objectives	• To review starting spots and strokes
	• To review prior letters (*L, T, I, H, F, E, A, Z, N, M*)
	• To introduce proper formation of uppercase *V, W,* and *X*

Materials	**1. Review Prior Letters**
	Display of the uppercase letters on the board
	Large Letter Formation Guidelines (on board for teacher)
	Grab Bag with Flashcards for uppercase letters: *L, T, I, H, F, E, A, Z, N, M*
	2. New Letters: *V, W, X*
	Alphabet Frieze
	Display of the uppercase letters on the board
	Large Letter Formation Guidelines (on board for teacher)
	3. Independent Thinking: Strokes and Letters: *V, W, X* (Small-Group Activity)
	Grab Bag with Flashcards for uppercase letters: *L, T, I, H, F, E, A, Z, N, M*
	Uppercase Letter Writing Practice Sheet: *V, W, X* (one for each student)
	Pencils (one for each student)
	Crayons
	Personal Activity Folder for each child (including Uppercase Alphabet Fill-In from the prior lesson)

ACTIVITIES

1. Review Prior Letters

   1.1. Review: *N, M*

   - Direct the children's attention to the display of the uppercase letters on the board.
     - Ask the children to name and find the letters taught in the last lesson (*N, M*).
     - Quickly review the formation of each of these two new letters, writing them with sound effects on the Large Letter Formation Guidelines and, with the children, in the air.

   1.2. Grab Bag Review

   - The Grab Bag should contain a Flashcard for each letter that has already been taught: *L, T, I, H, F, E, A, Z, N, M.*
   - Call on a child to choose a letter from the Grab Bag, and to
     - Signal for every one to name the chosen letter (Don't forget wait time!)
     - Lead everyone in air-writing it together with sound effects

---

TEACHER TIP

At least in early lessons, offer to accompany the child, side by side, in leading the air-writing.

- If you see any hesitation or uncertainty,
  - Repeat the air-writing
  - Put the card back in the bag so that it may be drawn again during the session
- Call on another child to choose and lead the response for the next letter.
- Repeat until at least five letters have been reviewed.

2. New Letters: *V, W, X*

2.1. Uppercase *V*

- Ask the children to find the uppercase *V* in the display of uppercase letters on the board and the Alphabet Frieze.
- Demonstrate how to write the uppercase *V* on the board, as shown. The numbers indicate the order of the strokes. (*Note:* Do not draw the arrows or numbers on the board. They are just for your reference.)
  - Note that there is no need to lift the pencil between the first and second stroke.
- Write the uppercase *V* again on the board, this time with sound effects.
  - "Pttt!" for the starting spot
  - "Sssssp!" for the first, top-down slanted stroke
  - "Sssssp!" for the second, bottom-up slanted stroke
- Lead the children to practice making the uppercase *V* in the air with accompanying sound effects.

2.2. Uppercase *W*

- Ask the children to find the uppercase *W* in the display of uppercase letters on the board and the Alphabet Frieze.
- Demonstrate how to write the uppercase *W* on the board, as shown. The numbers indicate the order of the strokes. (*Note:* Do not draw the arrows or numbers on the board. They are just for your reference.)
  - Note that there is no need to lift the pencil between any of the strokes.
- Write the uppercase *W* again on the board, this time with sound effects.
  - "Pttt!" for the starting spot
  - "Sssssp!" for the first slanted stroke
  - "Sssssp!" for the second slanted stroke
  - "Sssssp!" for the third slanted stroke
  - "Sssssp!" for the fourth slanted stroke
- Lead the children to practice making the uppercase *W* in the air with accompanying sound effects.

2.3. Uppercase *X*

- Ask the children to find the uppercase *X* in the display of uppercase letters on the board and the Alphabet Frieze.

- Demonstrate how to write the uppercase *X* on the board, as shown. The numbers indicate the order of the strokes. (*Note:* Do not draw the arrows or numbers on the board. They are just for your reference.)
  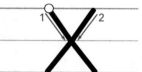

  - Note how the marker must be lifted between the strokes.

- Write the uppercase *X* again on the board, this time with sound effects.

  - "Pttt!" for the starting spot

  - "Sssssp!" for the first, top-down slanted stroke

  - "Tk!" when lifting your marker

  - "Sssssp!" for the second, top-down slanted stroke

- Lead the children to practice making the uppercase *X* in the air with accompanying sound effects.

2.4. Keeping Track of Letters

- Ask the children to find the *V, W,* and *X* on the display of uppercase letters on the board.

- Rewrite or otherwise tag each of the letters to show that they have been taught.

3. Independent Thinking: Strokes and Letters: *V, W, X*

- Gather the children into groups of three or four.

- Make sure every child has

  - Personal Activity Folder

  - Uppercase Letter Writing Practice Sheet: *V, W, X*

  - Uppercase Alphabet Fill-In activity sheet

3.1. Dictation Plus Writing New Letters: *V, W, X*

- Uppercase Letter Dictation

  - Remind the children that the top row of their Uppercase Letter Writing Practice Sheet is for dictation.

    - You will name a letter.

    - They will write the letter you name.

  - Dictate five letters from among those taught in previous lessons.

    - Choose the letters one by one from the Grab Bag.

    - Give the children time to write each letter before dictating the next.

- New Letters: *V, W, X*

  - Remind the children how to complete the rest of Uppercase Letter Writing Practice Sheet: *V, W, X.*

    - A child in each group directs the tracing and accompanying sound effects for the first (dotted) letter.

- The next child is then in charge of directing the rewriting of that letter in the second box in the row.
    - The turn-taking and writing continues until all boxes of the activity sheet are filled in.
- Remind the children that when they have completed the sheet, they will choose their very best letter for each row.
    - To mark the *one best letter* in each row, they choose a crayon and draw a frame around the outside of the square in which it appears.

3.2. Uppercase Alphabet Fill-In

- Remind the children that their Uppercase Alphabet Fill-In activity sheets are in their Personal Activity Folders.
- Tell the children that when they have completed the Uppercase Letter Writing Practice Sheets, they should work together to add today's new letters, *V, W,* and *X,* where they belong in their Uppercase Alphabet Fill-In activity sheets.

3.3. Cleaning Up

- Ask the children to put *both* of the activity sheets into their Personal Activity Folders.

> **LESSON 4** ## Uppercase Letters with Slanted Strokes: *Y, K*

Objectives
- To review starting spots and strokes
- To review prior letters (*L, T, I, H, F, E, A, Z, N, M, V, W, X*)
- To introduce proper formation of uppercase *Y* and *K*

Materials

1. **Review Prior Letters**

   Display of the uppercase letters on the board

   Large Letter Formation Guidelines (on board for teacher)

   Grab Bag with Flashcards for uppercase letters: *L, T, I, H, F, E, A, Z, N, M, V, W, X*

2. **New Letters: *Y, K***

   Alphabet Frieze

   Display of the uppercase letters on the board

   Large Letter Formation Guidelines (on board for teacher)

3. **Independent Thinking: Strokes and Letters: *Y, K* (Small-Group Activity)**

   Grab Bag with Flashcards for uppercase letters: *L, T, I, H, F, E, A, Z, N, M, V, W, X*

   Uppercase Letter Writing Practice Sheet: *Y, K* (one for each student)

   Pencils (one for each student)

   Crayons

   Personal Activity Folder for each child (including Uppercase Alphabet Fill-In from the prior lesson)

ACTIVITIES

1. Review Prior Letters

    1.1. Review *V, W, X*

    - Direct the children's attention to the display of uppercase letters on the board.
      - Ask the children to name and find the letters taught in the last lesson (*V, W, X*).
      - Quickly review the formation of each of these three new letters, writing them with sound effects on the Large Letter Formation Guidelines and, with the children, in the air.

    1.2. Grab Bag Review

    - The Grab Bag should contain a card for each letter that has already been taught: *L, T, I, H, F, E, A, Z, N, M, V, W, X.*
    - Call on a child to choose a letter from the Grab Bag, and to
      - Signal for every one to name the chosen letter (Don't forget wait time!)
      - Lead everyone in air-writing it together with sound effects
    - If you see any hesitation or uncertainty,
      - Repeat the air-writing

- Put the card back in the bag so that it may be drawn again during the session
- Call on another child to choose and lead the response for the next letter.
- Repeat until at least five letters have been reviewed.

> TEACHER TIP
> At least in early lessons, offer to accompany the child, side by side, in leading the air-writing.

2. New Letters: *Y, K*

2.1. Uppercase *Y*

- Ask the children to find the uppercase *Y* in the display of uppercase letters on the board and the Alphabet Frieze.
- Demonstrate how to write the uppercase *Y* on the board, as shown. The numbers indicate the order of the strokes. (*Note:* Do not draw the arrows or numbers on the board. They are just for your reference.)

  - Point out that the first slanted stroke ends exactly halfway to the baseline, which is also where the second and third strokes begin.
- Write the uppercase *Y* again on the board, this time with sound effects.
  - "Pttt!" for the starting spot
  - "Sssssp!" for the first, top-down slanted stroke
  - "Tk!" when lifting your marker
  - "Sssssp!" for the second, top-down slanted stroke
  - "F-f-f-f-f-t!" for the vertical stroke that forms the base of the *Y*
- Lead the children to practice making the uppercase *Y* in the air with accompanying sound effects.

2.2. Uppercase *K*

- Ask the children to find the uppercase *K* in the display of uppercase letters on the board and the Alphabet Frieze.
- Demonstrate how to write the uppercase *K* on the board, as shown. The numbers indicate the order of the strokes. (*Note:* Do not draw the arrows or numbers on the board. They are just for your reference.)

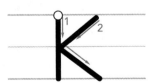

  - Remind the children that when there is a top-to-bottom stroke, it always comes first.
  - Point out that the first slanted stroke ends exactly halfway down, which also is where the second slanted stroke begins.
- Write the uppercase *K* again on the board, this time with sound effects.
  - "Pttt!" for the starting spot

- "F-f-f-f-f-t!" for the top-to-bottom vertical stroke
- "Tk!" when lifting your marker
- "Sssssp!" for the slanted stroke from the topline to the midline
- "Sssssp!" for the slanted stroke from the midline to the baseline

- Lead the children to practice making the uppercase *K* in the air with accompanying sound effects.

2.3. Keeping Track of Letters

- Ask the children to find the *Y* and *K* on the display of uppercase letters on the board.
- Rewrite or otherwise tag each of these letters to show that they have been taught.

3. Independent Thinking: Strokes and Letters: *Y, K*

- Gather the children into groups of three or four.
- Make sure every child has
  - Personal Activity Folder
  - Uppercase Letter Writing Practice Sheet: *Y, K*
  - Uppercase Alphabet Fill-In activity sheet

3.1. Dictation Plus Writing New Letters: *Y, K*

- Uppercase Letter Dictation
  - Remind the children that the top row of their Uppercase Letter Writing Practice Sheet is for dictation.
    - You will name a letter.
    - They will write the letter you name.
  - Dictate five letters from among those taught in previous lessons.
    - Choose the letters one by one from the Grab Bag.
    - Give the children time to write each letter before dictating the next.
- New Letters: *Y, K*
  - Remind the children how to complete the rest of Uppercase Letter Writing Practice Sheet: *Y, K.*
    - A child in each group directs the tracing and accompanying sound effects for the first (dotted) letter.
    - The next child is then in charge of directing the rewriting of that letter in the second box in the row.
    - The turn-taking and writing continues until all boxes of the activity sheet are filled in.
  - Remind the children that when they have completed the sheet, they will choose their very best letter for each row.
    - To mark the *one best letter* in each row, they choose a crayon and draw a frame around the outside of the square in which it appears.

3.2. Uppercase Alphabet Fill-In

- Remind the children that their Uppercase Alphabet Fill-In activity sheets are in their Personal Activity Folders.

- Tell the children that when they have completed the Uppercase Letter Writing Practice Sheets, they should work together to add today's new letters, *Y* and *K,* where they belong in their Uppercase Alphabet Fill-In activity sheets.

3.3. Cleaning Up

- Ask the children to put *both* of the activity sheets into their Personal Activity Folders.

Uppercase Letters with Loops, Humps, and Troughs

LESSON 1 ## Uppercase Letters with Loops, Humps, and Troughs: *D, B*

Objectives

- To review starting spots and strokes
- To review prior letters (*L, T, I, H, F, E, A, Z, N, M, V, W, X, Y, K*)
- To introduce proper formation of uppercase *D* and *B*

Materials

1. **Review Prior Letters**

   Display of the uppercase letters on the board

   Large Letter Formation Guidelines (on board for teacher)

   Smaller Letter Formation Guidelines (on board for students)

   Grab Bag with Flashcards for uppercase letters: *L, T, I, H, F, E, A, Z, N, M, V, W, X, Y, K*

2. **Introducing Loops, Humps, and Troughs**

   Large Letter Formation Guidelines (on board for teacher)

3. **New Letters: *D, B***

   Alphabet Frieze

   Display of the uppercase letters on the board

   Large Letter Formation Guidelines (on board for teacher)

4. **Independent Thinking: Strokes and Letters: *D, B* (Small-Group Activity)**

   Grab Bag with Flashcards for uppercase letters: *L, T, I, H, F, E, A, Z, N, M, V, W, X, Y, K*

   Uppercase Letter Writing Practice Sheet: *D, B* (one for each student)

   Pencils (one for each student)

   Crayons

   Personal Activity Folder for each child (including Uppercase Alphabet Fill-In from the prior lesson)

ACTIVITIES

1. **Review Prior Letters**

    1.1. **Review:** *Y, K*
        - Direct the children's attention to the display of uppercase letters on the board.
            - Ask the children to name and find the letters taught in the last lesson (*Y, K*).
            - Quickly review the formation of each of these letters, writing them with sound effects on the Large Letter Formation Guidelines and, with the children, in the air.

    1.2. **Team Grab Bag**
        - The Grab Bag should contain a Flashcard for each letter that has already been taught: *L, T, I, H, F, E, A, Z, N, M, V, W, X, Y, K.*
        - Divide the children into teams of three to five.
        - Each team should make a line facing the board.
        - Choose one of the letters from the Grab Bag, and name it.
            - Lead the children to write the letter with sound effects.
                - The first child in each line writes the letter on the board on the Smaller Letter Formation Guidelines.
                - The others air-write the letter.
                - When the first child has finished, he or she goes to the back of the line.
            - Repeat until every child has had a chance to write on the board.

2. **Introducing Loops, Humps, and Troughs**
    - Tell the children that many of the letters have loopy parts.
    - Tell them that sometimes the strokes loop in one direction and sometimes in another.
    - Demonstrate each on the board.
        - For some of the uppercase letters, the loop goes sideways.
        - For other uppercase letters, the loop is on the bottom, like a trough that holds water.
        - For other letters, the loop is upside down so that it looks like a hump.
    - Ask the children to air-write each version of stroke with you with the new sound effect.
        - "Pttt!" for the starting spot
        - "L-l-l-l-oop!" for the curved stroke

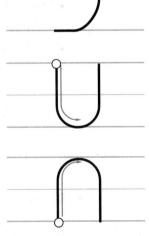

3. New Letters: *D, B*

   3.1. Uppercase *D*

   - Ask the children to find the uppercase *D* in the display of uppercase letters on the board and the Alphabet Frieze.

   - Demonstrate how to write the uppercase *D* on the board, as shown. The numbers indicate the order of the strokes. (*Note:* Do not draw the arrows or numbers on the board. They are just for your reference.)

     - Remind the children that when one of the strokes is a straight, top-to-bottom stroke, it always comes first.

   - Write the uppercase *D* again on the board, this time with sound effects.

     - "Pttt!" for the starting spot

     - "F-f-f-f-f-t!" for the vertical line

     - "Tk!" when lifting your marker

     - "L-l-l-l-oop!" for the curved stroke

   - Lead the children to practice making the uppercase *D* in the air with accompanying sound effects.

   3.2. Uppercase *B*

   - Ask the children to find the uppercase *B* in the display of uppercase letters on the board and the Alphabet Frieze.

   - Demonstrate how to write the uppercase *B* on the board, as shown. The numbers indicate the order of the strokes. (*Note:* Do not draw the arrows or numbers on the board. They are just for your reference.)

   - Write the uppercase *B* again on the board, this time with sound effects.

     - "Pttt!" for the starting spot

     - "F-f-f-f-t!" for the vertical line

     - "Tk!" when lifting your marker

     - "L-l-l-l-oop!" for the top curved stroke

     - "L-l-l-l-oop!" for the bottom curved stroke

   - Lead the children to practice making the uppercase *B* in the air with accompanying sound effects.

   3.3. Keeping Track of Letters

   - Ask the children to find the *D* and *B* on the display of uppercase letters on the board.

   - Rewrite or otherwise tag each of these letters to show that they have been taught.

4. Independent Thinking: Strokes and Letters: *D, B*

   - Gather the children into groups of three or four.

   - Make sure every child has

- Personal Activity Folder
- Uppercase Letter Writing Practice Sheet: *D, B*
- Uppercase Alphabet Fill-In activity sheet

4.1. Dictation Plus Writing New Letters: *D, B*

- Uppercase Letter Dictation
  - Remind the children that the top row of their Uppercase Letter Writing Practice Sheet is for dictation.
    - You will name a letter.
    - They will write the letter you name.
  - Dictate five letters from among those taught in previous lessons.
    - Choose the letters one by one from the Grab Bag.
    - Give the children time to write each letter before dictating the next.
- New Letters: *D, B*
  - Remind the children how to complete the rest of Uppercase Letter Writing Practice Sheet: *D, B*.
    - A child in each group directs the tracing and accompanying sound effects for the first (dotted) letter.
    - The next child is then in charge of directing the rewriting of that letter in the second box in the row.
    - The turn-taking and writing continues until all boxes of the activity sheet are filled in.
  - Remind the children that when they have completed the sheet, they will choose their very best letter for each row.
    - To mark the *one best letter* in each row, they choose a crayon and draw a frame around the outside of the square in which it appears.

4.2. Uppercase Alphabet Fill-In

- Remind the children that their Uppercase Alphabet Fill-In activity sheets are in their Personal Activity Folders.
- Tell the children that when they have completed the Uppercase Letter Writing Practice Sheets, they should work together to add today's new letters, *D* and *B*, where they belong in their Uppercase Alphabet Fill-In activity sheets.

4.3. Cleaning Up

- Ask the children to put *both* of the activity sheets into their Personal Activity Folders.

LESSON 2 Uppercase Letters with Loops, Humps, and Troughs: *P, R*

Objectives
- To review starting spots and strokes
- To review prior letters (*L, T, I, H, F, E, A, Z, N, M, V, W, X, Y, K, D, B*)
- To introduce proper formation of uppercase *P* and *R*

Materials
1. **Review Prior Letters**

   Display of the uppercase letters on the board

   Large Letter Formation Guidelines (on board for teacher)

   Smaller Letter Formation Guidelines (on board for students)

   Grab Bag with Flashcards for uppercase letters: *L, T, I, H, F, E, A, Z, N, M, V, W, X, Y, K, D, B*

2. **New Letters: *P, R***

   Alphabet Frieze

   Display of the uppercase letters on the board

   Large Letter Formation Guidelines (on board for teacher)

3. **Independent Thinking: Strokes and Letters: *P, R* (Small-Group Activity)**

   Grab Bag with Flashcards for uppercase letters: *L, T, I, H, F, E, A, Z, N, M, V, W, X, Y, K, D, B*

   Uppercase Letter Writing Practice Sheet: *P, R* (one for each student)

   Pencils (one for each student)

   Crayons

   Personal Activity Folder for each child (including Uppercase Alphabet Fill-In from the prior lesson)

ACTIVITIES

1. Review Prior Letters

   1.1. Review: *D, B*

   - Direct the children's attention to the display of uppercase letters on the board.
     - Ask the children to name and find the letters taught in the last lesson (*D, B*).
     - Quickly review the formation of each of these two new letters, writing them with sound effects on the Large Letter Formation Guidelines and, with the children, in the air.

   1.2. Team Grab Bag

   - The Grab Bag should now contain a Flashcard for each letter that has already been taught: *L, T, I, H, F, E, A, Z, N, M, V, W, X, Y, K, D, B*.
   - Divide the children into teams of three to five.
   - Each team should make a line facing the board.
   - Choose one of the letters from the Grab Bag, and name it.
     - Lead the children to write the letter in time with its sound effects.

- The first child in each line writes the letter on the board on the Smaller Letter Formation Guidelines.
- The others air-write the letter.
- When the first child has finished, he or she goes to the back of the line.
- Repeat until every child has had a chance to write on the board.

2. New Letters: *P, R*

2.1. Uppercase *P*

- Ask the children to find the uppercase *P* on the display of uppercase letters on the board and the Alphabet Frieze.
- Demonstrate how to write the uppercase *P* on the board, as shown. The numbers indicate the order of the strokes. (*Note:* Do not draw the arrows or numbers on the board. They are just for your reference.)
- Write the uppercase *P* again on the board, this time with sound effects.
  - "Pttt!" for the starting spot
  - "F-f-f-f-f-t!" for the vertical line
  - "Tk!" when lifting your marker
  - "L-l-l-l-oop!" for the curved stroke
- Lead the children to practice making the uppercase *P* in the air with accompanying sound effects.

2.2. Uppercase *R*

- Ask the children to find the uppercase *R* in the display of uppercase letters on the board and the Alphabet Frieze.
- Demonstrate how to write the uppercase *R* on the board, as shown. The numbers indicate the order of the strokes. (*Note:* Do not draw the arrows or numbers on the board. They are just for your reference.)
- Write the uppercase *R* again on the board, this time with sound effects.
  - "Pttt!" for the starting spot
  - "F-f-f-f-f-t!" for the vertical line
  - "Tk!" when lifting your marker
  - "L-l-l-l-oop!" for the curved stroke
  - "Ssssp!" for the slanted stroke
- Lead the children to practice making the uppercase *R* in the air with accompanying sound effects.

2.3. Keeping Track of Letters

- Ask the children to find the *P* and *R* on the display of uppercase letters on the board.
- Rewrite or otherwise tag each of these letters to show that they have been taught.

3. Independent Thinking: Strokes and Letters: *P, R*

- Gather the children into groups of three or four.
- Make sure every child has
  - Personal Activity Folder
  - Uppercase Letter Writing Practice Sheet: *P, R*
  - Uppercase Alphabet Fill-In activity sheet

3.1. Dictation Plus Writing New Letters: *P, R*

- Uppercase Letter Dictation
  - Remind the children that the top row of their Uppercase Letter Writing Practice Sheet is for dictation.
    - You will name a letter.
    - They will write the letter you name.
  - Dictate five letters from among those taught in previous lessons.
    - Choose the letters one by one from the Grab Bag.
    - Give the children time to write each letter before dictating the next.
- New Letters: *P, R*
  - Remind the children how to complete the rest of Uppercase Letter Writing Practice Sheet: *P, R*.
    - A child in each group directs the tracing and accompanying sound effects for the first (dotted) letter.
    - The next child is then in charge of directing the rewriting of that letter in the second box in the row.
    - The turn-taking and writing continues until all boxes of the activity sheet are filled in.
  - Remind the children that when they have completed the sheet, they will choose their very best letter for each row.
    - To mark the *one best letter* in each row, they choose a crayon and draw a frame around the outside of the square in which it appears.

3.2. Uppercase Alphabet Fill-In

- Remind the children that their Uppercase Alphabet Fill-In activity sheets are in their Personal Activity Folders.
- Tell the children that when they have completed the Uppercase Letter Writing Practice Sheets, they should work together to add today's new letters, *P* and *R*, where they belong in their Uppercase Alphabet Fill-In activity sheets.

3.3. Cleaning Up

- Ask the children to put *both* of the activity sheets into their Personal Activity Folders.

 **LESSON 3** ## Uppercase Letters with Loops, Humps, and Troughs: *U, J*

Objectives
- To review starting spots and strokes
- To review prior letters (*L, T, I, H, F, E, A, Z, N, M, V, W, X, Y, K, D, B, P, R*)
- To introduce proper formation of uppercase *U* and *J*

Materials

1. **Review Prior Letters**

   Display of the uppercase letters on the board

   Large Letter Formation Guidelines (on board for teacher)

   Smaller Letter Formation Guidelines (on board for students)

   Grab Bag with Flashcards for uppercase letters: *L, T, I, H, F, E, A, Z, N, M, V, W, X, Y, K, D, B, P, R*

2. **New Letters: *U, J***

   Alphabet Frieze

   Display of the uppercase letters on the board

   Large Letter Formation Guidelines (on board for teacher)

3. **Independent Thinking: Strokes and Letters: *U, J* (Small-Group Activity)**

   Grab Bag with Flashcards for uppercase letters: *L, T, I, H, F, E, A, Z, N, M, V, W, X, Y, K, D, B, P, R*

   Uppercase Letter Writing Practice Sheet: *U, J* (one for each student)

   Pencils (one for each student)

   Crayons

   Personal Activity Folder for each child (including Uppercase Alphabet Fill-In from the prior lesson)

ACTIVITIES

1. Review Prior Letters

   1.1. Review: *P, R*

   - Direct the children's attention to the display of uppercase letters on the board.
     - Ask them to name and find the letters taught in the last lesson (*P, R*).
     - Quickly review the formation of each of these two new letters, writing them with sound effects on the Large Letter Formation Guidelines and, with the children, in the air.

   1.2. Team Grab Bag

   - The Grab Bag should now contain a Flashcard for each letter that has already been taught: *L, T, I, H, F, E, A, Z, N, M, V, W, X, Y, K, D, B, P, R*.
   - Divide the children into teams of three to five.
   - Each team should make a line facing the board.
   - Choose one of the letters from the Grab Bag, and name it.
     - Lead the children to write the letter in time with its sound effects.

- The first child in each line writes the letter on the board on the Smaller Letter Formation Guidelines.
- The others air-write the letter.
- When the first child has finished, he or she goes to the back of the line.
- Repeat until every child has had a chance to write on the board.

2. New Letters: *U, J*

2.1. Uppercase *U*

- Ask the children to find the uppercase *U* in the display of uppercase letters on the board and the Alphabet Frieze.

- Demonstrate how to write the uppercase *U* on the board, as shown. The numbers indicate the order of the strokes. (*Note:* Do not draw the arrows or numbers on the board. They are just for your reference.)

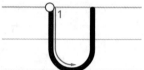

  - Point out that for this letter, the loops go on the bottom.
    - If desired, tell the children that **troughs** are things that hold or catch water.
    - Sometimes the word **trough** is used for bottom loops because that's what they look like.

- Write the uppercase *U* again on the board, this time with sound effects.
  - "Pttt!" for the starting spot
  - "L-l-l-l-oop!" for the bucket-shaped loop

- Lead the children to practice making the uppercase *U* in the air with accompanying sound effects.

2.2. Uppercase *J*

- Ask the children to find the uppercase *J* in the display of uppercase letters on the board and the Alphabet Frieze.

- Demonstrate how to write the uppercase *J* on the board, as shown. The numbers indicate the order of the strokes. (*Note:* Do not draw the arrows or numbers on the board. They are just for your reference.)

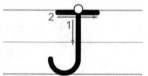

- Write the uppercase *J* again on the board, this time with sound effects.
  - "Pttt!" for the starting spot
  - "F-f-f-f-ft!" for the top-to-bottom stroke
  - "L-l-l-l-oop!" for the curl at the bottom
  - "Tk!" when lifting your marker
  - "T-ch-ch-cht!" for the horizontal stroke that makes the line on top

- Lead the children to practice making the uppercase *J* in the air with accompanying sound effects.

2.3. Keeping Track of Letters

- Ask the children to find the *U* and *J* on the display of uppercase letters on the board.
- Rewrite or otherwise mark each of these letters to show that they have been taught.

3. Independent Thinking: Strokes and Letters: *U, J*

- Gather the children into groups of three or four.
- Make sure every child has
  - Personal Activity Folder
  - Uppercase Letter Writing Practice Sheet: *U, J*
  - Uppercase Alphabet Fill-In activity sheet

3.1. Dictation Plus Writing New Letters: *U, J*

- Uppercase Letter Dictation
  - Remind the children that the top row of their Uppercase Letter Writing Practice Sheet is for dictation.
    - You will name a letter.
  - They will write the letter you name.
  - Dictate five letters from among those taught in previous lessons.
    - Choose the letters one by one from the Grab Bag.
    - Give the children time to write each letter before dictating the next.
- New Letters: *U, J*
  - Remind the children how to complete the rest of Uppercase Letter Writing Practice Sheet: *U, J*.
    - A child in each group directs the tracing and accompanying sound effects for the first (dotted) letter.
    - The next child is then in charge of directing the rewriting of that letter in the second box in the row.
    - The turn-taking and writing continues until all boxes of the activity sheet are filled in.
  - Remind the children that when they have completed the sheet, they will choose their very best letter for each row.
    - To mark the *one best letter* in each row, they choose a crayon and draw a frame around the outside of the square in which it appears.

3.2. Uppercase Alphabet Fill-In

- Remind the children that their Uppercase Alphabet Fill-In activity sheets are in their Personal Activity Folders.
- Tell the children that when they have completed the Uppercase Letter Writing Practice Sheets, they should work together to add today's new letters, *U* and *J*, where they belong in their Uppercase Alphabet Fill-In activity sheets.

3.3. Cleaning Up

- Ask the children to put *both* of the activity sheets into their Personal Activity Folders.

Uppercase Letters that Start at 2 o'Clock

....

LESSON 1

Uppercase Letters that Start at 2 o'Clock: *O, C*

Objectives
- To review starting spots and strokes
- To review prior letters (*L, T, I, H, F, E, A, Z, N, M, V, W, X, Y, K, D, B, P, R, U, J*)
- To introduce proper formation of uppercase *O* and *C*

Materials

1. **Review Prior Letters**

   Display of the uppercase letters on the board

   Large Letter Formation Guidelines (on board for teacher)

   Smaller Letter Formation Guidelines (on board for students)

   Grab Bag with Flashcards for uppercase letters: *L, T, I, H, F, E, A, Z, N, M, V, W, X, Y, K, D, B, P, R, U, J*

2. **Introducing 2 o'Clock Strokes**

   Large Letter Formation Guidelines (on board for teacher)

3. **New Letters: *O, C***

   Alphabet Frieze

   Display of the uppercase letters on the board

   Large Letter Formation Guidelines (on board for teacher)

4. **Independent Thinking: Strokes and Letters: *O, C* (Small-Group Activity)**

   Grab Bag with Flashcards for uppercase letters: *L, T, I, H, F, E, A, Z, N, M, V, W, X, Y, K, D, B, P, R, U, J*

   Uppercase Letter Writing Practice Sheet: *O, C* (one for each student)

   Pencils (one for each student)

   Crayons

   Personal Activity Folder for each child (including Uppercase Alphabet Fill-In from the prior lesson)

ACTIVITIES

1. **Review Prior Letters**

    1.1. Review: *U, J*

         - Direct the children's attention to the display of uppercase letters on the board.
             - Ask the children to name and find the letters taught in the last lesson (*U, J*).
             - Quickly review the formation of each of these two new letters, writing them with sound effects on the Large Letter Formation Guidelines and, with the children, in the air.

    1.2. Team Grab Bag

         - The Grab Bag should now contain a Flashcard for each letter that has already been taught: *L, T, I, H, F, E, A, Z, N, M, V, W, X, Y, K, D, B, P, R, U, J.*
         - Divide the children into teams of three to five.
             - Each team should make a line facing the board.
             - Choose one of the letters from the Grab Bag, and name it.
                 - Lead the children to write the letter in time with its sound effects.
                 - The first child in each line writes the letter on the board on the Smaller Letter Formation Guidelines.
                 - The others air-write the letter.
                 - When the child at the board has finished, he or she goes to the back of the line.
         - Repeat until every child has had a chance to write on the board.

2. **Introducing 2 o'Clock Strokes**

    - Tell the children that many of the letters are made of circles or parts of circles.
    - Tell them that for all of these letters, the starting point is the same. Some people call them *2 o'clock letters* because the starting point is right where the 2 is on a round clock.

    - Demonstrate on the board with sound effects for the starting point and the circular stroke.
        - "Pttt!" for the starting spot
        - "Wheeooo!" for the circular stroke (*Hint:* Whisper "wheeooo" so it sounds like a whistle.)
    - Ask the children to air-write the stroke with you with sound effects.

3. **New Letters: *O, C***

    3.1. Uppercase *O*

         - Ask the children to find the uppercase *O* in the display of uppercase letters on the board and the Alphabet Frieze.

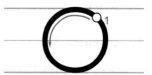

- Demonstrate how to write the uppercase *O* on the board, as shown. The numbers indicate the order of the strokes. (*Note:* Do not draw the arrows or numbers on the board. They are just for your reference.)

- Write the uppercase *O* again on the board, this time with sound effects.

  - "Pttt!" for the starting spot at 2 o'clock

  - "Wheeooo!" for the circular stroke

- Ask the children to air-write the uppercase *O* with you with sound effects.

  - Ask the children where the starting point goes. (2 o'clock)

3.2. Uppercase *C*

- Ask the children to find the uppercase *C* in the display of uppercase letters on the board and the Alphabet Frieze.

- Demonstrate how to write the uppercase *C* on the board, as shown. The numbers indicate the order of the strokes. (*Note:* Do not draw the arrows or numbers on the board. They are just for your reference.)

- Ask the children where the starting point goes. (2 o'clock)

  - Ask the children how the shape of the uppercase *C* differs from that of the uppercase *O*. (The *C* doesn't go all the way around.)

- Write the uppercase *C* again on the board, this time with sound effects.

  - "Pttt!" for the starting spot at 2 o'clock

  - "Wheeooo!" for the circular stroke

- Ask the children to air-write the uppercase *C* with you with sound effects.

3.3. Keeping Track of Letters

- Ask the children to find the *O* and *C* on the display of uppercase letters on the board .

- Rewrite or otherwise mark each of these letters to show that they have been taught.

4. Independent Thinking: Strokes and Letters: *O*, *C*

- Gather the children into groups of three or four.

- Make sure every child has

  - Personal Activity Folder

  - Uppercase Letter Writing Practice Sheet: *O*, *C*

  - Uppercase Alphabet Fill-In activity sheet

4.1. Dictation Plus Writing New Letters: *O*, *C*

  - Uppercase Letter Dictation

- Remind the children that the top row of their Uppercase Letter Writing Practice Sheet is for dictation.
  - You will name a letter.
  - They will write the letter you name.
- Dictate five letters from among those taught in previous lessons.
  - Choose the letters one by one from the Grab Bag.
  - Give the children time to write each letter before dictating the next.
- New Letters: *O, C*
  - Remind the children how to complete the rest of Uppercase Letter Writing Practice Sheet: *O, C.*
    - A child in each group directs the tracing and accompanying sound effects for the first (dotted) letter.
    - The next child is then in charge of directing the rewriting of that letter in the second box in the row.
    - The turn-taking and writing continues until all boxes of the activity sheet are filled in.
  - Remind the children that when they have completed the sheet, they will choose their very best letter for each row.
    - To mark the *one best letter* in each row, they choose a crayon and draw a frame around the outside of the square in which it appears.

4.2. Uppercase Alphabet Fill-In

- Remind the children that their Uppercase Alphabet Fill-In activity sheets are in their Personal Activity Folders.
- Tell the children that when they have completed the Uppercase Letter Writing Practice Sheets, they should work together to add today's new letters, *O, C,* where they belong in their Uppercase Alphabet Fill-In activity sheets.

4.3. Cleaning Up

- Ask the children to put *both* of the activity sheets into their Personal Activity Folders.

LESSON 2 Uppercase Letters that
Start at 2 o'Clock: *Q, G*

Objectives
- To review starting spots and strokes
- To review prior letters (*L, T, I, H, F, E, A, Z, N, M, V, W, X, Y, K, D, B, P, R, U, J, O, C*)
- To introduce proper formation of uppercase *Q* and *G*

Materials
1. **Review Prior Letters**
   Display of the uppercase letters on the board
   Large Letter Formation Guidelines (on board for teacher)
   Smaller Letter Formation Guidelines (on board for students)
   Grab Bag with Flashcards for uppercase letters: *L, T, I, H, F, E, A, Z, N, M, V, W, X, Y, K, D, B, P, R, U, J, O, C*

2. **New Letters: *Q, G***
   Alphabet Frieze
   Display of the uppercase letters on the board
   Large Letter Formation Guidelines (on board for teacher)

3. **Independent Thinking: Strokes and Letters: *Q, G* (Small-Group Activity)**
   Grab Bag with Flashcards for uppercase letters: *L, T, I, H, F, E, A, Z, N, M, V, W, X, Y, K, D, B, P, R, U, J, O, C*
   Uppercase Letter Writing Practice Sheet: *Q, G* (one for each student)
   Pencils (one for each student)
   Crayons
   Personal Activity Folder for each child (including Uppercase Alphabet Fill-In from the prior lesson)

ACTIVITIES

1. Review Prior Letters

    1.1. Review: *O, C*

    - Direct the children's attention to the display of uppercase letters on the board.
    - Ask them to name and find the letters taught in the last lesson. (*O, C*)
      - Ask the children where the starting point is for these letters. (2 o'clock)
      - Quickly review the formation of each of these two new letters, writing them with sound effects on the Large Letter Formation Guidelines and, with the children, in the air.

    1.2. Team Grab Bag

    - The Grab Bag should now contain a Flashcard for each letter that has already been taught: *L, T, I, H, F, E, A, Z, N, M, V, W, X, Y, K, D, B, P, R, U, J, O, C.*
    - Divide the children into teams of three to five.
      - Each team should make a line facing the board.

110

- Choose one of the letters from the Grab Bag, and name it.
    - Lead the children to write the letter in time with its sound effects.
    - The first child in each line writes the letter on the board on the Smaller Letter Formation Guidelines.
    - The others air-write the letter.
    - When the child at the board has finished, he or she goes to the back of the line.
- Repeat until every child has had a chance to write on the board.

2. New Letters: *Q, G*

2.1. Uppercase *Q*

- Ask the children to find the uppercase Q in the display of uppercase letters on the board and the Alphabet Frieze.
- Demonstrate how to write the uppercase Q on the board, as shown. The numbers indicate the order of the strokes. (*Note:* Do not draw the arrows or numbers on the board. They are just for your reference.)

- In demonstrating how to write the uppercase Q on the board,
    - Ask the children where the starting point goes (2 o'clock)
    - Ask the children how the letter Q differs from the letter O (it has a tail)
- Write the uppercase Q again on the board, this time with sound effects.
- Ask the children where the starting point goes. (2 o'clock)
    - "Pttt!" for the starting spot at 2 o'clock
    - "Wheeooo!" for the circular stroke
    - "Tk!" when lifting your marker
    - "Sssssp!" for the tail of the Q
- Lead the children to practice making the uppercase Q in the air with accompanying sound effects.

2.2. Uppercase *G*

- Ask the children to find the uppercase G in the display of uppercase letters on the board and the Alphabet Frieze.
- Demonstrate how to write the uppercase G on the board, as shown. The numbers indicate the order of the strokes. (*Note:* Do not draw the arrows or numbers on the board. They are just for your reference.)

- In demonstrating how to write the uppercase G on the board,
    - Ask the children where the starting point goes (2 o'clock)
    - Ask the children how the letter G differs from the letter C (it has a bar on its mouth)
- Write the uppercase G again on the board, this time with sound effects.

- "Pttt!" for the starting spot at 2 o'clock
- "Wheeooo!" for the circular stroke
- "Tk!" when lifting your marker
- "T-ch-ch-cht!" for the serif of the *G*
- Lead the children to practice making the uppercase *G* in the air with accompanying sound effects.

2.3. Keeping Track of Letters

- Ask the children to find the *Q* and *G* on the display of uppercase letters on the board.
- Rewrite or otherwise tag each of these letters to show that they have been taught.

3. Independent Thinking: Strokes and Letters: *Q, G*

- Gather the children into groups of three or four.
- Make sure every child has
  - Personal Activity Folder
  - Uppercase Letter Writing Practice Sheet: *Q, G*
  - Uppercase Alphabet Fill-In activity sheet

3.1. Dictation Plus Writing New Letters: *Q, G*

- Uppercase Letter Dictation
  - Remind the children that the top row of their Uppercase Letter Writing Practice Sheet is for dictation.
    - You will name a letter.
    - They will write the letter you name.
  - Dictate five letters from among those taught in previous lessons.
    - Choose the letters one by one from the Grab Bag.
    - Give the children time to write each letter before dictating the next.
- New Letters: *Q, G*
  - Remind the children how to complete the rest of Uppercase Letter Writing Practice Sheet: *Q, G.*
    - A child in each group directs the tracing and accompanying sound effects for the first (dotted) letter.
    - The next child is then in charge of directing the rewriting of that letter in the second box in the row.
    - The turn-taking and writing continues until all boxes of the activity sheet are filled in.
  - Remind the children that when they have completed the sheet, they will choose their very best job of writing the letter for each row.
  - To mark the *one best letter* in each row, they choose a crayon and draw a frame around the outside of the square in which it appears.

3.2. Uppercase Alphabet Fill-In

- Remind the children that their Uppercase Alphabet Fill-In activity sheets are in their Personal Activity Folders.

- Tell the children that when they have completed the Uppercase Letter Writing Practice Sheets, they should work together to add today's new letters, Q and G, where they belong in their Uppercase Alphabet Fill-In activity sheets.

3.3. Cleaning Up

- Ask the children to put *both* of the activity sheets into their Personal Activity Folders.

 **LESSON 3** # Uppercase Letters that Start at 2 o'Clock: *S*

Objectives	• To review starting spots and strokes
	• To review prior letters (*L, T, I, H, F, E, A, Z, N, M, V, W, X, Y, K, D, B, P, R, U, J, O, C, Q, G*)
	• To introduce proper formation of uppercase *S*
Materials	**1. Review Prior Letters**
	Display of the uppercase letters on the board
	Large Letter Formation Guidelines (on board for teacher)
	Smaller Letter Formation Guidelines (on board for students)
	Grab Bag with Flashcards for uppercase letters: *L, T, I, H, F, E, A, Z, N, M, V, W, X, Y, K, D, B, P, R, U, J, O, C, Q, G*
	2. New Letter: *S*
	Alphabet Frieze
	Display of the uppercase letters on the board
	Large Letter Formation Guidelines (on board for teacher)
	3. Independent Thinking: Strokes and Letters: *S* (Small-Group Activity)
	Uppercase Letter Writing Practice Sheet: *S* (one for each student)
	Pencils (one for each student)
	Crayons
	Personal Activity Folder for each child (including Uppercase Alphabet Fill-In from the prior lesson)

ACTIVITIES

1. Review Prior Letters

    1.1. Review: *Q, G*

    • Direct the children's attention to the display of uppercase letters on the board.

    • Ask them to name and find the letters taught in the last lesson. (*Q, G*)

        • Ask the children where the starting point is for these letters. (2 o'clock)

        • Quickly review the formation of each of these two new letters, writing them with sound effects on the Large Letter Formation Guidelines and, with the children, in the air.

    1.2. Team Grab Bag

    • The Grab Bag should now contain a Flashcard for each letter already taught: *L, T, I, H, F, E, A, Z, N, M, V, W, X, Y, K, D, B, P, R, U, J, O, C, Q, G.*

    • Divide the children into teams of three to five.

        • Each team should make a line facing the board.

        • Choose one of the letters from the Grab Bag, and name it.

            • Lead the children to write the letter in time with its sound effects.

- The first child in each line writes the letter on the board on the Smaller Letter Formation Guidelines.
  - The others air-write the letter.
  - When the child at the board has finished, he or she goes to the back of the line.
- Repeat until every child has had a chance to write on the board.

2. New Letter: *S*

   2.1. Uppercase *S*

   - Point out that there is only one uppercase letter that the children haven't learned yet. Ask them what letter it is. (*S*)
   - Demonstrate how to write the uppercase *S* on the board, as shown. The numbers indicate the order of the strokes. (*Note:* Do not draw the arrows or numbers on the board. They are just for your reference.)

   - In demonstrating how to write the uppercase *S* on the board,
     - Ask the children where the starting point goes (2 o'clock)
     - Point out that the letter *S* is special—it curls twice, like a snake!
   - Write the uppercase *S* again on the board, this time with sound effects.
     - "Pttt!" for the starting spot at two o'clock
     - "Wheeooo!" for the top circular stroke
     - "Wheeooo!" for the bottom circular stroke
   - Lead the children to practice making the uppercase *S* in the air with accompanying sound effects.

   2.2. Keeping Track of Letters

   - Rewrite or otherwise mark the uppercase *S* in the display of uppercase letters on the board to show that it has been taught.

3. Independent Thinking: Strokes and Letters: *S*

   - Gather the children into groups of three or four.
   - Make sure every child has
     - Personal Activity Folder
     - Uppercase Letter Writing Practice Sheet: *S*
     - Uppercase Alphabet Fill-In activity sheet
   - Point out to the children that their Uppercase Letter Writing Practice Sheet looks a little bit different today.
     - The first row is for practicing their new letter, *S*, as usual.
     - The rest of the boxes are for writing the whole uppercase alphabet.
   - When their group has completed the row for their new letter, *S*, the children will work together to write the whole alphabet, from *A* to *Z*.
     - Demonstrate on the board:

- Write the letter *A*, and ask the children what letter comes next.
- Write the letter *B*, and ask what letter comes next.
- At letter *E*, pause and recite the "Alphabet Song" to affirm that the next letter is *F*.
- When working with their groups, the children should take turns going around the circle saying which letter comes next.
- Whenever they are unsure of what letter comes next, they should point to each letter they have already written while singing the "Alphabet Song."

3.1. New Letter: *S*

- Remind the children how to complete the first row of Uppercase Letter Writing Practice Sheet: *S*:
  - A child in each group directs the tracing and accompanying sound effects for the first (dotted) letter.
  - The next child is then in charge of directing the rewriting of that letter in the second box in the row.
  - The turn-taking and writing continues until the first line of boxes on the activity sheet is filled in.
- Remind the children that when they have completed the sheet, they will choose their very best letter *S*.
  - To mark the *one best letter S*, they choose a crayon and draw a frame around the outside of the square in which it appears.

3.2. Writing the Uppercase Alphabet

- Remind the children that when their group finishes the first row of Uppercase Letter Writing Practice Sheet: *S*, they will work together to write the whole uppercase alphabet.
- Rotate through the groups and remind them
  - To take turns, going around the circle, saying what letter comes next
  - To use the "Alphabet Song" as an organizer and mnemonic whenever they are unsure of what letter comes next

3.3. Uppercase Alphabet Fill-In

- Remind the children that their Uppercase Alphabet Fill-In activity sheets are in their Personal Activity Folders.
- Tell the children that when they have completed the Uppercase Letter Writing Practice Sheets, they should add today's new letter, *S*, where it belongs in their Uppercase Alphabet Fill-In activity sheets.
- Their Uppercase Alphabet Fill-In activity sheet is now complete!

3.4. Cleaning Up

- Ask the children to put *both* of the activity sheets into their Personal Activity Folders.
- Collect their Personal Activity Folders.

TEACHER TIP
To encourage the children to write the alphabet fairly often, invite them to do it on the board on rainy days or during other open activity moments.

LESSON 4 Write Your Own Name

ASSESSMENT ALERT: The Progress-Check Uppercase Letter Writing assessment is administered during this lesson to evaluate students' progress.

Objectives
- To administer the Uppercase Letter Writing assessment
- To celebrate finishing the uppercase alphabet by making Name Displays

Materials
1. **Progress-Check Uppercase Letter Writing Assessment**

   Uppercase Letter Writing assessment form (see Appendix A.2)

   Pencil (one for each child)

2. **Write Your Own Name Using Uppercase Letters**

   Write Your Own Name (Uppercase) activity sheet (one for each child; see Appendix B.5 or online)

   Pencil (one for each child)

   List of Name Poems (for teacher reference)

   Finished Name Display to show the children what they will make

3. **Making Name Displays**

   Materials for creating Name Displays
   - Scissors for cutting out *best name*
   - Colored mats sized for mounting the names (e.g., 9" × 4", three per sheet of 9" × 12" construction paper)
   - Paste for affixing the names to the mats
   - Highlighting markers for tracing over the names
   - Variety of stickers for decorating the mats

ACTIVITIES

1. Progress-Check Uppercase Letter Writing Assessment
   - Tell the children that you have something for them to work on before they make their Name Displays.
   - Hold up the Uppercase Letter Writing assessment form, and ask if it looks familiar.
     - Affirm that it looks just like their Uppercase Alphabet Fill-In activity sheets except that none of the uppercase letters have yet been filled in.
     - Tell them that today they will fill in all of the uppercase letters on this sheet.
   - Explain that this is not a group activity: They will work by themselves.
     - They will each get a copy, and their job is to fill in as many of the uppercase letters as they can.
     - You will give them 5 minutes to complete the sheet. (For younger or less sophisticated students, allow 10 minutes.)
     - If they finish early, they can turn the sheet over and write the whole alphabet as many times as they can.

• Tell the children that it is important for them to do as good a job as they can because you want to save the sheet and share it with their parents.

TEACHER TIP
When collecting the children's Uppercase Letter Writing assessment, add the children's names and any notes, such as whether they finished quickly or at long length. Review each child's effort carefully, and make time to provide additional help and practice with the uppercase alphabet for the class as a whole or for those children who need extra help as indicated by their performance.

2. Write Your Own Name Using Uppercase Letters

   2.1. Remembering Name Poems
      • Ask the children to raise their hands if they remember their Name Poems.
      • Call on a few students to recite their Name Poems.
      • Tell the children that, now that they know how to write all of the letters, they can use their Name Poems to write their own names!
      • Demonstrate how to do so.
         • Call on a child to recite his or her Name Poem.
            • Ask the child to recite just the letters of his or her name.
            • Ask the child to recite the letters again, slowly, as you write them on the board.
            • Recite the child's Name Poem again, this time while pointing to the letters written on the board.
         • Repeat at least once more with another child.

   2.2. Write Your Own Name Activity Sheet
      • Tell the children that their next challenge today is to write their own names.
         • Give each child an individualized copy of the Write Your Own Name (Uppercase) activity sheet. (See Unit II, Introduction, Instructions: Special Materials and Preparation.)
         • Explain to the children that they will
            • Trace their names in the top row
            • Write their names four more times, once in each of the rows provided
            • Use their Name Poems to figure out how to spell their names when writing the names on their own.
      • Tell the children that when they have finished, they will
         • Choose their best name
         • Cut it out and use it to make their own Name Display
      • Hold up the finished Name Display as an example.
      • Show the children where the materials are for them to make their Name Displays.

3. Making Name Displays

- The children are welcome to work together in constructing their Name Displays.
- Tell them to do the following:
    - Choose their *best name* from the Write Your Own Name (Uppercase) activity sheet.
    - Cut out the best name.
    - Choose a mat.
    - Paste the cut-out name on the mat.
    - Decorate the mat as desired.

Writing Lowercase Letters

ASSESSMENT ALERT: **The Progress-Check Uppercase Letter Writing assessment should be completed for every child before beginning this unit.**

By the end of this unit, children should be able to

■ Recognize the lowercase letters with greater speed, accuracy, and confidence

■ Write most of the lowercase letters from memory or dictation

The lowercase letters are far more difficult to learn than the uppercase letters. In the first lesson of this unit, students complete the Entry-Level Lowercase Letter Writing assessment. The students' scores on this assessment will most likely be lower than they were for the Entry-Level Uppercase Letter Writing assessment. In the last lesson of the unit, the Progress-Check Lowercase Letter Writing assessment is administered to gauge students' progress. Although all students should be able to write most of the lowercase letters of the alphabet from memory or dictation by the end of the unit, their scores may be lower than scores received on the Progress-Check Uppercase Letter Writing assessment at the end of Unit II. Pay careful attention to these scores in order to give all students, individually or collectively, the help they need to become comfortable and confident with all of the lowercase letters. Their success with phonemic awareness, phonics, and reading depends on it.

As mentioned in the introduction to Unit II, visual representation of the letters is integrally bound to the movements that the hands make when writing them. But there is more. Although learning to recognize the uppercase letters is *hastened* by learning to write them, research indicates that learning to recognize the lowercase letters *depends* on learning to write them. The reason is that, for survival purposes, the visual system itself is preprogrammed to ignore differences in the orientation of objects; yet, orientation is integral to letter identity and, indeed, makes all the difference between b, p, q, and d and between n and u.

What matters is not just *writing* a letter, but linking its appearance to a common, habitual stroke sequence for its writing. Thus, the letter-writing lessons are designed to help the children write the letters such that each is represented by a consistent set of strokes, produced in a consistent order. You will be able to tell whether children are using the proper stroke sequence by examining their written work. The tendency to write letters backwards is a strong indication that children are not adhering to recommended starting spots or stroke sequences, as is inconsistency in the rendering of a letter from one occasion to the next.

The unit is divided into four chapters, each focused on one of the four basic writing strokes:

- Chapter 8: Lowercase Letters that Start at 2 o'Clock
- Chapter 9: Lowercase Letters with Loops, Humps, and Troughs
- Chapter 10: Lowercase Letters with Slanted Strokes
- Chapter 11: Lowercase Letters with Straight Up-and-Down Strokes

Each chapter begins with a reminder of the focal stroke itself and then works through a set of letters that center on that stroke. In the last chapter, students wrap up the unit by learning to print their own names in uppercase and lowercase letters and by completing the Lowercase Letter Writing assessment (Progress Check) again to gauge their growth and progress.

ASSESSMENT

The Lowercase Letter Writing assessment (Entry Level) is completed in the first lesson of this unit and then readministered (Progress Check) in the last lesson of the unit to gauge progress and continuing needs.

When	Assessment	How	Resource
Chapter 8, Lesson 1	Entry-Level Lowercase Letter Writing	Whole group	Appendix A.3
Chapter 11, Lesson 2	Progress-Check Lowercase Letter Writing	Whole group	Appendix A.3

HANDS-ON GAMES AND INDIVIDUAL DIFFERENCES

During Small-Group Sessions

During small-group activity sessions in this unit, the primary activity for the students is practice in writing the lowercase letters. Some of your time will be spent moving from group to group to offer encouragement and guidance on proper conduct. Otherwise, use this time to work with small groups or individuals who need extra support.

Give first priority to those students who are still having difficulty learning to recognize their letters. Although it is important not to short shrift letter-writing practice with these children, make sure to include extra work on letter recognition.

As the lessons in this unit progress, children who need closer help specifically with writing the letters, including extra attention to proper stroke sequences, will become more obvious.

Between Small-Group Sessions

Between lessons, it is important to find time to go through the children's Personal Activity Folders. Keep track of progress and needs using the Whole-Class Record Form and the Individual Record Form as explained in the Unit II Introduction. Again, the Whole-Class Record Form is for summarizing progress for the whole class, so only one copy is needed for the unit. The Individual Record Form is for keeping notes on the needs and progress of individual students, including particular issues that have warranted special attention and follow-up, so one form is needed per student.

Again, feel free to affix acclaim stickers (e.g., blue, red, or silver stars) to the children's activity sheets as an easy and pleasing way to let each child know that you have reviewed his or her work.

LESSON MATERIALS AND RESOURCES

The following table summarizes the materials and resources needed for both whole-group and small-group activities. *Note:* This book contains online materials (refer to About the Online Materials at the beginning of this book for more information). In the Notes column, *online* indicates that the materials are only provided online. The Notes column also indicates whether materials require additional assembly, or *special preparation.* Instructions for special preparation are provided following the table.

Chapter	Material	Use	Notes
8, 9, 10, and 11	Board, easel, or projection system	Displaying activity-specific materials	Special preparation
8, 9, 10, and 11	Alphabet Frieze	Whole group	From Unit I
8, 9, 10, and 11	Display of lowercase letters on the board	Whole group	Special preparation
8, 9, 10, and 11	Large Letter Formation Guidelines (on board, for teacher use)	Modeling/teaching letter formation	Special preparation
10 and 11	Smaller Letter Formation Guidelines (on board, for student use, one per team)	Team Grab Bag	Special preparation
8, 9, 10, and 11	Lowercase Flashcards	Whole group	Special preparation
8, 9, 10, and 11	Grab Bag	Whole group	From Unit II
8, 9, 10, and 11	Popsicle stick mug	Optional	From Unit II (Use as desired. For clarification, use is described in Chapters 8 and 9.)
8, 9, 10, and 11	Links to music for the "Alphabet Song," "Alphabet Bounce," and "Vowel Name Song"	Whole group	Online
8, 9, 10, and 11	Personal Activity Folders (labeled, one per child)	Individual portfolios	From Unit II
8, 9, 10, and 11	Lowercase Alphabet Fill-In (one per child for entire unit)	Small group	Appendix B.4
8, 9, 10, and 11	Lowercase Letter Writing Practice (one per child per lesson)	Small group	Appendix B.4
8, 9, 10, and 11	Pencils for children	Small group	None
8, 9, 10, and 11	Crayons	Small group	None
11	Write Your Own Name (Lowercase) activity sheet	Individual	Special preparation
11	Name Poems	As needed	From Unit I
11	Materials to create Name Display	Whole group	Special preparation
8, 9, 10, and 11	Scissors for cutting out best letters	Optional	None
8, 9, 10, and 11	Baggies for storing best letters	Optional	None
8, 9, 10, and 11	Whole-Class Record Form and Individual Record Forms	For keeping track of progress and needs	From Unit II
8 and 11	Lowercase Letter Writing assessment	Individual activity	Appendix A.3

Note: Appendix B materials are also available online, organized by unit.

INSTRUCTIONS: SPECIAL MATERIALS AND PREPARATION

Board, Easel, or Projection System

Each of the lessons in this unit requires teacher demonstration of the stroke sequence for the different letters that are taught or reviewed. The instructions are based on the assumption that a board or easel is used.

■ When making the letters manually in the air and on the board, do not face the children or the letters will be backward.

■ When making strokes and letters in the air, stand in various places in the classroom to make sure that all students have a good opportunity to see.

■ At the board, model each stroke or letter at least twice—once standing to the right of the writing and once standing to the left—to give all students a good view.

A suitable projection system, such as an interactive tablet and whiteboard or an overhead projector, may be used instead of a board or easel. Such technologies have the advantage of projecting what is written from a distance without getting in the way. Just make sure that each stroke and letter appears large and in proper orientation on the projection surface.

Display of Lowercase Letters

The display of lowercase letters is principally for referring to letters during whole-group activities and for keeping track of those letters that have been taught already. As with the display of uppercase letters in Unit II, write the whole alphabet in lowercase letters only, on chart paper or on the board where it will not be erased. During each lesson, mark the letters taught (e.g., rewrite them in green) to give the children a sense of progress and to reinforce their growing sense of the alphabet as a whole. You may choose to use a different color to distinguish letters taught in the most recent lesson.

Large Letter Formation Guidelines (for Teacher)

The lessons in this unit, as well as Units II and IV, require writing or modeling the formation of the letters with Letter Formation Guidelines: a topline, a midline, and a baseline. Leave at least 12" between the midline and baseline and again between the midline and topline so that letters will be big enough. In other words, the distance from the topline to the baseline should be at least 2 feet. In addition, take care to leave enough room beneath the baseline for letters that have tails.

Writing directly on a board requires the ability to write and erase letters without having to redraw the guidelines over and over. Two suggestions for making the guidelines follow:

■ *Permanent marker:* The easiest way to make the guidelines is with a nonerasable marker and a straight edge. *Warning:* Before doing this, make sure that you can erase the guidelines when you are done with them. Permanent marker will usually erase from a white board with solvent or lemon juice or by coloring over it with a dry erase marker; however, the operative word here is *usually*. Some white board surfaces are more absorbent than others, and some become less erasable with time. Before using permanent marker on the white board, test its short-term (e.g., a few minutes) removability and, if that works, its long-term (e.g., a week) removability.

■ *Whiteboard tape:* A safer way to make the guidelines is by using tape. A number of manufacturers make removable tape for whiteboards (or blackboards). You will want tape that is about ¼" wide. To make the set of three guidelines (topline, midline, and baseline) 2 feet long, use a roll of tape that is at least 6 feet (or 2 yards) long.

Smaller Letter Formation Guidelines (for Students)

The Team Grab Bag games in Chapters 10 and 11 use Letter Formation Guidelines on the board for the students' use. These Smaller Letter Formation Guidelines will need to be smaller and closer to the bottom on the board so that they are within reach of all of the students. Leave about 6" between the midline and the baseline and another 6" between the midline and the topline so that the distance from the baseline to the topline is about 12". Be sure to leave enough room beneath the baseline for letters with tails.

Because the students need to be able to write and erase letters without having to redraw the guidelines, make the guidelines with whiteboard tape or a nonerasable marker (see instructions for Large Letter Formation Guidelines).

One option is to make a separate set of guidelines for each team. In that case, make as many Letter Formation Guidelines as you have teams; for example, if the students are in six teams, create six sets of guidelines. An alternative is to make a single set of guidelines—baseline, midline, and topline— that stretches all the way across the board.

If the board is wide enough, ask the children to add new letters to their team's list without erasing those already written by their team members. This allows good review of the whole set.

Lowercase Flashcards

Throughout the unit, Flashcards will be used for reviewing letter recognition and letter formation. To make the Flashcards, print each of the lowercase letters on a card (e.g., an index card). Use a bold marker and make sure that the letters are easy to see from all corners of the classroom. The letters needed for each activity are specified in the lessons.

Write Your Own Name (Lowercase) Activity Sheet

The Write Your Own Name (Lowercase) Activity Sheet is available as an online application and as a blank, photocopiable form in Appendix B.6. The application allows you to provide a printed letter model for each child's name. If you choose to use the blank form in Appendix B.6, photocopy enough copies for each child to have one. In the first row of each child's activity sheet, hand-write his or her name with an initial uppercase letter followed by lowercase letters. Leave the remaining four rows blank. Please create these individualized activity sheets prior to Lesson 2 in Chapter 11.

Other Small-Group Material

Conducting the small-group activities also requires

- Pencil for each child (pencils with erasers are fine if you think they are appropriate)
- Crayons (at least one for each group)
- Name Poems (for your reference, in case anybody has forgotten)
- Craft materials for making Name Displays (e.g., colored mats, stickers, art supplies for decorating the mats, glue for affixing the names to the mats)

Lowercase Letters that Start at 2 o'Clock

ASSESSMENT ALERT: The Entry-Level Lowercase Letter Writing assessment should be completed for all children at the end of Lesson 1, prior to beginning Lesson 2.

LESSON 1 Introducing Lowercase Letters

Objective
- To give an overview of the differences in the shapes of the uppercase and lowercase letters
- To give an overview of the differences in the use of uppercase and lowercase letters
- To benchmark the children's ability to write the lowercase letters

Materials

1. **Why Do We Need to Learn Both?**

   Alphabet Frieze

   A short poem in which uppercase letters are used for the first letter of each word in the title, of the author's name, and of the first word of each line
   - *Note:* To ease discussion, do not choose a poem in which any word is written entirely in uppercase letters.

   Samples of print for contrasting the use of uppercase and lowercase letters
   - *Note:* The print must be visible for all of the children (e.g., big book, easel).
   - Covers versus text pages of books
   - Product names on packages
   - Titles versus text in the newspaper
   - Safety signs (e.g., STOP, WALK, EXIT)
   - *Note:* It is fine if some words on these samples are printed entirely in uppercase letters; point out that they are especially important words.

   (Optional) Removable highlighter tape
   - *Note:* This is very useful for highlighting words or letters in books; it is like tinted, see-through sticky notes. It comes in a tape dispenser, so it is easy to cut to the right length.

2. **Looking over the Lowercase Letters**

   Display of the lowercase letters on the board

   Alphabet Frieze

   Large Letter Formation Guidelines (on board for teacher)

3. **Entry-Level Lowercase Letter Writing Assessment**

   Lowercase Letter Writing assessment form (one for each child; see Appendix A.3)

   Pencils (one for each student)

ACTIVITIES

1. Why Do We Need to Learn Both?

1.1. Remembering the Lowercase Letters

- Direct the children's attention to the Alphabet Frieze, and remind the children that every letter has two forms, the **uppercase** and the **lowercase.**
    - Explain that most words can be written with either uppercase or lowercase letters. If the words are spelled the same, they say the same thing.
    - Demonstrate with a few words, such as *NO–no, SEE–see, BUS–bus,* and *YOU–you.*
- Tell the children that, as they shall see, there is a good reason for having two shapes for every letter.

1.2. Exploring Uppercase and Lowercase Usage

- Direct the children's attention to the short *poem.*
- Ask the children to examine the page and see how many **uppercase** letters they can find.
    - Ask the children to point to (and name) all the *uppercase* letters on the page.
    - If using highlighter tape, place a piece of tape on each found uppercase letter to highlight it.
    - Ask the children to count all of the *uppercase* letters they found on the page.
- Ask the children to examine the page and see how many **lowercase** letters they can find.
    - Ask the children to point to and name some of the *lowercase* letters on the page.
    - Challenge the children to count the *lowercase* letters in the poem. (Feel free to stop as soon as it is clear that there are many more *lowercase* than *uppercase* letters.)
- Ask the children whether there are more **uppercase** or **lowercase** letters on the page, engaging them to be sure they see that there are lots and lots of lowercase letters.

1.3. Why Uppercase Letters?

- Return the children's attention to words in the poem that contain uppercase letters, asking them to examine each one they find.
- "Are all of the letters in the word uppercase?"
    - If not,
        - "How many letters in the word are uppercase?" (just one)
        - "Which one?"
        - "Is the uppercase letter always the first letter of the word?"
- Tell the children that, in writing, it is customary to use an uppercase letter as the first letter of words that are very important or special.
    - Lead the children in examining the instances of uppercase letters in the poem to convey to them that uppercase letters are used for the first letter of
        - Important words in the **title** or **name** of the poem
        - People's names (e.g., author, illustrator)
        - The first word of every line of the poem
    - All of the rest of the letters are lowercase.

- Summarize that uppercase letters are usually used to alert readers that a word is especially important.
  - Share a few more (typical) samples of print with them to affirm that
    - Most of the letters in text are lowercase letters
    - Uppercase letters are used for important words, such as (share as many as desired)
      - Titles or names of publication
      - Titles of selections or articles
      - People's names (including authors)
      - Product and company names
      - Names of cities, states, countries
      - Names of days and months
      - The first word in every sentence or of every line in a poem
      - Safety signs (e.g., EXIT, STOP, WALK)

TEACHER TIP

Throughout the year, direct the children's attention to other conventionally important words that begin with uppercase letters, such as the first word of each sentence and the names of people, streets, cities, states, countries, months, and days of the week.

- Lead the children to summarize why it is important to know both uppercase and lowercase letters.
  - "Why is it important for readers to know all of the **lowercase** letters?" (because most of the letters in print are *lowercase*)
  - "Why is it important for readers to know all of the **uppercase** letters?" (because the most important words begin with *uppercase* letters)

2. Looking over the Lowercase Letters

- Remind the children that most of the letters in what they read and write will be in lowercase letters. That means that it's very important to learn to recognize and write the lowercase letters very well.
- Beneath the Large Letter Formation Guidelines on the board (from Unit II), add a line below the baseline for lowercase letters with tails.
- Point out that many of the lowercase letters look quite **different** from their uppercase partners.
  - Share a few examples (e.g., *Aa, Bb, Dd, Ee, Gg, Qq, Rr*) in the display of lowercase letters written on the board and the Alphabet Frieze.
- Point out that some of the lowercase letters look very **similar** to their uppercase partners.

- Lead the children to examine a few examples (e.g., *Cc, Oo, Ss, Tt, Uu, Vv, Ww, Xx, Zz*) in the display of lowercase letters written on the board and the Alphabet Frieze.
- Point out that these lowercase letters are only half as tall as their uppercase partners.
  - Explain that, for this reason, the lowercase letters are sometimes called the **small letters**.

3. Entry-Level Lowercase Letter Writing Assessment

- Tell the children that their next challenge will be to learn how to write *all* of the lowercase letters.
  - They will start that challenge today by showing how many lowercase letters they can already write.
- Explain the task.
  - Hold up a blank copy of the Lowercase Letter Writing assessment form, and ask if it looks familiar.
  - Affirm that it looks just like their Uppercase Alphabet Fill-In activity sheets, except that the *lowercase* letters are missing.
  - Tell the children that each of them will fill in all of the *lowercase* letters that they can on this sheet.
- Explain that this is not a group activity: They will work by themselves.
  - Give each child a separate copy of the Lowercase Letter Writing assessment.
  - Each child works independently to fill in as many of the *lowercase* letters as possible.
  - When the children are finished, they should raise their hands so that you can collect their work.

TEACHER TIP

When collecting the children's Entry-Level Lowercase Letter Writing assessment sheets, add their names, the date, and any notes, such as whether they finished quickly or took a long time. For details on scoring, see the instructions in Appendix A.3.

Lowercase Letters
that Start at 2 o'Clock: *o, c*

> ASSESSMENT ALERT: **The Entry-Level Lowercase Letter Writing assessment should be completed prior to beginning this lesson.**

Objectives
- To remind children of the 2 o'clock (circular) strokes
- To introduce proper formation of lowercase o and c

Materials
1. **Flashcard Review: Lowercase Letters (*o, c, a, d, g, q, s, f*)**
   Flashcards for 2 o'clock lowercase letters: *o, c, a, d, g, q, s, f*
   (*Optional*) Mug and labeled Popsicle sticks

2. **Remembering 2 o'Clock Strokes**
   Large Letter Formation Guidelines (on board for teacher)

3. **New Letters: *o, c***
   Alphabet Frieze
   Display of the lowercase letters on the board
   Large Letter Formation Guidelines (on board for teacher)

4. **Independent Thinking: Strokes and Letters: *o, c* (Small-Group Activity)**
   Lowercase Letter Writing Practice Sheet: o, c (one for each child)
   Lowercase Alphabet Fill-In activity sheet (one for each child)
   Pencils (one for each child)
   Crayons
   Personal Activity Folder for each child

ACTIVITIES

1. Flashcard Review: Lowercase Letters (*o, c, a, d, g, q, s, f*)
   - The stack of Flashcards should include all of the 2 o'clock lowercase letters: *o, c, a, d, g, q, s, f.*
   - Remind the children how to play the game.
     - There is one lowercase letter on each Flashcard.
     - When you hold up a card, the children think of the name of the letter shown.
     - The children do not say anything until you give the signal.
   - When the response sounds hesitant or confused, slip the letter back into the unused part of the stack, just a few cards down, so that it will quickly show up again.
   - Review the entire stack at least once.

TEACHER TIP: POPSICLE STICK ROUTINE

Once the children are comfortable with the Flashcard game, it is wise to switch unpredictably between requesting the response from the whole group and calling on individuals (in surprise order).

A handy technique for managing whole-group response sessions is to use the Popsicle Stick Routine:

- Write each of the children's names on a Popsicle stick.
- Write "all" on several sticks (roughly one third as many as there are children in the class).
- Put all of the Popsicle sticks, name-side down, in a mug.
- Instead of choosing someone to call on, select a stick and read it.
- After reading a stick, replace it in the mug, allowing it be chosen again at any time.

Among the benefits of the Popsicle Stick Routine is that it enforces the wait time. Better still, it encourages every child to prepare a response because any name can be drawn.

2. Remembering 2 o'Clock Strokes

- Tell the children that all of the **lowercase** letters are made up of the same kinds of strokes that they learned for the **uppercase** letters.
- Announce that they will begin with **lowercase** letters that are made of circles or parts of circles.
  - Remind them that for all of these letters, the starting point is the same. Some people call them **2 o'clock letters** because the **magic starting spot** is right where the **2** is on the face of a round clock.
  - Clarify the 2 o'clock position with a graphic and, ideally, by pointing out the location of the 2 on a real clock.

- Demonstrate on the board with sound effects for the starting point and the circular stroke.
  - "Pttt!" for the starting spot at the *2 o'clock* position
  - "Wheeooo!" for the circular stroke (*Hint:* Whisper "wheeooo" so it sounds like a whistle.)

INSTRUCTIONAL ALERT

When making these strokes manually on the board, take care to shift from one side to the other while writing so that all of the children will get a good view of the board.

- Ask the children to air-write the stroke with you with sound effects.
- Remind the children that the key to writing every stroke is to respect its *magic starting spot*.

UH-OH ALERT
Do not be tempted to face the children while modeling air-writing or the actions will look backward to the them.

3. New Letters: *o, c*

- The Large Letter Formation Guidelines on the board should include a baseline, a midline, and a topline, as well as a line beneath the baseline as guidance for lowercase letters with tails.

3.1. Lowercase *o*

- Ask the children to find the lowercase *o*
  - In the display of lowercase letters on the board
  - In the Alphabet Frieze
- Lead the children to compare
  - The shapes of the capital *O* and lowercase *o*, noticing their similarity
  - The sizes of the capital *O* and lowercase *o*, making sure they notice that the lowercase *o* is only half as tall
- Demonstrate how to write the lowercase *o* on the board, as shown. (*Note:* Do not draw the arrows or numbers on the board. They are just for your reference.)

- Make sure the children notice that the top of the lowercase *o* is at the *midline*. It is only half as tall as the uppercase *O*.
- Write the lowercase *o* again on the board, this time with sound effects.
  - "Pttt!" for the starting spot at *2 o'clock*
  - "Wheeooo!" for the circular stroke
- Lead the children to practice making the lowercase *o* in the air with sound effects.
- Repeat several times.

3.2. Lowercase *c*

- Ask the children to find the lowercase *c* in the display of lowercase letters on the board and the Alphabet Frieze.
- Lead the children to compare
  - The shapes of the uppercase *C* and lowercase *c*
  - The sizes of the uppercase *C* and lowercase *c*, making sure they notice that the lowercase *c* is only half as tall, reaching only to the midline

- Demonstrate how to write the lowercase *c* on the board, as shown. (*Note:* Do not draw the arrows or numbers on the board. They are just for your reference.)
- Write the lowercase *c* again on the board, this time with sound effects.

- • "Pttt!" for the starting spot at *2 o'clock*
- • "Wheeooo!" for the circular stroke
- Lead the children to practice making the lowercase *c* in the air with sound effects.
- Repeat several times.

3.3. Keeping Track of Letters

- Ask the children to find the *o* and the *c* in the display of lowercase letters on the board.
- Rewrite or otherwise mark the letters, *o* and *c*, to show that they have been taught.

4. Independent Thinking: Strokes and Letters: *o, c*

- Gather the children into groups of three or four.
- Make sure every child has his or her Personal Activity Folder, including a copy of the Lowercase Letter Writing Practice Sheet: *o, c* (see Appendix B.4) and the Lowercase Alphabet Fill-In Sheet (also in Appendix B.4).

TEACHER TIP: GROUPING

For this activity, it is best that the number of children in each group not be five. Otherwise, the same child will end up conducting only the tracing box for each letter.

4.1. Labeling Your Own Work

- Tell the children that, from now on, they will write their names on their activity sheets.
  - Point out the name blank in the upper right corner of their Lowercase Letter Writing Practice Sheet.
  - Ask them to print their name (in uppercase letters) in the name blank.

TEACHER TIP

Beyond the activity sheets in this program, it is a good idea to ask the children to write their names on all their work from now on.

4.2. Writing Uppercase *O*, *C* and New Letters: *o, c*

- Tell the children that for the first two rows on their activity sheet they will write uppercase letters. Ask which two uppercase letters. (*O, C*)
- Ask the children how the third and fourth rows are different from the first two rows. (They will write the lowercase letters, *o* and *c*.)
- Explain how the activity is conducted.
  - A child in each group directs the tracing, providing the accompanying sound effects for the first (dotted) letter.
  - The next child is then in charge of directing the rewriting of that letter in the second box in the row.
  - The turn taking and writing continue until all boxes of the activity sheet are filled in.
  - Remind the children that they must begin each letter at its *magic starting spot*.

- When they have completed the sheet, they will choose their very best letter for each row.
  - To mark the *one best letter* in each row, they choose a crayon and draw a frame around the outside of the square in which the letter appears.

EXTENSION: LOWERCASE LETTER COLLAGE
When this unit is finished, have the children celebrate by creating a Lowercase Letter Collage with their best letters. Ask the children to cut out their best letter from each row at the end of each day and to store them in a personally labeled baggie or envelope.

4.3. Lowercase Alphabet Fill-In

- Distribute a copy of the Lowercase Alphabet Fill-In to each child.
- Ask the children to write their names in the space provided in the top right corner of the page.
- Guide the children in filling in the Lowercase Alphabet Fill-In activity sheet with the letters of the day.
  - Ask them what they see on this activity sheet.
    - Affirm that it shows the entire **uppercase** alphabet.
  - Point out that there is a writing box before each letter, and ask them what that might be for.
    - Affirm that what's missing on this sheet are the **lowercase** letters.
  - Explain that every day they will fill in their new, *lowercase* letters on this sheet.
  - Remind the children that one of today's letters is the lowercase o.
    - Ask them where they think the lowercase o should be added to this page.
    - Affirm that it belongs in the space before the uppercase O.
    - Ask the children to find and point to that spot on their own sheets and to make sure that everybody in their group agrees on where it is.
  - Ask the children to work with their groups
    - To figure out where the lowercase c belongs
    - To write the lowercase c in that spot

4.4. Cleaning Up

- Ask the children to put *both* of the activity sheets into their Personal Activity folders.

LESSON 3 | Lowercase Letters that Start at 2 o'Clock: *a, d*

Objectives
- To review prior lowercase letters (*o, c*)
- To introduce proper formation of lowercase *a* and *d*

Materials
1. **Flashcard Review: Lowercase Letters (*o, c, a, d, g, q, s, f*)**
   Flashcards for 2 o'clock lowercase letters: *o, c, a, d, g, q, s, f*
   (*Optional*) Mug and labeled Popsicle sticks

2. **Review Prior Letters**
   Display of the lowercase letters on the board (with prior letters marked)
   Large Letter Formation Guidelines (on board for teacher)

3. **New Letters: *a, d***
   Alphabet Frieze
   Display of the lowercase letters on the board
   Large Letter Formation Guidelines (on board for teacher)

4. **Independent Thinking: Strokes and Letters: *a, d* (Small-Group Activity)**
   Lowercase Letter Writing Practice Sheet: *a, d* (one for each child)
   Lowercase Alphabet Fill-In activity sheet (one for each child)
   Pencils (one for each child)
   Crayons
   Personal Activity Folder for each child (including Lowercase Alphabet Fill-In from the prior lesson)

ACTIVITIES

1. Flashcard Review: Lowercase Letters (*o, c, a, d, g, q, s, f*)
   - The stack of Flashcards should include all of the 2 o'clock lowercase letters: *o, c, a, d, g, q, s, f*.
   - Remind the children how to play the game.
     - There is one lowercase letter on each card.
     - When you hold up a card, the children think of the name of the letter shown.
     - The children do not say anything until you give the signal.
   - When the response sounds hesitant or confused, slip the letter back into the unused part of the stack, just a few cards down, so that it will quickly show up again.
   - Review the entire stack at least once.

> TEACHER TIP: POPSICLE STICK ROUTINE
> Once the children are comfortable with the Flashcard game, use the Popsicle Stick Routine to reinforce wait time while switching unpredictably between requesting the response from the whole group and calling on individuals (in surprise order).

2. Review Prior Letters

- Direct the children's attention to the display of lowercase letters on the board.
  - Ask the children to find and name the letters that they learned how to write in the last lesson.
  - Make sure that all children notice how these two letters are specially marked as having been taught in the display.

UH-OH ALERT

Do not be tempted to face the children while modeling air-writing or the actions will look backward to them.

2.1. Review: *o*

- Ask the children where the *magic starting spot* is for the lowercase *o*. (2 o'clock)
- Write the lowercase letter *o* on the board with sound effects.
  - "Pttt!" for the starting spot at *2 o'clock*
  - "Wheeooo!" for the circular stroke
- Ask the children to join you in air-writing the letter *o* several times.
  - Remind them to make the baseline for the letters with their idle arm.
  - Make sure they make the sound effects as they write to help them remember the strokes.

2.2. Review: *c*

- Write the lowercase letter *c* on the board with sound effects.
  - "Pttt!" for the starting spot at *2 o'clock*
  - "Wheeooo!" for the circular stroke
- Ask the children to join you in air-writing the letter *c* several times

---

INSTRUCTIONAL ALERT

When writing on the board, take care to shift from one side to the other while writing so that all of the children will get a good view of the board.

---

3. New Letters: *a, d*

3.1. Lowercase *a*

- Ask the children to find the lowercase *a*
  - In the display of lowercase letters on the board
  - In the Alphabet Frieze
- Demonstrate how to write the lowercase *a* on the board, as shown. The numbers indicate the order of the strokes. (*Note:* Do not draw the arrows and numbers on the board. They are just for your reference.)
  - Point out that the first stroke

- Begins at 2 o'clock
- Is shaped like the lowercase letter *c*
- Write the lowercase *a* again on the board, this time with sound effects.
  - First the circular stroke, forming the shape of the letter *c*
    - "Pttt!" for the starting spot at *2 o'clock*
    - "Wheeooo!" for the circular, *c*-shaped stroke
    - "Tk!" when lifting your marker
    - "F-f-f-f-f-t!" for the vertical, top-down stroke.
- Remind the children that the up-and-down, straight strokes are always made from top to bottom.
- Lead the children to practice making the lowercase *a* in the air with sound effects.

3.2. Lowercase *d*

- Ask the children to find the lowercase *d*
  - In the display of lowercase letters on the board
  - In the Alphabet Frieze
- Demonstrate how to write the lowercase *d* on the board, as shown. The numbers indicate the order of the strokes. (*Note:* Do not draw the arrows and numbers on the board. They are just for your reference.)

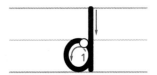

  - Point out that the *first* stroke
    - Begins at 2 o'clock
    - Is shaped like the lowercase letter *c*
- Write the lowercase *d* again on the board, this time with sound effects.
  - "Pttt!" for the starting spot at *2 o'clock*
  - "Wheeooo!" for the circular, *c*-shaped stroke
  - "Tk!" when lifting your marker
  - "F-f-f-f-f-t!" for the vertical, top-down stroke.
- Lead the children to practice making the lowercase *d* in the air with sound effects.

3.3. Keeping Track of Letters

- Ask the children to find the *a* and the *d* in the display of lowercase letters on the board.
- Rewrite or otherwise mark the letters to show that they have been taught.

4. Independent Thinking: Strokes and Letters: *a, d*

- Gather the children into groups of three or four.
- Make sure every child has
  - Personal Activity Folder
  - Lowercase Letter Writing Practice Sheet: *a, d*
  - Lowercase Alphabet Fill-In activity sheet

4.1. Dictation Plus Writing New Letters: *a, d*

- Ask the children to print their names (in uppercase letters) in the name blank at the upper right corner of the Lowercase Letter Writing Practice Sheet.

- Lowercase Letter Dictation

  - Point out that today's writing sheet is almost the same as the last one except that the top row is blank boxes only.

  - Explain that you are going to dictate lowercase letters for the top row.

  - ***Dictate*** means that you will name a letter, and they will write the letter you name.

  - Dictate the following, giving the children time to write each letter before saying the next:

    o   c   c   o   c

- New Letters: *a, d*

  - Remind the children how to complete the rest of Lowercase Letter Writing Practice Sheet: *a, d*.

    - A child in each group directs the tracing and accompanying sound effects for the first (dotted) letter.

    - The next child is then in charge of directing the rewriting of that letter in the second box in the row.

    - The turn taking and writing continue until all boxes of the activity sheet are filled in.

  - Remind the children that they must

    - Begin each line or letter at its *magic starting spot*

    - Write all vertical lines from top to bottom

  - Remind the children that when they have completed the sheet, each of them will choose their very best letter for each row.

    - To mark the *one best letter* in each row, they choose a crayon and draw a frame around the outside of the square in which the letter appears.

4.2. Lowercase Alphabet Fill-In

- Remind the children that their Lowercase Alphabet Fill-In activity sheets are in their Personal Activity Folders.

- Tell the children that when they have completed the Lowercase Letter Writing Practice Sheets, they should work together to add today's new letters, *a* and *d*, where they belong in their Lowercase Alphabet Fill-In activity sheets.

4.3. Cleaning Up

- Ask the children to put *both* of the activity sheets into their Personal Activity Folders.

Lowercase Letters
that Start at 2 o'Clock: *g*, *q*

Objectives
- To review prior lowercase letters (*o*, *c*, *a*, *d*)
- To introduce proper formation of lowercase *g* and *q*

Materials

1. **Flashcard Review: Lowercase Letters (*o*, *c*, *a*, *d*, *g*, *q*, *s*, *f*)**
   Flashcards for 2 o'clock lowercase letters: *o*, *c*, *a*, *d*, *g*, *q*, *s*, *f*
   (*Optional*) Mug and labeled Popsicle sticks

2. **Review Prior Letters**
   Display of the lowercase letters on the board (with prior letters marked)
   Large Letter Formation Guidelines (on board for teacher)

3. **New Letters: *g*, *q***
   Alphabet Frieze
   Display of the lowercase letters on the board
   Large Letter Formation Guidelines (on board for teacher)

4. **Independent Thinking: Strokes and Letters: *g*, *q* (Small-Group Activity)**
   Lowercase Letter Writing Practice Sheet: *g*, *q* (one for each child)
   Lowercase Alphabet Fill-In activity sheet (one for each child)
   Pencils (one for each child)
   Crayons
   Personal Activity Folder for each child (including Lowercase Alphabet Fill-In
   from the prior lesson)

ACTIVITIES

1. Flashcard Review: Lowercase Letters (*o*, *c*, *a*, *d*, *g*, *q*, *s*, *f*)
   - The stack of Flashcards should include all of the 2 o'clock lowercase letters: *o*, *c*, *a*, *d*, *g*, *q*, *s*, *f*.
   - Remind the children how to play the game.
     - There is one letter on each card.
     - When you hold up a card, the children think of the name of the letter shown.
     - The children do not say anything until you give the signal.
   - As always, use the Popsicle Stick Routine if desired.
   - When the response sounds hesitant or confused, slip the letter back into the unused part of the stack, just a few cards down, so that it will quickly show up again.
   - Review the entire stack at least once.

2. Review Prior Letters
   - Direct the children's attention to the display of lowercase letters on the board.
     - Ask the children to find and name the lowercase letters that they have learned how to write already (*o*, *c*, *a*, *d*).

- Make sure that all children notice how these letters are specially marked as having been taught in the display.
- For each of these previously taught letters *(o, c, a, d)*
  - Ask the children to join you in air-writing it with sound effects
  - Write the letter on the board with sound effects, reminding the children of anything special about the letter
  - Repeat and revisit the letter's air-writing as deemed useful

3. New Letters: *g, q*

3.1. Lowercase *g*

- Ask the children to find the lowercase *g* in the display of lowercase letters on the board and the Alphabet Frieze.
- Demonstrate how to write the lowercase *g* on the board, as shown. The numbers indicate the order of the strokes. (*Note:* Do not draw the arrows and numbers on the board. They are just for your reference.)
- Point out that
  - The *magic starting spot* is at 2 o'clock
  - The first stroke is again like the lowercase letter *c*
  - The second stroke hangs beneath the baseline, curling under the *g*'s body
- Write the lowercase *g* again on the board, this time with sound effects.
  - "Pttt!" for the starting spot
  - "Wheeeooo!" for the circular stroke
  - "F-f-f-f-f-l-l-l-l-oop!" for the second stroke
    - "F-f-f-f-f-!" for the top-down part of the stroke
    - "L-l-l-l-oop!" for the curved part of the second stroke
- Lead the children to practice making the lowercase *g* in the air with sound effects.

3.2. Lowercase *q*

- Ask the children to find the lowercase *q* in the display of lowercase letters on the board and the Alphabet Frieze.
- Demonstrate how to write the lowercase *q* on the board, as shown.
- Write the lowercase *q* again on the board, this time with sound effects.
  - "Pttt!" for the starting spot
  - "Wheeeooo!" for the circular stroke
  - "F-f-f-f-f-t-cht!" for the second stroke
    - "F-f-f-f-f-t!" for the top-down part of the stroke

- "T-cht!" for the little tail of the *q*
- Lead the children in air-writing the lowercase *q* in the air with accompanying sound effects.

3.3. Keeping Track of Letters

- Ask the children to find the *g* and the *q* in the display of lowercase letters on the board.
- Rewrite or otherwise mark the letters to show that they have been taught.

4. Independent Thinking: Strokes and Letters: *g, q*

- Gather the children into groups of three or four.
- Make sure every child has
  - Personal Activity Folder
  - Lowercase Letter Writing Practice Sheet: *g, q*
  - Lowercase Alphabet Fill-In activity sheet

4.1. Dictation Plus Writing New Letters: *g, q*

- Ask the children to print their names (in uppercase letters) in the name blank at the upper right corner of their Lowercase Letter Writing Practice Sheet.
- Lowercase Letter Dictation
  - Remind the children that the top row of their Lowercase Letter Writing Practice Sheet is for dictation.
    - You will name a letter.
    - They will write the letter you name.
  - Dictate the following, giving the children time to write each letter before saying the next:

        o   c   a   d   c

- New Letters: *g, q*
  - Remind the children how to complete the rest of Lowercase Letter Writing Practice Sheet: *g, q*:
    - A child in each group directs the tracing and accompanying sound effects for the first (dotted) letter.
    - The next child is then in charge of directing the rewriting of that letter in the second box in the row.
    - The turn taking and writing continue until all boxes of the activity sheet are filled in.
  - Remind the children that when they have completed the sheet, they will choose their very best letter for each row.
    - To mark the *one best letter* in each row, they choose a crayon and draw a frame around the outside of the square in which the letter appears.

4.2. Lowercase Alphabet Fill-In

- Remind the children that their Lowercase Alphabet Fill-In activity sheets are in their Personal Activity Folders.

- Tell the children that when they have completed the Lowercase Letter Writing Practice Sheets, they should work together to add today's new letters, *g* and *q*, where they belong in their Lowercase Alphabet Fill-In activity sheets.

4.3. Cleaning Up

- Ask the children to put *both* of the activity sheets into their Personal Activity Folders.

Lowercase Letters
that Start at 2 o'Clock: *s, f*

Objectives
- To review names and shapes of lowercase letters that start at the 2 o'clock
- To review prior lowercase letters (*o, c, a, d, g, q*)
- To introduce proper formation of lowercase *s* and *f*

Materials
1. **Flashcard Review: Lowercase Letters (*o, c, a, d, g, q, s, f*)**
   Flashcards for 2 o'clock lowercase letters: *o, c, a, d, g, q, s, f*
   (*Optional*) Mug and labeled Popsicle sticks

2. **Review Prior Letters**
   Display of the lowercase letters on the board (with prior letters marked)
   Large Letter Formation Guidelines (on board for teacher)

3. **New Letters: *s, f***
   Alphabet Frieze
   Display of the lowercase letters on the board
   Large Letter Formation Guidelines (on board for teacher)

4. **Independent Thinking: Strokes and Letters: *s, f* (Small-Group Activity)**
   Lowercase Letter Writing Practice Sheet: *s, f* (one for each child)
   Lowercase Alphabet Fill-In activity sheet (one for each child)
   Pencils (one for each child)
   Crayons
   Personal Activity Folder for each child (including Lowercase Alphabet Fill-In from the prior lesson)

ACTIVITIES

1. Flashcard Review: Lowercase Letters (*o, c, a, d, g, q, s, f*)
   - The stack of Flashcards should include all of the 2 o'clock lowercase letters: *o, c, a, d, g, q, s, f*.
   - Remind the children how to play the game.
     - There is one letter on each card.
     - When you hold up a card, the children think of the name of the letter shown.
     - The children do not say anything until you give the signal.
   - Use the Popsicle Stick Routine if desired.
   - When the response sounds hesitant or confused, slip the letter back into the unused part of the stack, just a few cards down, so that it will quickly show up again.
   - Review the entire stack at least once.

2. Review Prior Letters
   - Direct the children's attention to the display of lowercase letters on the board.

- Ask the children to find and name the lowercase letters that they have learned how to write already: *o, c, a, d, g, q.*
- Make sure that all children notice how these letters are specially marked as having been taught in the display.

- For each of these previously taught lowercase letters (*o, c, a, d, g, q*)
  - Ask the children to join you in air-writing it with sound effects
  - Write the letter on the board with sound effects, reminding the children of anything special about the letter
  - Repeat and revisit the letter's air-writing as deemed useful

3. New Letters: *s, f*

  3.1. Lowercase *s*

  - Ask the children to find the lowercase *s* in the display of lowercase letters on the board and the Alphabet Frieze.
  - Demonstrate how to write the lowercase *s* on the board, as shown. The numbers indicate the order of the strokes. (*Note:* Do not draw the arrows and numbers on the board. They are just for your reference.)
  - Point out that
    - The *magic starting spot* is at 2 o'clock
    - The first stroke is like the lowercase letter *c* but smaller, and when it gets to the bottom, it curls back in the other direction like a snake
    - Write the lowercase *s* again on the board, this time with sound effects.
      - "Pttt!" for the starting spot
      - "Wheeeoooeee!" for the entire, double circular stroke
    - Lead the children to practice making the lowercase *s* in the air with sound effects.

  3.2. Lowercase *f*

  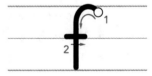

  - Ask the children to find the lowercase *f* in the display of lowercase letters on the board and the Alphabet Frieze.
  - Demonstrate how to write the lowercase *f* on the board, as shown. The numbers indicate the order of the strokes. (*Note:* Do not draw the arrows and numbers on the board. They are just for your reference.)
    - Point out that even though this is a lowercase letter, this letter reaches all the way to the top line.
    - Write the lowercase *f* again on the board, this time with sound effects.
    - "Pttt!" for the magic starting spot at 2 o'clock
    - "Wheeoof-f-f-f-t!" for the first stroke
      - "Wheeeooo!" for the first, curved part of the stroke

- "F-f-f-f-f-t!" for the top-down bar, reaching all the way to the baseline
  - "Tk!" when lifting your marker
  - "T-ch-cht!" for the horizontal strokes that makes the bar on the midline
- Lead the children in air-writing the lowercase *f* in the air with accompanying sound effects.

3.3. Keeping Track of Letters

- Ask the children to find the *s* and the *f* in the display of lowercase letters on the board.
- Rewrite or otherwise mark the letters to show that they have been taught.

4. Independent Thinking: Strokes and Letters: *s, f*

- Gather the children into groups of three or four.
- Make sure every child has
  - Personal Activity Folder
  - Lowercase Letter Writing Practice Sheet: *s, f*
  - Lowercase Alphabet Fill-In activity sheet

4.1. Dictation Plus Writing New Letters: *s, f*

- Ask the children to print their names (in uppercase letters) in the name blank at the upper right corner of the Lowercase Letter Writing Practice Sheet.
- Lowercase Letter Dictation
  - Remind the children that the top row of their Lowercase Letter Writing Practice Sheet is for dictation.
    - You will name a letter.
    - They will write the letter you name.
  - Dictate the following, giving the children time to write each letter before saying the next:

      o   a   d   g   q

- New Letters: *s, f*
  - Remind the children of how to complete the rest of Lowercase Letter Writing Practice Sheet: *s, f*.
    - A child in each group directs the tracing and accompanying sound effects for the first (dotted) letter.
    - The next child is then in charge of directing the rewriting of that letter in the second box in the row.
    - The turn taking and writing continue until all boxes of the activity sheet are filled in.
  - Remind the children that when they have completed the sheet, they will choose their very best letter for each row.
    - To mark the *one best letter* in each row, they choose a crayon and draw a frame around the outside of the square in which the letter appears.

4.2. Lowercase Alphabet Fill-In

- Remind the children that their Lowercase Alphabet Fill-In activity sheets are in their Personal Activity Folders.

- Tell the children that when they have completed the Lowercase Letter Writing Practice Sheets, they should work together to add today's new letters, *s* and *f*, where they belong in their Lowercase Alphabet Fill-In activity sheets.

4.3. Cleaning Up

- Ask the children to put *both* of the activity sheets into their Personal Activity Folders.

Lowercase Letters with Loops, Humps, and Troughs

LESSON 1 Lowercase Letters with Loops, Humps, and Troughs: *b, p*

Objectives
- To review formation of 2 o'clock letters (*o, c, a, d, g, q, s, f*)
- To review names and shapes of lowercase letters with loops, humps, and troughs (*b, p, m, n, r, h, u, j, e*).
- To introduce proper formation of lowercase *b* and *p*

Materials

1. **Review Prior Letters**

   Display of the lowercase letters on the board

   Large Letter Formation Guidelines (on board for teacher)

   Grab Bag with Flashcards for previously taught letters: *o, c, a, d, g, q, s, f*

2. **Flashcard Review: Lowercase Letters with Loops, Humps, and Troughs**

   Flashcard stack for letters with loops, humps, and troughs: *b, p, m, n, r, h, u, j, e*

3. **Remembering Loops, Humps, and Troughs**

   Large Letter Formation Guidelines (on board for teacher)

4. **New Letters: *b, p***

   Alphabet Frieze

   Display of the lowercase letters on the board

   Large Letter Formation Guidelines (on board for teacher)

5. **Independent Thinking: Strokes and Letters: *b, p* (Small-Group Activity)**

   Grab Bag with Flashcards for previously taught letters: *o, c, a, d, g, q, s, f*

   Lowercase Letter Writing Practice Sheet: *b, p* (one for each child).

   Pencils (one for each child)

   Crayons

   Personal Activity Folder (including Lowercase Alphabet Fill-In from the prior lesson)

ACTIVITIES

1. **Review Prior Letters**

    1.1. **Review: *s, f***

        - Direct the children's attention to the display of the lowercase letters on the board.
            - Ask them to name and find the lowercase letters taught in the last lesson (*s, f*).
            - Quickly review the formation of each of these two new letters, writing them with sound effects on the Large Letter Formation Guidelines and, with the children, in the air.

    1.2. **Grab Bag Review**

        - The Grab Bag should contain a Flashcard for each letter already taught: *o, c, a, d, g, q, s, f*.
            - Call on a child to choose a letter from the Grab Bag and to
                - Signal for everyone to name the chosen letter (Don't forget wait time!)
                - Lead everyone in air-writing the letter together with sound effects

---

UH-OH ALERT

Make sure the child models the letter with his or her back to the others so that the actions do not look backward to the children.

        - If you notice any hesitation or uncertainty,
            - Repeat the air-writing
            - Put the card back in the bag so that it may be drawn again during the session
        - Call on another child to choose and lead the response for the next letter.
        - Repeat until at least five letters have been reviewed.

2. **Flashcard Review: Lowercase Letters with Loops, Humps, and Troughs**

    - The stack of Flashcards should include all of the lowercase letters with loops, humps, and troughs: *b, p, m, n, r, h, u, j, e*.
    - Tell the children that they have now completed the lowercase letters that start at 2 o'clock, so it's time to start on lowercase letters with loops, humps, and troughs.
    - To refresh their memories of these letters, start with the Flashcard game.
    - Remind the children of how to play the game.
        - There is one letter on each card.
        - When you hold up a card, the children think of the name of the letter shown.
        - The children do not say anything until you give the signal.
    - As always, use the Popsicle Stick Routine if desired.
    - When the response sounds hesitant or confused, slip the letter back into the unused part of the stack, just a few cards down, so that it will quickly show up again.
    - Review the entire stack at least once.

3. Remembering Loops, Humps, and Troughs

- Tell the children that many of the letters have loopy parts.
- Tell them that sometimes the strokes loop in one direction and sometimes in another.
- Demonstrate each on the board.
  - For some of the lowercase letters, the loop goes sideways.
  - For other lowercase letters, the loop is on the bottom, like a trough that holds water.
  - For other letters, the loop is upside down so that it looks like a hump.
- Ask the children to air-write each version of stroke with you with the new sound effect.
  - "Pttt!" for the starting spot
  - "L-l-l-l-oop!" for the curved stroke

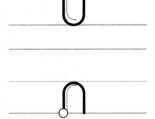

4. New Letters: *b*, *p*

  4.1. Lowercase *b*

- Ask the children to find the lowercase *b* in the display of lowercase letters on the board and the Alphabet Frieze.
- Demonstrate how to write the lowercase *b* on the board, as shown. The numbers indicate the order of the strokes. (*Note:* Do not draw the arrows or numbers on the board. They are just for your reference.)

- Point out that
  - The up-down bar reaches all the way from the topline to the baseline
  - The loop sits between the midline and the baseline
- Write the lowercase *b* again on the board, this time with sound effects.
  - "Pttt!" for the magic starting spot
  - "F-f-f-f-f-t!" for the top-down bar
  - "L-l-l-l-oop!" for the curved stroke, the belly of the *b*
- Lead the children to practice making the lowercase *b* in the air with accompanying sound effects.

  4.2. Lowercase *p*

- Ask the children to find the lowercase *p* in the display of lowercase letters on the board and the Alphabet Frieze.
- Demonstrate how to write the lowercase *p* on the board, as shown. (*Note:* Do not draw the arrows or numbers on the board. They are just for your reference.)
  - Point out that

- The up-down bar begins at the midline and extends below the baseline
- The top of the loop fits between the midline and the baseline
- Write the lowercase *p* again on the board, this time with sound effects.
    - "Pttt!" for the magic starting spot
    - "F-f-f-f-f-t!" for the top-down bar
    - "L-l-l-l-oop!" for the curved stroke, the belly of the *p*
- Lead the children to practice making the lowercase *p* in the air with accompanying sound effects.

4.3. Keeping Track of Letters

- Ask the children to find the *b* and the *p* on the display of lowercase letters on the board.
- Rewrite or otherwise mark the letters to show that they have been taught.

5. Independent Thinking: Strokes and Letters: *b, p*

- Gather the children into groups of three or four.
- Make sure every child has
    - Personal Activity Folder
    - Lowercase Letter Writing Practice Sheet: *b, p*
    - Lowercase Alphabet Fill-In activity sheet

5.1. Dictation Plus Writing New Letters: *b, p*

- Remind the children to print their names (in uppercase letters) in the name blank at the upper right corner of the Lowercase Letter Writing Practice Sheet.
- Lowercase Letter Dictation
    - Remind the children that the top row of their Lowercase Letter Writing Practice Sheet is for dictation.
        - You will name a letter.
        - They will write the letter you name.
    - Choose five letters from among those taught in previous lessons.
        - The Grab Bag should contain only those letters.
        - Give the children time to write each letter before dictating the next.
- New Letters: *b, p*
    - Remind the children how to complete the rest of Lowercase Letter Writing Practice Sheet: *b, p*.
        - A child in each group directs the tracing and accompanying sound effects for the first (dotted) letter.
        - The next child is then in charge of directing the rewriting of that letter in the second box in the row.
        - The turn taking and writing continue until all boxes of the activity sheet are filled in.

- Remind the children that when they have completed the sheet, they will choose their very best letter for each row.
  - To mark the *one best letter* in each row, they choose a crayon and draw a frame around the outside of the square in which the letter appears.

5.2. Lowercase Alphabet Fill-In

- Remind the children that their Lowercase Alphabet Fill-In activity sheets are in their Personal Activity folders.
- Tell the children that when they have completed the Lowercase Letter Writing Practice Sheets, they should work together to add today's new letters, *b* and *p*, where they belong in their Lowercase Alphabet Fill-In activity sheets.

5.3. Cleaning Up

- Ask the children to put *both* of the activity sheets into their Personal Activity Folders.

LESSON 2 Lowercase Letters with
Loops, Humps, and Troughs: *n, m*

Objectives
- To review names and shapes of lowercase letters with loops, humps, and troughs (*b, p, m, n, r, h, u, j, e*)
- To review formation of previously taught letters (*o, c, a, d, g, q, s, f, b, p*)
- To introduce proper formation of lowercase *m* and *n*

Materials
1. **Review Prior Letters**
   Display of the lowercase letters on the board
   Large Letter Formation Guidelines (on board for teacher)
   Grab Bag with Flashcards for prior letters: *o, c, a, d, g, q, s, f, b, p*

2. **Flashcard Review: Lowercase Letters with Loops, Humps, and Troughs**
   Flashcard stack with letters with loops, humps, and troughs: *b, p, m, n, r, h, u, j, e*

3. **New Letters: *n, m***
   Alphabet Frieze
   Display of the lowercase letters on the board
   Large Letter Formation Guidelines (on board for teacher)

4. **Independent Thinking: Strokes and Letters: *n, m* (Small-Group Activity)**
   Grab Bag with Flashcards for prior letters: *o, c, a, d, g, q, s, f, b, p*
   Lowercase Letter Writing Practice Sheet: *n, m* (one for each child)
   Pencils (one for each child)
   Crayons
   Personal Activity Folder for each child (including Lowercase Alphabet Fill-In from the prior lesson)

ACTIVITIES

1. Review Prior Letters

   1.1. Review: *b, p*

   - Direct the children's attention to the display of lowercase letters on the board.
     - Ask them to name and find the two letters taught in the last lesson (*b, p*).
     - Quickly review the formation of each of these two new letters, writing them with sound effects on the Large Letter Formation Guidelines and, with the children, in the air.

   1.2. Grab Bag Review

   - The Grab Bag should contain a Flashcard for each letter that has already been taught: *o, c, a, d, g, q, s, f, b, p*.
   - Call on a child to choose a letter from the Grab Bag and to
     - Signal for everyone to name the chosen letter (Don't forget wait time!)
     - Lead everyone in air-writing the letter together with sound effects

- If you notice any hesitation or uncertainty,
  - Repeat the air-writing
  - Put the card back in the bag so that it may be drawn again during the session
- Call on another child to choose and lead the response for the next letter.
- Repeat until at least five letters have been reviewed.

2. Flashcard Review: Lowercase Letters with Loops, Humps, and Troughs

- The stack of Flashcards should include all of the lowercase letters with loops, humps, and troughs: *b, p, m, n, r, h, u, j, e.*
- Remind the children how to play the game.
  - There is one lowercase letter on each card.
  - When you hold up a card, the children think of the name of the letter shown.
  - The children do not say anything until you give the signal.
- As always, use the Popsicle Stick Routine if desired.
- When the response sounds hesitant or confused, slip the letter back into the unused part of the stack, just a few cards down, so that it will quickly show up again.
- Review the entire stack at least once.

3. New Letters: *n, m*

- Remind the children that they are now working on lowercase letters with loops, humps, and troughs.
  - Both of today's letters have humps.
  - Remind the children of the proper formation of the hump stroke (as shown).

3.1. Lowercase *n*

- Ask the children to find the lowercase *n* in the display of lowercase letters on the board and the Alphabet Frieze.
- Demonstrate how to write the lowercase *n* on the board, as shown. (*Note:* Do not draw the arrows or numbers on the board. They are just for your reference.)

  - Point out that the there is no need to lift the marker after the first stroke because the second stroke is made from bottom to top.
- Write the lowercase *n* again on the board, this time with sound effects.
  - "Pttt!" for the starting spot
  - "F-f-f-f-f-t!" for the first vertical stroke, from top to bottom
  - "L-l-l-l-oop!" for the curved stroke, the hump of the *n*

- Lead the children to practice making the lowercase *n* in the air with accompanying sound effects.

3.2. Lowercase *m*

- Ask the children to find the lowercase *m* in the display of lowercase letters on the board and the Alphabet Frieze.

- Demonstrate how to write the lowercase *m* on the board, as shown. (*Note:* Do not draw the arrows or numbers on the board. They are just for your reference.)

- Write the lowercase *m* again on the board, this time with sound effects.

  - "Pttt!" for the starting spot

  - "F-f-f-f-f-t!" for the first vertical stroke, from top to bottom

  - "L-l-l-l-oop!" for the curved stroke, the first hump of the *m*

  - "L-l-l-l-oop!" for the curved stroke, the second hump of the *m*

- Lead the children to practice making the lowercase *m* in the air with accompanying sound effects.

3.3. Keeping Track of Letters

- Ask the children to find the *n* and the *m* on the display of lowercase letters on the board.

- Rewrite or otherwise mark the new letters to show that they have been taught.

4. Independent Thinking: Strokes and Letters: *n, m*

- Gather the children into groups of three or four.

- Make sure every child has

  - Personal Activity Folder

  - Lowercase Letter Writing Practice Sheet: *n, m*

  - Lowercase Alphabet Fill-In activity sheet

4.1. Dictation Plus Writing New Letters: *n, m*

- Remind the children to print their names (in uppercase letters) in the name blank at the upper right corner of their Lowercase Letter Writing Practice Sheet.

- Lowercase Letter Dictation

  - Remind the children that the top row of their Lowercase Letter Writing Practice Sheet is for dictation.

    - You will name a letter.

    - They will write the letter you name.

  - Dictate five letters from among those taught in previous lessons.

    - Choose the letters one by one from the Grab Bag.

    - Give the children time to write each letter before dictating the next.

- New Letters: *n, m*

  - Remind the children of how to complete the rest of Lowercase Letter Writing Practice Sheet: *n, m*.

- A child in each group directs the tracing and accompanying sound effects for the first (dotted) letter.
- The next child is then in charge of directing the rewriting of that letter in the second box in the row.
- The turn taking and writing continue until all boxes of the activity sheet are filled in.
- Remind the children that when they have completed the sheet, they will choose their very best letter for each row.
  - To mark the *one best letter* in each row, they choose a crayon and draw a frame around the outside of the square in which the letter appears.

4.2. Lowercase Alphabet Fill-In

- Remind the children that their Lowercase Alphabet Fill-In activity sheets are in their Personal Activity Folders.
- Tell the children that when they have completed the Lowercase Letter Writing Practice Sheets, they should work together to add today's new letters, *n* and *m*, where they belong in their Lowercase Alphabet Fill-In activity sheets.

4.3. Cleaning Up

- Ask the children to put *both* of the activity sheets into their Personal Activity Folders.

Lowercase Letters with Loops, Humps, and Troughs: *r, h*

Objectives
- To review formation of previously taught letters (*o, c, a, d, g, q, s, f, b, p, m, n*)
- To review names and shapes of lowercase letters with loops, humps, and troughs
- To introduce proper formation of lowercase *r* and *h*

Materials

1. **Review Prior Letters**

   Display of the lowercase letters on the board

   Large Letter Formation Guidelines (on board for teacher)

   Grab Bag with Flashcards for prior letters: *o, c, a, d, g, q, s, f, b, p, m, n*

2. **Flashcard Review: Lowercase Letters with Loops, Humps, and Troughs**

   Flashcard stack with letters with loops, humps, and troughs: *b, p, m, n, r, h, u, j, e*

3. **New Letters: *r, h***

   Alphabet Frieze

   Display of the lowercase letters on the board

   Large Letter Formation Guidelines (on board for teacher)

4. **Independent Thinking: Strokes and Letters: *r, h* (Small-Group Activity)**

   Grab Bag with Flashcards for prior letters: *o, c, a, d, g, q, s, f, b, p, m, n*

   Lowercase Letter Writing Practice Sheet: *r, h* (one for each child)

   Pencils (one for each child)

   Crayons

   Personal Activity Folder for each child (including Lowercase Alphabet Fill-In from the prior lesson)

ACTIVITIES

1. Review Prior Letters

   1.1. Review: *n, m*
   - Direct the children's attention to the display of lowercase letters on the board.
     - Ask them to name and find the letters taught in the last lesson (*n, m*).
     - Quickly review the formatio n of each of these two new letters, writing them with sound effects on the Large Letter Formation Guidelines and, with the children, in the air.

   1.2. Grab Bag Review
   - The Grab Bag should contain a card for each letter that has already been taught: *o, c, a, d, g, q, s, f, b, p, m, n*.
   - Call on a child to choose a letter from the Grab Bag and to
     - Signal for everyone to name the chosen letter (Don't forget wait time!)
     - Lead everyone in air-writing the letter together with sound effects

> **UH-OH ALERT**
> Make sure the child models the letter with his or her back to the others so that the actions do not look backward to the children.

- If you notice any hesitation or uncertainty,
  - Repeat the air-writing
  - Put the card back in the bag so that it may be drawn again during the session
- Call on another child to choose and lead the response for the next letter
- Repeat until at least five letters have been reviewed.

2. Flashcard Review: Lowercase Letters with Loops, Humps, and Troughs

- The stack of Flashcards should include all of the lowercase letters with loops, humps, and troughs: *b, p, m, n, r, h, u, j, e.*
- Remind the children of how to play the game.
  - There is one lowercase letter on each card.
  - When you hold up a card, the children think of the name of the letter shown.
  - The children do not say anything until you give the signal.
- When the response sounds hesitant or confused, slip the letter back into the unused part of the stack, just a few cards down, so that it will quickly show up again.
- Review the entire stack at least once.

3. New Letters: *r, h*

3.1. Lowercase *r*

- Ask the children to find the lowercase *r* in the display of lowercase letters on the board and the Alphabet Frieze.
- Demonstrate how to write the lowercase *r* on the board, as shown. (*Note:* Do not draw the arrows or numbers on the board. They are just for your reference.)

  - Note that there is no need to lift the pencil between the first and second stroke.
- Write the lowercase *r* again on the board, this time with sound effects.
  - "Pttt!" for the starting spot
  - "F-f-f-f-f-t!" for the top-down bar
  - "L-l-l-l-oop!" for the curved stroke
- Lead the children to practice making the lowercase *r* in the air with accompanying sound effects.

3.2. Lowercase *h*

- Ask the children to find the lowercase *h* in the display of lowercase letters on the board and the Alphabet Frieze.

- Demonstrate how to write the lowercase *h* on the board, as shown. (*Note:* Do not draw the arrows or numbers on the board. They are just for your reference.)
  - Note that there is no need to lift the pencil between any of the strokes.
- Write the lowercase *h* again on the board, this time with sound effects.
  - "Ptttt!" for the starting spot
  - "F-f-f-f-f-t!" for the top-down bar
  - "L-l-l-l-oop!" for the curved stroke
- Lead the children to practice making the lowercase *h* in the air with accompanying sound effects.

3.3. Keeping Track of Letters

- Ask the children to find the *r* and *h* on the display of lowercase letters on the board.
- Rewrite or otherwise tag each of the letters to show that they have been taught.

4. Independent Thinking: Strokes and Letters: *r, h*

- Gather the children into groups of three or four.
- Make sure every child has
  - Personal Activity Folder
  - Lowercase Letter Writing Practice Sheet: *r, h*
  - Lowercase Alphabet Fill-In activity sheet

4.1. Dictation Plus Writing New Letters: *r, h*

- Remind the children to print their names (in uppercase letters) in the name blank at the upper right corner of their Lowercase Letter Writing Practice Sheet.
- Lowercase Letter Dictation
  - Remind the children that the top row of their Lowercase Letter Writing Practice Sheet is for dictation.
    - You will name a letter.
    - They will write the letter you name.
  - Dictate five letters from among those taught in previous lessons.
    - Choose the letters one by one from the Grab Bag.
    - Give the children time to write each letter before dictating the next.
- New Letters: *r, h*
  - Remind the children how to complete the rest of Lowercase Letter Writing Practice Sheet: *r, h*.
    - A child in each group directs the tracing and accompanying sound effects for the first (dotted) letter.
    - The next child is then in charge of directing the rewriting of that letter in the second box in the row.

- The turn taking and writing continue until all boxes of the activity sheet are filled in.
- Remind the children that when they have completed the sheet, they will choose their very best letter for each row.
  - To mark the *one best letter* in each row, they choose a crayon and draw a frame around the outside of the square in which the letter appears.

4.2. Lowercase Alphabet Fill-In

- Remind the children that their Lowercase Alphabet Fill-In activity sheets are in their Personal Activity Folders.
- Tell the children that when they have completed the Lowercase Letter Writing Practice Sheets, they should work together to add today's new letters, *r* and *h*, where they belong in their Lowercase Alphabet Fill-In activity sheets.

4.3. Cleaning Up

- Ask the children to put *both* of the activity sheets into their Personal Activity Folders.

 **LESSON 4** Lowercase Letters with
Loops, Humps, and Troughs: *u, j, e*

Objectives
- To review formation of prior letters (*o, c, a, d, g, q, s, f, b, p, m, n, r, h*)
- To review recognition of letters with loops, humps, and troughs
- To introduce proper formation of lowercase *u, j,* and *e*

Materials
1. **Review Prior Letters**

   Display of the lowercase letters on the board

   Large Letter Formation Guidelines (on board for teacher)

   Grab Bag with Flashcards for prior letters: *o, c, a, d, g, q, s, f, b, p, m, n, r, h*

2. **Flashcard Review: Lowercase Letters with Loops, Humps, and Troughs**

   Flashcard stack with letters with loops, humps, and troughs: *b, p, m, n, r, h, u, j, e*

3. **New Letters: *u, j,* and *e***

   Alphabet Frieze

   Display of the lowercase letters on the board

   Large Letter Formation Guidelines (on board for teacher)

4. **Independent Thinking: Strokes and Letters: *u, j, e* (Small-Group Activity)**

   Grab Bag with Flashcards for prior letters: *o, c, a, d, g, q, s, f, b, p, m, n, r, h*

   Lowercase Letter Writing Practice Sheet: *u, j, e* (one for each child)

   Pencils (one for each child)

   Crayons

   Personal Activity Folder for each child (including Lowercase Alphabet Fill-In from the prior lesson)

ACTIVITIES

1. Review Prior Letters

   1.1. Review: *r, h*

   - Direct the children's attention to the display of lowercase letters on the board.
     - Ask them to name and find the letters taught in the last lesson (*r, h*).
     - Quickly review the formation of the new letters, writing them with sound effects on the Large Letter Formation Guidelines and, with the children, in the air.

   1.2. Grab Bag Review

   - The Grab Bag should contain a card for each letter that has already been taught: *o, c, a, d, g, q, s, f, b, p, m, n, r, h*.
   - Call on a child to choose a letter from the Grab Bag and to
     - Signal for everyone to name the chosen letter (Don't forget wait time!)
     - Lead everyone in air-writing it together with sound effects

- If you notice any hesitation or uncertainty,
  - Repeat the air-writing
  - Put the card back in the bag so that it may be drawn again during the session
- Call on another child to choose and lead the response for the next letter.
- Repeat until at least five letters have been reviewed.

2. Flashcard Review: Lowercase Letters with Loops, Humps, and Troughs
- The stack of Flashcards should include all of the lowercase letters with loops, humps, and troughs: *b, p, m, n, r, h, u, j, e.*
- Remind the children of how to play the game:
  - There is one lowercase letter on each card.
  - When you hold up a card, the children think of the name of the letter shown.
  - The children do not say anything until you give the signal.
- When the response sounds hesitant or confused, slip the letter back into the unused part of the stack, just a few cards down, so that it will quickly show up again.
- Review the entire stack at least once.

3. New Letters: *u, j, e*
- Tell the children that there are three new lowercase letters today.
  - The first two have troughs—the loops go on the bottom.
  - The third one is special. It is different from any other letter.

3.1. Lowercase *u*
- Ask the children to find the lowercase *u* in the display of lowercase letters on the board and the Alphabet Frieze.
- Demonstrate how to write the lowercase *u* on the board, as shown. (*Note:* Do not draw the arrows or numbers on the board. They are just for your reference.)

  - Point out that the curve sits on the baseline, making a little bucket or trough.
- Write the lowercase *u* again on the board, this time with sound effects.
  - "Pttt!" for the starting spot
  - "L-l-l-l-oop!" for the curved stroke
  - "F-f-f-f-f-t!" for the top-down bar
- Lead the children to practice making the lowercase *u* in the air with accompanying sound effects.

161

3.2. Lowercase *j*

- Ask the children to find the lowercase *j* in the display of lowercase letters on the board and the Alphabet Frieze.
- Demonstrate how to write the lowercase *j* on the board, as shown. (*Note:* Do not draw the arrows or numbers on the board. They are just for your reference.)
  - Point out that the trough hangs below the baseline like a little hook.
  - Point out that there is a dot over the top of the lowercase *j*.
- Write the lowercase *j* again on the board, this time with sound effects.
  - "Pttt!" for the starting spot
  - "F-f-f-f-f-l-l-l-l-oop!" for the body of the *j* stroke
    - "F-f-f-f-!" for the top-down part of the stroke
    - "L-l-l-l-oop!" for the little curved part that hangs down
  - "Ding!" for the dot
- Lead the children to practice making the lowercase *j* in the air with accompanying sound effects.

3.3. Lowercase *e*

- Ask the children to find the lowercase *e* in the display of lowercase letters on the board and the Alphabet Frieze.
- Demonstrate how to write the lowercase *e* on the board, as shown. (*Note:* Do not draw the arrows or numbers on the board. They are just for your reference.)
  - Point out that the first stroke of the lowercase *e* is very special: It is a little bar that lies between the midline and the baseline.
- Write the lowercase *e* again on the board, this time with sound effects.
  - "Pttt!" for the starting spot
  - "T-ch-cht!" for the horizontal stroke
  - "Wheeooo!" for the circular stroke
- Lead the children to practice making the lowercase *e* in the air with accompanying sound effects.

3.4. Keeping Track of Letters

- Ask the children to find the *u*, *j*, and *e* on the display of lowercase letters on the board.
- Rewrite or otherwise tag these letters to show that they have been taught.

4. Independent Thinking: Strokes and Letters: *u, j, e*

- Gather the children into groups of three or four.

- Make sure every child has
  - Personal Activity Folder
  - Lowercase Letter Writing Practice Sheet: *u, j, e*
  - Lowercase Alphabet Fill-In activity sheet

4.1. Dictation Plus Writing New Letters: *u, j, e*

- Remind the children to print their names (in uppercase letters) in the name blank at the upper right corner of their Lowercase Letter Writing Practice Sheet.
- Lowercase Letter Dictation
  - Remind the children that the top row of their Lowercase Letter Writing Practice Sheet is for dictation.
    - You will name a letter.
    - They will write the letter you name.
  - Dictate five letters from among those taught in previous lessons.
    - Choose the letters one by one from the Grab Bag.
    - Give the children time to write each letter before dictating the next.
- New Letters: *u, j, e*
  - Remind the children of how to complete the rest of Lowercase Letter Writing Practice Sheet: *u, j, e.*
    - A child in each group directs the tracing and accompanying sound effects for the first (dotted) letter.
    - The next child is then in charge of directing the rewriting of that letter in the second box in the row.
    - The turn taking and writing continue until all boxes of the activity sheet are filled in.
  - Remind the children that when they have completed the sheet, they will choose their very best letter for each row.
    - To mark the one best letter in each row, they choose a crayon and draw a frame around the outside of the square in which the letter appears.

4.2. Lowercase Alphabet Fill-In

- Remind the children that their Lowercase Alphabet Fill-In activity sheets are in their Personal Activity Folders.
- Tell the children that when they have completed the Lowercase Letter Writing Practice Sheets, they should work together to add today's new letters, *u, j,* and *e,* where they belong in their Lowercase Alphabet Fill-In activity sheets.

4.3. Cleaning Up

- Ask the children to put *both* of the activity sheets into their Personal Activity Folders.

Lowercase Letters with Slanted Strokes

· ·

LESSON 1 Lowercase Letters
with Slanted Strokes: *v, w*

Objectives
- To review formation of previously taught letters (*o, c, a, d, g, q, s, f, b, p, m, n, r, h, u, j, e*)
- To review names and shapes of lowercase letters with slanted strokes
- To introduce proper formation of lowercase *v* and *w*

Materials
1. **Review Prior Letters**

   Display of the lowercase letters on the board

   Large Letter Formation Guidelines (on board for teacher)

   Smaller Letter Formation Guidelines (on board for students)

   Grab Bag with Flashcards for prior letters: *o, c, a, d, g, q, s, f, b, p, m, n, r, h, u, j, e*

2. **Remembering Slanted Strokes**

   Large Letter Formation Guidelines (on board for teacher)

3. **Flashcard Review: Lowercase Letters with Slanted Strokes**

   Flashcard Stack with *v, w, x, z, k, y*

4. **New Letters: *v, w***

   Alphabet Frieze

   Display of the lowercase letters on the board

   Large Letter Formation Guidelines (on board for teacher)

5. **Independent Thinking: Strokes and Letters: *v, w* (Small-Group Activity)**

   Grab Bag with Flashcards for prior letters: *o, c, a, d, g, q, s, f, b, p, m, n, r, h, u, j, e*

   Lowercase Letter Writing Practice Sheet: *v, w* (one for each child)

   Pencils (one for each child)

   Crayons

   Personal Activity Folder for each child (including Lowercase Alphabet Fill-In from the prior lesson)

ACTIVITIES

1. Review Prior Letters

1.1. Review: *u, j, e*

- Direct the children's attention to the display of lowercase letters on the board.
  - Ask them to name and find the letters taught in the last lesson (*u, j, e*).
  - Quickly review the formation of each of these two new letters, writing them with sound effects on the Lowercase Letter Formation Guidelines and, with the children, in the air.

1.2. Team Grab Bag

- The Grab Bag should contain a Flashcard for each letter that has already been taught: *o, c, a, d, g, q, s, f, b, p, m, n, r, h, u, j, e.*
- Divide the children into teams of three to five.
- Each team should make a line facing the board.
- Choose one of the letters from the Grab Bag, and name it.
  - Lead the children to write the letter with sound effects.
    - The first child in each line writes the letter on the board on the Smaller Letter Formation Guidelines.
    - The others air-write the letter.
    - When the first child has finished, he or she goes to the back of the line.
- Repeat until every child has had a chance to write on the board.

2. Remembering Slanted Strokes

- Tell the children that many of the letters have strokes that **slant**.
- Tell them that
  - Sometimes the strokes slant to the right
  - For lowercase letters, the slants are often short
- Demonstrate on the board. (*Note:* Do not draw the arrows or numbers on the board. They are just for your reference.)

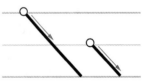

- Ask the children to air-write the stroke with you.
  - "Pttt!" for the starting spot
  - "Ssssp!" for the slanted stroke
- Tell the children that sometimes the strokes slant to the left.
- Demonstrate on the board. (*Note:* Do not draw the arrows or numbers on the board. They are just for your reference.)

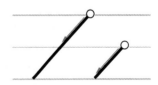

- Ask the children to air-write the stroke with you.
  - "Pttt!" for the starting spot
  - "Ssssp!" for the slanted stroke

3. Flashcard Review: Lowercase Letters with Slanted Strokes

- The stack of Flashcards should include all of the lowercase letters with slanted strokes: *v, w, x, z, k, y.*
- Remind the children of how to play the game.
    - There is one lowercase letter on each card.
    - When you hold up a card, the children think of the name of the letter shown.
    - The children do not say anything until you give the signal.
- When the response sounds hesitant or confused, slip the letter back into the unused part of the stack, just a few cards down, so that it will quickly show up again.
- Review the entire stack at least once.

4. New Letters: *v, w*

4.1. Lowercase *v*

- Ask the children to find the lowercase *v* in the display of lowercase letters on the board and the Alphabet Frieze.
- Demonstrate how to write the lowercase *v* on the board, as shown. (*Note:* Do not draw the arrows or numbers on the board. They are just for your reference.)
    - Point out that it's the same as the uppercase *V* but only reaches to the *midline.*
- Write the lowercase *v* again on the board, this time with sound effects.
    - "Pttt!" for the starting spot
    - "Sssssp! Sssssp!" for the two slanted strokes
- Lead the children to practice making the lowercase *v* in the air with accompanying sound effects.

4.2. Lowercase *w*

- Ask the children to find the lowercase *w* in the display of lowercase letters on the board and the Alphabet Frieze.
- Demonstrate how to write the lowercase *w* on the board, as shown. (*Note:* Do not draw the arrows or numbers on the board. They are just for your reference.)
    - Point out that it's the same as the uppercase *W* but only reaches to the midline.
- Write the lowercase *w* again on the board, this time with sound effects.
    - "Pttt!" for the starting spot
    - "Sssssp! Sssssp! Sssssp! Sssssp!" for the four slanted strokes
- Lead the children to practice making the lowercase *w* in the air with accompanying sound effects.

4.3. Keeping Track of Letters

- Ask the children to find the *v* and *w* on the display of lowercase letters on the board.
- Rewrite or otherwise tag these letters to show that they have been taught.

5. Independent Thinking: Strokes and Letters: *v, w*

- Gather the children into groups of three or four.
- Make sure every child has
  - Personal Activity Folder
  - Lowercase Letter Writing Practice Sheet: *v, w*
  - Lowercase Alphabet Fill-In activity sheet

5.1. Dictation Plus Writing New Letters: *v, w*

- Remind the children to print their names (in uppercase letters) in the name blank at the upper right corner of their Lowercase Letter Writing Practice Sheet.
- Lowercase Letter Dictation
  - Remind the children that the top row of their Lowercase Letter Writing Practice Sheet is for dictation.
    - You will name a letter.
    - They will write the letter you name.
  - Dictate five letters from among those taught in previous lessons.
    - Choose the letters one by one from the Grab Bag.
    - Give the children time to write each letter before dictating the next.
- New Letters: *v, w*
  - Remind the children of how to complete the rest of Lowercase Letter Writing Practice Sheet: *v, w*.
    - A child in each group directs the tracing and accompanying sound effects for the first (dotted) letter.
    - The next child is then in charge of directing the rewriting of that letter in the second box in the row.
    - The turn taking and writing continue until all boxes of the activity sheet are filled in.
  - Remind the children that when they have completed the sheet, they will choose their very best letter for each row.
    - To mark the *one best letter* in each row, they choose a crayon and draw a frame around the outside of the square in which the letter appears.

5.2. Lowercase Alphabet Fill-In

- Remind the children that their Lowercase Alphabet Fill-In activity sheets are in their Personal Activity Folders.

- Tell the children that when they have completed the Lowercase Letter Writing Practice Sheets, they should work together to add today's new letters, *v* and *w*, where they belong in their Lowercase Alphabet Fill-In activity sheets.

5.3. Cleaning Up

- Ask the children to put *both* of the activity sheets into their Personal Activity Folders.

Lowercase Letters
with Slanted Strokes: x, z

Objectives
- To review formation of previously taught letters (o, c, a, d, g, q, s, f, b, p, m, n, r, h, u, j, e, v, w)
- To review names and shapes of lowercase letters with slanted strokes
- To introduce proper formation of lowercase x and z

Materials

1. **Review Prior Letters**

   Display of the lowercase letters on the board

   Large Letter Formation Guidelines (on board for teacher)

   Smaller Letter Formation Guidelines (on board for students)

   Grab Bag with Flashcards for prior letters: o, c, a, d, g, q, s, f, b, p, m, n, r, h, u, j, e, v, w

2. **Flashcard Review: Lowercase Letters with Slanted Strokes**

   Flashcard Stack with v, w, x, z, k, y

3. **New Letters: x, z**

   Alphabet Frieze

   Display of the lowercase letters on the board

   Large Letter Formation Guidelines (on board for teacher)

4. **Independent Thinking: Strokes and Letters: x, z (Small-Group Activity)**

   Grab Bag with Flashcards for prior letters: o, c, a, d, g, q, s, f, b, p, m, n, r, h, u, j, e, v, w

   Lowercase Letter Writing Practice Sheet: x, z (one for each child)

   Pencils (one for each child)

   Crayons

   Personal Activity Folder for each child (including Lowercase Alphabet Fill-In from the prior lesson)

ACTIVITIES

1. Review Prior Letters

   1.1. Review: v, w

   - Direct the children's attention to the display of lowercase letters on the board.
     - Ask them to name and find the letters taught in the last lesson (v, w).
     - Quickly review the formation of each of these two new letters, writing them with sound effects on the Large Letter Formation Guidelines and, with the children, in the air.

   1.2 Team Grab Bag

   - The Grab Bag should now contain a Flashcard for each letter that has already been taught: o, c, a, d, g, q, s, f, b, p, m, n, r, h, u, j, e, v, w.
   - Divide the children into teams of three to five.

- Each team should make a line facing the board.
- Choose one of the letters from the Grab Bag, and name it.
  - Lead the children to write the letter with its sound effects.
    - The first child in each line writes the letter on the board on the Smaller Letter Formation Guidelines.
    - The others air-write the letter.
    - When the first child has finished, he or she goes to the back of the line.
  - Repeat until every child has had a chance to write on the board.

2. **Flashcard Review: Lowercase Letters with Slanted Strokes**

- The stack of Flashcards should include all of the lowercase letters with slanted strokes: *v, w, x, z, k, y.*
- Remind the children how to play the game.
  - There is one lowercase letter on each card.
  - When you hold up a card, the children think of the name of the letter shown.
  - The children do not say anything until you give the signal.
- When the response sounds hesitant or confused, slip the letter back into the unused part of the stack, just a few cards down, so that it will quickly show up again.
- Review the entire stack at least once.

3. **New Letters: *x, z***

3.1. **Lowercase *x***

- Ask the children to find the lowercase *x* on the display of lowercase letters on the board and the Alphabet Frieze.
- Demonstrate how to write the lowercase *x* on the board, as shown. (*Note*: Do not draw the arrows or numbers on the board. They are just for your reference.)

- Write the lowercase *x* again on the board, this time with sound effects.
  - "Pttt!" for the starting spot
  - "Sssssp!" for the first slanted stroke
  - "Tk!" when lifting your marker
  - "Sssssp!" for the second slanted stroke
- Lead the children to practice making the lowercase *x* in the air with accompanying sound effects.

3.2. **Lowercase *z***

- Ask the children to find the lowercase *z* in the display of lowercase letters on the board and the Alphabet Frieze.
- Demonstrate how to write the lowercase *z* on the board, as shown. (*Note*: Do not draw the arrows or numbers on the board. They are just for your reference.)

- Write the lowercase *z* again on the board, this time with sound effects.
  - "Pttt!" for the starting spot
  - "T-ch-cht!" for the first horizontal stroke
  - "Ssssp!" for the slanted stroke
  - "T-ch-cht!" for the second horizontal stroke
- Lead the children to practice making the lowercase *z* in the air with accompanying sound effects.

3.3. Keeping Track of Letters

- Ask the children to find the *x* and *z* on the display of lowercase letters on the board.
- Rewrite or otherwise mark these letters to show that they have been taught.

4. Independent Thinking: Strokes and Letters: *x, z*

- Gather the children into groups of three or four.
- Make sure every child has
  - Personal Activity Folder
  - Lowercase Letter Writing Practice Sheet: *x, z*
  - Lowercase Alphabet Fill-In activity sheet

4.1. Dictation Plus Writing New Letters: *x, z*

- Remind the children to print their names (in uppercase letters) in the name blank at the upper right corner of their Lowercase Letter Writing Practice Sheet.
- Lowercase Letter Dictation
  - Remind the children that the top row of their Lowercase Letter Writing Practice Sheet is for dictation.
    - You will name a letter.
    - They will write the letter you name.
  - Dictate five letters from among those taught in previous lessons.
    - Choose the letters one by one from the Grab Bag.
    - Give the children time to write each letter before dictating the next.
- New Letters: *x, z*
  - Remind the children how to complete the rest of Lowercase Letter Writing Practice Sheet: *x, z*.
    - A child in each group directs the tracing and accompanying sound effects for the first (dotted) letter.
    - The next child is then in charge of directing the rewriting of that letter in the second box in the row.
    - The turn taking and writing continue until all boxes of the activity sheet are filled in.
  - Remind the children that when they have completed the sheet, they will choose their very best letter for each row.

- To mark the *one best letter* in each row, they choose a crayon and draw a frame around the outside of the square in which the letter appears.

4.2. Lowercase Alphabet Fill-In

- Remind the children that their Lowercase Alphabet Fill-In activity sheets are in their Personal Activity Folders.

- Tell the children that when they have completed the Lowercase Letter Writing Practice Sheets, they should work together to add today's new letters, *x* and *z*, where they belong in their Lowercase Alphabet Fill-In activity sheets.

4.3. Cleaning Up

- Ask the children to put *both* of the activity sheets into their Personal Activity Folders.

Lowercase Letters
with Slanted Strokes: *k, y*

Objectives
- To review formation of previously taught letters (*o, c, a, d, g, q, s, f, b, p, m, n, r, h, u, j, e, v, w, x, z*)
- To review names and shapes of lowercase letters with slanted strokes
- To introduce proper formation of lowercase *k* and *y*

Materials

1. **Review Prior Letters**

   Display of the lowercase letters on the board

   Large Letter Formation Guidelines (on board for teacher)

   Smaller Letter Formation Guidelines (on board for students)

   Grab Bag with Flashcards for prior letters: *o, c, a, d, g, q, s, f, b, p, m, n, r, h, u, j, e, v, w, x, z*

2. **Flashcard Review: Lowercase Letters with Slanted Strokes**

   Flashcard Stack with *v, w, x, z, k, y*

3. **New Letters: *k, y***

   Alphabet Frieze

   Display of the lowercase letters on the board

   Large Letter Formation Guidelines (on board for teacher)

4. **Independent Thinking: Strokes and Letters: *k, y* (Small-Group Activity)**

   Grab Bag with Flashcards for prior letters: *o, c, a, d, g, q, s, f, b, p, m, n, r, h, u, j, e, v, w, x, z*

   Lowercase Letter Writing Practice Sheet: *k, y* (one for each child)

   Pencils (one for each child)

   Crayons

   Personal Activity Folder for each child (including Lowercase Alphabet Fill-In from the prior lesson)

ACTIVITIES

1. Review Prior Letters

  1.1. Review: *x, z*

    - Direct the children's attention to the display of lowercase letters on the board.
      - Ask them to name and find the letters taught in the last lesson (*x, z*).
      - Quickly review the formation of each of these two new letters, writing them with sound effects on the Large Letter Formation Guidelines and, with the children, in the air.

  1.2. Team Grab Bag

    - The Grab Bag should now contain a Flashcard for each letter that has already been taught: *o, c, a, d, g, q, s, f, b, p, m, n, r, h, u, j, e, v, w, x, z.*
    - Divide the children into teams of three to five.

- Each team should make a line facing the board.
- Choose one of the letters from the Grab Bag, and name it.
  - Lead the children to write the letter with its sound effects.
    - The first child in each line writes the letter on the board on the Smaller Letter Formation Guidelines.
    - The others in each line air-write the letter.
    - When the first child has finished, he or she goes to the back of the line.
  - Repeat until every child has had a chance to write on the board.

2. Flashcard Review: Lowercase Letters with Slanted Strokes

- The stack of Flashcards should include all of the lowercase letters with slanted strokes: *v, w, x, z, k, y.*
- Remind the children of how to play the game.
  - There is one lowercase letter on each card.
  - When you hold up a card, the children think of the name of the letter shown.
  - The children do not say anything until you give the signal.
- When the response sounds hesitant or confused, slip the letter back into the unused part of the stack, just a few cards down, so that it will quickly show up again.
- Review the entire stack at least once.

3. New Letters: *k, y*

3.1. Lowercase *k*

- Ask the children to find the lowercase *k* on the display of lowercase letters on the board and the Alphabet Frieze.
- Demonstrate how to write the lowercase *k* on the board, as shown. (*Note:* Do not draw the arrows or numbers on the board. They are just for your reference.)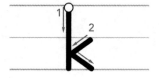
- Write the lowercase *k* again on the board, this time with sound effects.
  - "Pttt!" for the starting spot
  - "F-f-f-f-f-t!" for the top-to-bottom vertical stroke
  - "Tk!" when lifting your marker
  - "Sssssp! Sssssp!" for the two slanted strokes
- Lead the children to practice making the lowercase *k* in the air with accompanying sound effects.

3.2. Lowercase *y*

- Ask the children to find the lowercase *y* in the display of lowercase letters on the board and the Alphabet Frieze.
- Demonstrate how to write the lowercase *y* on the board, as shown. (*Note:* Do not draw the arrows or numbers on the board. They are just for your reference.)

- Write the lowercase *y* again on the board, this time with sound effects.
  - "Pttt!" for the starting spot
  - "Sssp!" for the first slanted stroke
  - "Tk!" when lifting your marker
  - "Sssssssp!" for the second slanted stroke
- Lead the children to practice making the lowercase *y* in the air with accompanying sound effects.

3.3. Keeping Track of Letters

- Ask the children to find the *k* and *y* on the display of lowercase letters on the board.
- Rewrite or otherwise mark these letters to show that they have been taught.

4. Independent Thinking: Strokes and Letters: *k, y*

- Gather the children into groups of three or four.
- Make sure every child has
  - Personal Activity Folder
  - Lowercase Letter Writing Practice Sheet: *k, y*
  - Lowercase Alphabet Fill-In activity sheet

4.1. Dictation Plus Writing New Letters: *k, y*

- Remind the children to print their names (in uppercase letters) in the name blank at the upper right corner of their Lowercase Letter Writing Practice Sheet.
- Lowercase Letter Dictation
  - Remind the children that the top row of their Lowercase Letter Writing Practice Sheet is for dictation.
    - You will name a letter.
    - They will write the letter you name.
  - Dictate five letters from among those taught in previous lessons.
    - Choose the letters one by one from the Grab Bag.
    - Give the children time to write each letter before dictating the next.
- New Letters: *k, y*
  - Remind the children how to complete the rest of Lowercase Letter Writing Practice Sheet: *k, y*.
    - A child in each group directs the tracing and accompanying sound effects for the first (dotted) letter.
    - The next child is then in charge of directing the rewriting of that letter in the second box in the row.
    - The turn taking and writing continue until all boxes of the activity sheet are filled in.
- Remind the children that when they have completed the sheet, they will choose their very best letter for each row.

- To mark the *one best letter* in each row, they choose a crayon and draw a frame around the outside of the square in which the letter appears.

4.2. Lowercase Alphabet Fill-In

- Remind the children that their Lowercase Alphabet Fill-In activity sheets are in their Personal Activity Folders.

- Tell the children that when they have completed the Lowercase Letter Writing Practice Sheets, they should work together to add today's new letters, *k* and *y*, where they belong in their Lowercase Alphabet Fill-In activity sheets.

4.3. Cleaning Up

- Ask the children to put *both* of the activity sheets into their Personal Activity Folders.

CHAPTER

11

Lowercase Letters with Straight Up-and-Down Strokes

· ·

LESSON 1 Lowercase Letters with
Straight Up-and-Down Strokes: *l, t, i*

Objectives
- To review formation of previously taught letters (*o, c, a, d, g, q, s, f, b, p, m, n, r, h, u, j, e, v, w, x, z, k, y*)
- To review names and shapes of lowercase letters with straight up-and-down strokes
- To introduce proper formation of lowercase *l, t,* and *i*

Materials
1. **Review Prior Letters**
   Display of the lowercase letters on the board
   Large Letter Formation Guidelines (on board for teacher)
   Smaller Letter Formation Guidelines (on board for students)
   Grab Bag with Flashcards for prior letters: *o, c, a, d, g, q, s, f, b, p, m, n, r, h, u, j, e, v, w, x, z, k, y*

2. **Remembering Vertical Strokes**
   Large Letter Formation Guidelines (on board for teacher)

3. **Flashcard Review: Letters with Straight Up-and-Down Strokes**
   Flashcard Stack with letters with straight up-and-down strokes: *l, t, i*

4. **New Letters: *l, t, i***
   Alphabet Frieze
   Display of the lowercase letters on the board
   Large Letter Formation Guidelines (on board for teacher)

5. **Independent Thinking: Strokes and Letters: *l, t, i* (Small-Group Activity)**
   Grab Bag with Flashcards for prior letters: *o, c, a, d, g, q, s, f, b, p, m, n, r, h, u, j, e, v, w, x, z, k, y*
   Lowercase Letter Writing Practice Sheet: *l, t, i* (one for each child)
   Pencils (one for each child)
   Crayons
   Personal Activity Folder for each child (including Lowercase Alphabet Fill-In from the prior lesson)

177

ACTIVITIES

1. **Review Prior Letters**

   1.1. **Review:** *k, y*
      - Direct the children's attention to the display of lowercase letters on the board.
        - Ask the children to name and find the letters taught in the last lesson (*k, y*).
        - Quickly review the formation of each of these two new letters, writing them with sound effects on the Large Letter Formation Guidelines and, with the children, in the air.

   1.2. **Team Grab Bag**
      - The Grab Bag should contain a card for each letter that has already been taught: *o, c, a, d, g, q, s, f, b, p, m, n, r, h, u, j, e, v, w, x, z, k, y.*
      - Divide the children into teams of three to five.
      - Each team should make a line facing the board.
      - Choose one of the letters from the Grab Bag, and name it.
        - Lead the children to write the letter with sound effects
          - The first child in each line writes the letter on the board on the Smaller Letter Formation Guidelines.
          - The others air-write the letter.
          - When the first child has finished, he or she goes to the back of the line.
        - Repeat until every child has had a chance to write on the board.

2. **Remembering Vertical Strokes**
   - Tell the children that the rest of the letters are centered on strokes that go straight up and down.
   - Demonstrate on the board, reminding them that straight up-and-down strokes always start at the top. (*Note:* Do not draw the arrows or numbers on the board. They are just for your reference.)
   - Ask the children to air-write the stroke with you.
     - "Pttt!" for the starting spot
     - "F-f-f-f-f-t!" for the vertical, top-down stroke

3. **Flashcard Review: Letters with Straight Up-and-Down Strokes**
   - The stack of Flashcards should include all of the straight up-and-down lowercase letters: *l, t, i.*
   - Remind the children how to play the game.
     - There is one lowercase letter on each card.
     - When you hold up a card, the children think of the name of the letter shown.
     - The children do not say anything until you give the signal.
   - When the response sounds hesitant or confused, slip the letter back into the unused part of the stack, just a few cards down, so that it will quickly show up again.
   - Review the entire stack at least twice.

4. New Letters: *l*, *t*, *i*

4.1. Lowercase *l*

- Ask the children to find the lowercase *l* in the display of lowercase letters on the board and the Alphabet Frieze.

- Demonstrate how to write the lowercase *l* on the board, as shown. (*Note:* Do not draw the arrows or numbers on the board. They are just for your reference.)

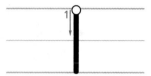

  - Point out that the lowercase *l* is one of the lowercase letters that reaches all the way from the topline to the baseline.

  - Remind the children that the stroke for straight up-and-down lines always begins at the top.

- Write the lowercase *l* again on the board, this time with sound effects.

  - "Pttt!" for the starting spot

  - "F-f-f-f-f-t!" for the vertical, top-down stroke

- Lead the children to practice making the lowercase *l* in the air with accompanying sound effects.

4.2. Lowercase *t*

- Ask the children to find the lowercase *t* in the display of the lowercase letters on the board and the Alphabet Frieze.

- Demonstrate how to write the lowercase *t* on the board, as shown. (*Note:* Do not draw the arrows or numbers on the board. They are just for your reference.)

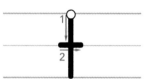

- Write the lowercase *t* again on the board, this time with sound effects.

  - "Pttt!" for the starting spot

  - "F-f-f-f-f-t!" for the top-to-bottom vertical stroke

  - "Tk!" when lifting your marker

  - "T-ch-ch!" for the horizontal stroke

- Lead the children to practice making the lowercase *t* in the air with accompanying sound effects.

4.3. Lowercase *i*

- Ask the children to find the lowercase *i* in the display of lowercase letters on the board and the Alphabet Frieze.

- Demonstrate how to write the lowercase *i* on the board, as shown. (*Note:* Do not draw the arrows or numbers on the board. They are just for your reference.)

- Write the lowercase *i* again on the board, this time with sound effects.

  - "Pttt!" for the starting spot

  - "F-f-f-f-f-t!" for the top-to-bottom vertical stroke

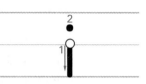

- "Tk!" when lifting your marker
- "Ding!" for the dot
- Lead the children to practice making the lowercase *i* in the air with accompanying sound effects.

4.4. Keeping Track of Letters

- Ask the children to find the *l*, *t*, and *i* on the display of lowercase letters on the board.
- Rewrite or otherwise tag these letters to show that they have been taught.

5. Independent Thinking: Strokes and Letters: *l, t, i*

- Gather the children into groups of three or four.
- Make sure every child has
  - Personal Activity Folder
  - Lowercase Letter Writing Practice Sheet: *l, t, i*
  - Lowercase Alphabet Fill-In activity sheet

5.1. Dictation Plus Writing New Letters: *l, t, i*

- Remind the children to print their names (in uppercase letters) in the name blank at the upper right corner of their Lowercase Letter Writing Practice Sheet.
- Lowercase Letter Dictation
  - Remind the children that the top row of their Lowercase Letter Writing Practice Sheet is for dictation.
    - You will name a letter.
    - They will write the letter you name.
  - Dictate five letters from among those taught in previous lessons.
    - Choose the letters one by one from the Grab Bag.
    - Give the children time to write each letter before dictating the next.
- New Letters: *l, t, i*
  - Remind the children how to complete the rest of Lowercase Letter Writing Practice Sheet: *l, t, i*.
    - A child in each group directs the tracing and accompanying sound effects for the first (dotted) letter.
    - The next child is then in charge of directing the rewriting of that letter in the second box in the row.
    - The turn taking and writing continue until all boxes of the activity sheet are filled in.
  - Remind the children that when they have completed the sheet, they will choose their very best letter for each row.
    - To mark the *one best letter* in each row, they choose a crayon and draw a frame around the outside of the square in which the letter appears.

5.2. Lowercase Alphabet Fill-In

- Remind the children that their Lowercase Alphabet Fill-In activity sheets are in their Personal Activity Folders.

- Tell the children that when they have completed the Lowercase Letter Writing Practice Sheets, they should work together to add today's new letters, *l, t,* and *i,* where they belong in their Lowercase Alphabet Fill-In activity sheets.

5.3. Cleaning Up

- Ask the children to put *both* of the activity sheets into their Personal Activity Folders.

 **LESSON 2** Lowercase Letter Wrap-Up

ASSESSMENT ALERT: The Progress-Check Lowercase Letter Writing assessment is administered during this lesson to evaluate students' progress.

Objectives
- To administer the Lowercase Letter Writing Assessment
- To celebrate finishing the lowercase alphabet by making a Name Display

Materials
1. **Progress-Check Lowercase Letter Writing Assessment**
   Lowercase Letter Writing Assessment form (see Appendix A.3)
   Pencil (one for every child)

2. **Write Your Own Name Using Lowercase Letters**
   Write Your Own Name (Lowercase) activity sheet (one for each child; see Appendix B.6 and online)
   Pencil (one for every child)
   Finished Name Display
   Materials for creating Name Displays
   - Scissors for cutting out "best" name
   - Colored mats sized for mounting the names (e.g., 9" × 4", three per sheet of 9" × 12" construction paper)
   - Paste for affixing the names to the mats
   - Highlighting markers for tracing over the names
   - Variety of stickers for decorating the mats

ACTIVITIES

1. Progress-Check Lowercase Letter Writing Assessment
   - Hold up an unfilled copy of the Lowercase Letter Writing assessment form, and ask if it looks familiar.
   - Affirm that it looks like their Lowercase Alphabet Fill-In activity sheets except that none of the lowercase letters have been filled in.
   - Tell the children that today each of them will fill in all of the lowercase letters on this sheet.
   - Explain that this is not a group activity: They will work by themselves.
     - Give each child a separate copy of the Progress-Check Lowercase Letter Writing assessment, and ask the children to fill in as many of the lowercase letters as they can.
     - Tell the children that it is important for them to do their best because you want to save the sheet and share it with their parents.
     - Remind the children to write their names where indicated in the top right corner of the page.
       - Explain that when they have finished, they will raise their hands so that you can collect (and make sure they have written their names on) their sheets.

2. Write Your Own Name Using Lowercase Letters

- Write the name of one of the children on the board in uppercase letters:

  JOCELYN

- Explain that when people usually write their names, they use lowercase letters for all but the first letter; write the name again to show them:

  JOCELYN

  Jocelyn

- Tell the children that they know how to write all the lowercase letters; it's time for them to learn to write their names the "grown-up" way.
  - Give each child an individualized copy of the Write Your Own Name (Lowercase) activity sheet. (See Unit III, Introduction, Instructions: Special Materials and Preparation.)
  - Explain to the children that they will
    - Trace their names in the top row
    - Write their names four more times, once in each of the rows provided
    - Use their Name Poems to figure out how to spell their names when writing the names on their own.
- When they are done, they will choose their favorite written name to make a new Name Display.
  - The children are welcome to work together in constructing their Name Displays.
  - Tell them to do the following:
    - Choose the best rendition of their name from the Write Your Own Name (Lowercase) activity sheet and cut it out.
    - Choose a mat.
    - Paste the cut-out name on the mat.
    - Decorate the mat as desired.

Introducing Letters and Sounds

By the end of this unit, children should be able to

■ Understand that letters represent sounds in spoken words

■ Recall and say the primary sound of most consonants

■ Distinguish the primary sounds of the consonants in word-initial position

■ Understand that vowels have long and short sounds

■ Name the two sounds for each vowel

■ Distinguish the long and short sounds of the vowels in real words

In the final unit of this program, attention is turned to the sounds of the letters. The unit is divided into two chapters:

■ Chapter 12: A Sound for Each Letter

■ Chapter 13: Long and Short Vowels

The goal of Chapter 12 is to convey to the children that the letters represent the sounds of spoken words. Beyond introducing a sound for each letter, the focus is on engaging children in voicing and hearing those sounds in real, meaningful words.

For letters that are consonants, children are introduced to the primary or most frequent sound; for example, the sound presented for the letter *c* is /k/. The consonant games are centered on hearing that sound in word-initial position, as research shows this to be the entry for developing consonant awareness (Duncan, Seymour, & Hill, 1997).

The vowels, by contrast, are exercised by having the children listen for such sounds as /ē/ when it occurs in the medial (*meet* versus *moat*) or final (*see* versus *sow*) position in words. This is a relatively difficult challenge. However, it is also an important one. Children must learn to hear vowels in the middle and end of words as they develop phonemic awareness and learn phonics and spelling. To make this challenge easier, only the *long* sounds of the vowels are introduced in Chapter 12. One advantage of the long vowels is that they require tensing of the mouth that must be held long enough to make a relatively clean and distinctive sound. A second is that the long sounds of the vowels are the same as their names. As such, each long vowel sound is already familiar to the children, allowing them to concentrate their attention on finding the sound within the words.

Awareness of vowel phonemes is notoriously difficult for young children. How many times do young spellers have to be reminded that every syllable must have a vowel? One reason is that consonants are intentional, ballistic movements. They are articulated, whereas the vowels are shapes of the mouth. Awareness of short vowels is especially difficult. Because they are short in duration and lax in pronunciation, the short vowels are hard to detect, and their sounds vary far more as a function of the phonemes that surround them than do those of the long vowels.

In Chapter 13, the short sounds of the vowels are introduced, and the games and activities are centered on contrasting the short and long sound of each vowel. Children will gradually gain command of the short vowels as they learn to read and spell. Nevertheless, by the time children finish Chapter 13, they should be able to name the two sounds of each vowel with confidence and often succeed in discerning them. Even more important, the children should have a firm understanding that, in English, every vowel has two primary sounds, long and short. Making sure that children know this from the start can prevent a lot of confusion later.

Although secure learning of the names and both sounds of the vowels is extremely helpful for all soon-to-be readers, it is especially important for English language learners. For one thing, most other languages sport only one primary sound per vowel, making transfer of expectations from their home language problematic. In addition, the names and long sounds of English vowels differ from the Latinate languages in befuddling ways. For example, the name and long sound of the English letter *Aa* is the same as the name and sound of the letter *Ee* in Spanish, and the name and long sound of the English letter *Ee* is the same as the name and sound of the Spanish letter *Ii*.

ASSESSMENT ALERTS

When	Assessment	How	Resource
Chapter 12, Lessons 2–9	Exit-Level Uppercase Letter Recognition	Individual	Appendix A.1
Chapter 12, Lessons 2–9	Exit-Level Lowercase Letter Recognition	Individual	Appendix A.1
Chapter 13, Lessons 1–4	Initial Consonant Sounds	Individual	Appendix A.4
Chapter 13, Lesson 5	Exit-Level Uppercase Letter Writing	Whole group	Appendix A.2
Chapter 13, Lesson 5	Exit-Level Lowercase Letter Writing	Whole group	Appendix A.3
At the end of Chapter 13	Vowel Identification and Sounds	Individual	Appendix A.5

Uppercase and Lowercase Letter Recognition Assessment

The Exit-Level Uppercase and Lowercase Letter Recognition assessments must be administered individually. They are completed over the course of Chapter 12 by calling children out from small-group sessions. Every child should be confident and accurate in recognizing all of the letters, both uppercase and lowercase. Additional forms (Extra Check 1, 2, and 3) are provided so that you can readminister these assessments with any children who need further work.

Initial Consonant Sounds Assessment

The Initial Consonant Sounds assessment requires 24 Initial Consonant Picture Cards (see Appendix A.4), which must be cut apart and, ideally, mounted and laminated for durability.

Vowel Identification and Sounds Assessment

The Vowel Identification and Sounds assessment is administered after Unit IV, Chapter 13. Be sure to provide extra instruction and practice to children in need because understanding the vowels is important. Bear in mind, too, that knowledge of the vowels and of their long and short sounds is required of kindergartners in the Common Core State Standards Initiative. In addition to the forms and instructions provided in Appendix A.5, you will need a subset of the Lowercase Letter Cards that the children used for small-group activities in Unit 1.

HANDS-ON GAMES AND INDIVIDUAL DIFFERENCES

During Small-Group Sessions

During small-group activity sessions in this unit, the primary activity for the children is practice working together to find newly taught letter sounds in words. In Chapter 12, the students work with consonant sounds. In Chapter 13, they work with long and short vowel sounds.

Across both chapters, most of your time is spent administering individual assessments:

- The Exit-Level Uppercase Letter Recognition and Exit-Level Lowercase Letter Recognition assessments are to be administered individually across the small-group sessions of Chapter 12.
- The Initial Consonant Sounds assessment is to be administered individually across the small-group sessions of Chapter 13.

Between Small-Group Sessions

Between lessons, it is important to find time to go through the children's Personal Activity Folders. While you are checking each child's activity sheet

- Make sure the child has written his or her name
- Enter completion notes on the Whole-Class Record Form
- Enter notes about specific needs and progress of each individual on Individual Record Forms (It is a good idea to add the student's name lest papers wander from folders.)
- Add stickers or notes to the children's activity sheets to let the children know you have reviewed their efforts

LESSON MATERIALS AND RESOURCES

The following table summarizes the materials and resources needed for both whole-group and small-group activities. *Note:* This book contains online materials (refer to About the Online Materials at the beginning of this book for more information). In the Notes column, *online* indicates that the materials are only provided online. The Notes column also indicates whether materials require additional assembly, or *special preparation*. Instructions for special preparation are provided following the table.

Chapters	Materials	Use	Notes
12 and 13	Alphabet Frieze	Whole group	From Unit I
12	Links to music for the "Vowel Name Song," "Apples and Bananas," and "Consonant Song"	Whole group	Online
12	Objects whose names begin with *Bb*	Lesson 1, Helicopter Game	None
12	Helicopter Game Picture Cards	Lessons 2–10, Helicopter Game	Online
12	Projection or display set-up	Lessons 2–10, Helicopter Game	Special preparation
12	Popsicle stick mug	Optional	From Unit II
12	Laser pointer	Optional	None
12	Ledger paper	Lesson 1	None
12	Lowercase Flashcards	Whole group	From Unit II
12	Consonant Sound Game Activity Sheets	Lessons 2–10	Appendix B.7

Chapters	Materials	Use	Notes
13	Links to music for "Consonant Song" and "Long and Short Vowel Song"	Whole group	Online
13	Long and Short Vowel Picture Cards	Small group	Special preparation
13	Long and Short Vowel Labels	Small group	Special preparation

Note: Appendix B materials are also available online.

INSTRUCTIONS: SPECIAL MATERIALS AND PREPARATION

Projection or Display Set-Up

The pictures needed for the Helicopter Game in Lessons 2–10 of Chapter 12 are provided online. How to display them depends on the available classroom resources.

One option is to make the pictures larger and stick them on the board.

Another option is to project them from a computer or an overhead projector. (*Note:* If screen is not back projected, then make sure to point to the pictures without occluding them.) Possibilities include a long metal or wooden pointer, a laser pointer, or the cursor on the computer. For SMART Boards, use the pointer tool provided.

Long and Short Vowel Picture Cards

The Long and Short Vowel Picture Cards needed for each small-group session in Chapter 13 are provided online. Cut out the individual cards from the template. If cards are printed in black and white, you may choose to project a color version on the board for children to use as clarification if needed. For each lesson, use as many sets of Long and Short Vowel Picture Cards as there are groups.

Long and Short Vowel Labels

In the small-group sessions in Chapter 13, the children sort pictures into two piles, one for long vowels and one for short vowels. To keep the sorting straight, each group will need a label for each pile. Please make two labels for each group for each lesson, one for the long vowel pile and one for the short vowel pile. Index cards are suitable. Because the word *long* is visually shorter than *short*, write stretched ("long") and squashed ("short") vowels on each card as shown:

Long *Aa*   **Short *Aa***

A Sound for Each Letter

ASSESSMENT ALERT: Begin the Exit-Level Uppercase Letter Recognition and Exit-Level Lowercase Letter Recognition assessments in Lesson 2 and complete them by Lesson 9.

LESSON 1 Introducing the
Sounds of the Letters: *Aa, Bb*

Objectives
- To introduce the idea that every letter represents a speech sound
- To introduce the long sound of the letter *Aa*
- To introduce the primary sound of the letter *Bb*

Materials
1. **Introducing Letter Sounds**
   Alphabet Frieze

2. **Introducing *Aa, /ā/***
   Alphabet Frieze
   (*Optional*) Music for the "Vowel Name Song" (see online materials for links)
   (*Optional*) Music for "Apples and Bananas" (see online materials for links)

3. **Introducing *Bb, /b/***
   Objects whose names begin with *Bb, /b/*
   Note: The Helicopter Game Picture Cards from the online materials may be used instead, but objects are recommended for this first lesson.

4. **Independent Thinking: Write the Whole Alphabet**
   Ledgered paper and pencil (for each child)

ACTIVITIES

1. Introducing Letter Sounds
   - Explain to the children that the way reading and spelling work is that the letters represent the sounds of words.
     - That means that in order to learn to read and spell, they must learn the sounds that each letter represents.
     - The next few sessions introduce the children to the sounds of the letters, starting with *Aa* and working through *Zz*.

2. Introducing *Aa*, /ā/

- Point to the letter *Aa* in the Alphabet Frieze.
  - Ask the children if they remember why the *Aa* is red, reminding them that **vowels** are special letters.
  - Challenge the children to name the five **vowels** of the alphabet.
  - Have the children sing the "Vowel Name Song" several times to refresh their memories.

Vowel Name Song

Five vowels in the alphabet,

I'll name them all for you:

A! E! I, O, U!

A! E! I, O, U!

A! E! I, O, U!

Now you can name them, too!

2.1. Listening for Vowels: /ā/

- Explain to the children that one of the reasons that vowels are special is that they often say their own names in words.
- Tell them that it is time to learn a new game called Listening for Vowels.
- Explain to the children that you will say a word, and they must listen carefully to decide whether it contains the /ā/ sound.
  - When they hear the sound /ā/ in a word, they should stand on their tiptoes, raise their arms to the sky, and repeat, "/ā/"!
  - If they do not hear the sound /ā/ in the word, they should *not* stand on their tiptoes, and they should place their hands on their chests.
- Go through several examples, providing support and feedback to make sure all children understand how to play.
  - *Play* (Children should rise on tiptoes, with arms stretched, and say, "/ā/.")
  - *Say* (Children should rise on tiptoes, with arms stretched, and say, "/ā/.")
  - *So* (Children should be silent, standing flat footed, with both hands on chest.)
  - *Ways* (Children should rise on tiptoes, with arms stretched, and say, "/ā/.")
  - *Wise* (Children should be silent, standing flat footed, with both hands on chest.)
- Continue through the following list, left to right. Words that contain the /ā/ sound are bolded.

way	**hay**	**day**	do	who	**lay**	low	**say**
see	me	**may**	moo	**made**	**make**	**bake**	bike
late	light	**lake**	like	**wake**	woke	**cake**	coke
coat	comb	**came**	aim	**same**	**tame**	time	type
tape	tube	tune	moon	**main**	brown	**brain**	rain

INSTRUCTIONAL TIP
Be on the lookout for children who may be having difficulty, and take care to work with them later so that they understand.

2.2. Introduce the Song "Apples and Bananas"

- Teach the song "Apples and Bananas."

Apples and Bananas

I like to eat, eat, eat apples and bananas!

I like to eat, eat, eat apples and bananas!

- Now, teach the children to sing the song substituting the sound, /ā/, in each occurrence of the words, *eat*, *apples*, and *bananas*, as shown:

I like to āt, āt, āt āpples and bānānās!

I like to āt, āt, āt āpples and bānānās!

3. Introducing *Bb*, /b/

- Turn the children's attention to the next letter of the alphabet, *Bb*.
  - Ask the children
    - Whether the letter *Bb* is a vowel (no)
    - How they can tell it's not a vowel (it's not red)
  - Tell them that letters that aren't vowels are called **consonants.** The letter *Bb* is a **consonant.**
- Tell the children that the sound of the letter *Bb* is /b/.
- Ask the children to repeat the /b/ sound with you: /b/–b/–/b/–/b/–...

3.1. Helicopter Game: *Bb*, /b/

NOTE TO TEACHER
Helicopter Game Picture Cards are conveniently provided online for every lesson, including this one. Even so, in this *first* lesson, it is a good idea to use real objects instead of pictures. Using real objects helps to convey to children that letter–sound correspondence pertains not just to curriculum words but also to words of all kinds.

- Helicopter Game set-up
  - Display the *four* objects chosen for /b/.
    - As examples, useable objects include a box, a ball, a boot, a bag, a bear, a book, and a bell. (The Helicopter Game Picture Cards are box, ball, bear, and boot.)
    - Make sure all objects are large enough to be easily seen by the children.
  - Explain that the words for everything displayed start with the letter *Bb*.
  - Point to each of the objects in turn, and make sure all of the children
    - Know the object's intended name
    - Notice that the first sound of its name is /b/

> **HELICOPTER GAME TIPS**
>
> This game is similar to the game of airplane when feeding a baby except that instead of flying a spoon into a baby's mouth, you fly your pointer finger or a laser pointer around until it alights on one of the objects displayed. (*Note:* The term *pointer* is used in this chapter to describe either your finger or a laser pointer.)
>
> As in playing airplane with a baby, it is important to move the pointer in ways that surprise and engage: Let it move through the air slowly or zip by. Let it ascend or descend straight up and down like a helicopter. Let it circle, zoom, swoop, or hover. Let it dither, even changing its mind at the last moment. Occasionally, let it get caught shifting back and forth between two of the objects or return to the same object over and over.
>
> When landing on an object, be sure to dwell for a moment so that all of the children have time to think and learn.

- Helicopter Game play
  - Explain to the students that, in this game, the pointer will move over the objects, like a helicopter. When the pointer lands on one of the objects, they must announce the name of the object.
    - When the children announce each word, they will emphasize the initial sound as much as they can: They will make the /b/ sound as loud and strong as they can.
      - Give the children practice in naming each of the objects.
      - Have them name the objects again while emphasizing the initial /b/ sound.
  - As you move the pointer through the air, the students recite the target phoneme to make the helicopter sound: "/b/–/b/–/b/–/b/–/b/–/b/–/b/–...."
    - As an example, if the objects displayed are a box, a ball, a boot, and a bear, then depending how the pointer behaves, the students might sound like this:

      "/b/–/b/–/b/–/b/–/b/–/b/–/b/–BOX! /b/–/b/–/b/–/b/–/b/–/b/–BALL! /b/–/b/–/b/–/b/–/b/–BOOT! /b/–/b/–BEAR! /b/–/b/–BOOT! /b/–/b/–BALL! /b/–/b/–/b/–/b/–/b/–/b/–BOX! /b/–/b/–BOX! /b/–/b/–BOX! /b/–/b/–/b/– /b/–/b/–/b/–BOX! /b/–/b/–BALL! /b/–/b/–/b/–/b/–BOOT! /b/–/b/–/b/– /b/–/b/–/b/–/b/–...."

3.2. **I'm Thinking of Something that Starts with:** *Bb*

- In this version of the game, the goal is to cover a lot of words that start with the target letter in relatively little time. Clue sets can be shorter and more pointed.
- Explain to the children that you are going to think of things that start with the sound of the letter *Bb*.
  - You will give them hints.
  - While they are thinking, they will recite the sound of the letter /b/.
  - When they know the answer, they will raise their hands.
- For each word, continue repeating or adding clues until all of the children have raised their hands.

> **TEACHER TIP**
>
> It is a good idea to use the Popsicle stick mug when calling for each answer. In addition to a stick with each child's name, include a number of sticks labeled "all," "girls," and "boys."

- Begin play by announcing, "I'm thinking of something that starts with the letter *Bb*."
  - Say, "What's the sound of the letter *Bb*?"
  - "Chant it while I give you hints: /b/–/b/–/b/–...."
  - "Raise your hand when you think you know."

INSTRUCTIONAL NOTE

After providing each hint, pause to give the children ample time to think of, alter, or refine their hypotheses about what the word might be based on the hints.

- Suggested target words

  blue   bird   brown   butterfly   black   book

- Sample hints
  - *Blue:* It's a color. It's the color of the sky on a sunny day. This word rhymes with *flew* and *glue.*
  - *Bird:* It's something that's alive. It has wings. It has feathers. It tweets and sings.
  - *Brown:* It's a color. It's a dark color. It's the color of chocolate. It's the color of coffee. This word rhymes with *down, clown,* and *frown.*
  - *Butterfly:* It is an insect. It can fly. It has large, beautiful wings. It begins life as a caterpillar. This word has three syllables (clap out three syllables).
  - *Black:* It's a color that's even darker than brown. It's as dark as night. It's the color of my shoes. It's the opposite of *white.* This word rhymes with *tack, snack,* and *back.*
  - *Book:* It is something you read. It has lots of pages inside. We have lots of them on the shelf over there. This word rhymes with *look, hook,* and *took.*

4. Independent Thinking: Write the Whole Alphabet
   - Give each child the sheet of ledgered writing paper.
     - Ask the children to print their name at the top of the paper.
   - Tell the children you have a special challenge for them.
     - On the front side of this sheet of paper, they will do their best to write the whole lowercase alphabet, *a* through *z.*
     - Tell them that if they get stuck, they should sing the "Alphabet Song" to themselves, and write down the letter that goes with every letter they say.
   - When they have finished with the lowercase alphabet, they should
     - Turn the sheet over
     - Write the whole uppercase alphabet, from *A* to *Z*

WORD TO THE WISE

Every child needs to be confident and comfortable with the alphabet—the more so, the better. The goal, after all, is not just that they learn the letters well enough to write them correctly today, but that they learn them so well that they will know them tomorrow, next week, and next year— forever!

- Feel free to repeat this activity, and find ways to celebrate progress and success.

Introducing the
Sounds of the Letters: *Cc, Dd*

Objectives
- To remind the children about the sounds of the letters *Aa* and *Bb*
- To introduce the primary sounds of the letters *Cc* and *Dd*

Materials
1. **Warm-Up and Review**
   Alphabet Frieze
   (*Optional*) Music for the "Vowel Name Song" (see online materials for links)
2. **Introducing *Cc*, /k/**
   Alphabet Frieze
   Helicopter Game Picture Cards or objects for *Cc*, /k/ (online)
3. **Introducing *Dd*, /d/**
   Alphabet Frieze
   Helicopter Game Picture Cards or objects for *Dd*, /d/ (online)
4. **Independent Thinking: Consonant Sound Game (Small-Group Activity)**
   Consonant Sound Game Activity Sheet: *Bb, Cc* (one for each child, see Appendix B.7)
   Uppercase Letter Recognition assessment (one for each child; see Appendix A.1)
   Lowercase Letter Recognition assessment (one for each child; see Appendix A.1)
   Pencils (one for each child)

ACTIVITIES

1. Warm-Up and Review

   1.1. Remembering *Aa*, /ā/
   - Point to the *Aa* on the Alphabet Frieze, and ask the children to
     - Name the letter
     - Tell you its sound
   - Ask the children if they remember why the *Aa* is red, reminding them that *Aa* is a **vowel.**
   - Challenge the children to name the five **vowels** of the alphabet.
   - Have the children sing the "Vowel Name Song" to remember the five vowels.

     Vowel Name Song
     Five vowels in the alphabet,
     I'll name them all for you:
     A! E! I, O, U!
     A! E! I, O, U!
     A! E! I, O, U!
     Now you can name them, too!
   - Remind the children that one of the reasons that vowels are special is that they often say their own names in words.

194

- Ask them to play a quick round of the Listening for Vowels game with /ā/.
- Remind the children that you will say a word, and they must listen carefully to decide whether it contains the /ā/ sound.
  - When they hear the sound /ā/ in a word, they should stand on their tiptoes, raise their arms to the sky, and repeat, "/ā/"!
  - If they do *not* hear the sound /ā/ in the word, they should stand flat footed and place their hands on their chests.
- Use the following list, left to right. Words that contain the /ā/ sound are bolded.

pay	**way**	**say**	so	**gray**	grow	**lay**	low
lays	lies	**bays**	buys	tries	**trays**	**praise**	prize
raise	rose	nose	goes	**hay**	hose	**ace**	ice
race	rice	**face**	**space**	spice	nice	**lake**	like
bike	**bake**	**wake**	**ache**	food	**fade**	mood	**made**

1.2. Remembering *Bb*, /b/

- Point to the *Bb* on the Alphabet Frieze and ask the children to
  - Name the letter
  - Tell you its sound
- Ask the children to repeat the sound of *Bb* with you: /b/–/b/–/b/–/b/–....
- Play a few rounds of the I'm Thinking of Something game with the letter *Bb*. (For instructions, see Lesson 1, Activity 3.2.)
  - Remind the children how to play.
    - You will think of things that start with the sound of the letter *Bb*.
    - You will give them hints.
    - While they are thinking, they will recite the sound of the letter *Bb*: /b/.
    - When they know the answer, they will raise their hands.
  - For each word, continue repeating or adding clues until all of the children have raised their hands.
- Suggested target words

  bib   bed   bus
- Sample hints
  - *Bib:* It's something for a baby. The baby wears this when eating. It keeps the baby from getting food all over her clothes. This word rhymes with *rib*.
  - *Bed:* It's a kind of furniture. It's where you sleep. It has a mattress and covers. This word rhymes with *head* and *red*.
  - *Bus:* It is a vehicle, like a car only much bigger. Lots of people can ride in it at the same time. Some of you ride one to school. This word rhymes with *us* and *fuss*.

2. Introducing *Cc*, /k/

- Turn the children's attention to the next letter of the alphabet, *Cc*, and ask the children to give its name.
- Ask the children
  - Whether the letter *Cc* is a *vowel* or a *consonant*

- How they can tell that *Cc* is a *consonant* (it's not red)
- Tell the children that the sound of the letter *Cc* is /k/.
- Ask the children to repeat the /k/ sound with you: /k/–/k/–/k/–/k/–....

2.1. Helicopter Game: *Cc*, /k/

> **NOTE TO TEACHER**
> Helicopter Game Picture Cards are provided online. Tape the pictures on the board or use a conventional projection system, such as an overhead or computer LCD projector; use a laser pointer instead of your pointer finger as the "helicopter" to prevent blocking the images during play.

- Helicopter Game preparation: *Cc*, /k/
  - Direct the children's attention to the pictures for *Cc*:

        car   cake   comb   cow

  - Explain that the words for everything shown start with the letter *Cc*.
  - Point to each of the pictures or objects in turn, and make sure all of the children
    - Know its intended name
    - Notice that the first sound of its name is /k/
- Helicopter Game play: *Cc*, /k/
  - Tell the students that it's time to play the Helicopter Game with the letter *Cc*.
    - Remind the students that, in this game, the pointer will move over the objects, like a helicopter. Whenever the pointer lands on one of the objects, they must announce the name of the object.
      - When the children announce each word, they will emphasize the initial sound as much as they can: They will make the /k/ sound as loud and strong as they can.
    - Give the children practice saying the words while emphasizing the initial /k/ sound.
    - Remind the students that as you move the helicopter pointer through the air, they will recite the target phoneme to make the helicopter sound: "/k/–/k/–/k/–/k/–/k/–/k/–...."

2.2. I'm Thinking of Something that Starts with: *Cc*
- Remind the children how to play.
  - You will think of things that start with the sound of the letter *Cc*.
  - You will give them hints.
  - While they are thinking, they will recite the sound of the letter *Cc*: "/k/–/k/–/k/–...."
  - When they know the answer, they will raise their hands.
- For each word, continue repeating or adding clues until all of the children have raised their hands.

> **INSTRUCTIONAL NOTE**
> After providing each hint, pause to give the children ample time to think of, alter, or refine their hypotheses about what the word might be, based on the hints.

- Begin play by announcing, "I'm thinking of something that starts with the letter *Cc.*"
    - "What's the sound of the letter *Cc*?"
    - "Chant it while I give you hints: /k/–/k/–/k/–...."
    - "Raise your hand when you think you know the answer."
- Suggested target words

camera	cat	crayon	clock
coat	cold	comb	couch

- Sample hints
    - *Camera:* It is used to take pictures or photographs. To take a picture, you hold it like this, look through it to see the picture you're taking, and push a button. This word has three syllables (clap out three syllables).
    - *Cat:* It is alive. It is an animal. It is a kind of pet. It is soft and furry. It says, "Meow." It purrs when it's happy. This word rhymes with *hat, sat,* and *rat.*
    - *Crayon:* It's sort of like a pencil, but it's not a pencil. It is something used for coloring. It comes in many different colors. We have a box of them [location].
    - *Clock:* There's one on the wall in this room. It has numbers on it. It shows what time it is. This word rhymes with *sock, rock,* and *block.*
    - *Coat:* It's a kind of clothing. We wear it on top of all our other clothing. It keeps us warm, especially when we are outdoors. This word rhymes with *boat, note,* and *goat.*
    - *Cold:* This is a word that describes temperature. It is the opposite of *hot.* It describes the temperature of ice cream, snow, and the inside of the refrigerator. This word rhymes with *old, sold,* and *gold.*
    - *Comb:* This is something we use to smooth our hair. It is not a brush. A brush has lots of soft bristles, but this thing has just one long row of hard teeth. This word rhymes with *home, roam,* and *dome.*
    - *Couch:* This is a kind of furniture. I have one at home in my living room. It's something that we sit on. It is like a chair except that it is wide enough to hold more than one person. Another name for this thing is a *sofa.* This word rhymes with *vouch* and *ouch.*

3. Introducing *Dd,* /d/

- Turn the children's attention to the next letter of the alphabet, *Dd,* and ask the children to give its name.
    - Ask the children
        - Whether the letter *Dd* is a *vowel* or a *consonant*
        - How they can tell that *Dd* is a *consonant* (it's not red)
- Tell the children that the sound of the letter *Dd* is /d/.
- Ask the children to repeat the /d/ sound with you: /d/–/d/–/d/–/d/–....

3.1. Helicopter Game: *Dd,* /d/

- Helicopter Game preparation
    - Direct the children's attention to the pictures for *Dd,* /d/:

dog	drum	deer	duck

    - Explain that the words for everything shown start with the letter *Dd.*

197

- Point to each of the pictures or objects in turn, and make sure all of the children
  - Know its intended name
  - Notice that the first sound of its name is /d/
- Helicopter Game play
  - Tell the students that it's time to play the Helicopter Game with the letter *Dd*.
  - Remind the students that when they announce each word, they will emphasize the initial sound as much as they can.
  - Give the children practice saying the words while emphasizing the initial /d/ sound.
  - Remind the students that as you move the helicopter pointer through the air, they will recite the target phoneme to make the helicopter sound: "/d/–/d/–/d/–/d/–/d/–/d/–/d/–...."

3.2. I'm Thinking of Something that Starts with: *Dd*

- Begin play by announcing, "I'm thinking of something that starts with the letter *Dd*."
  - "What's the sound of the letter *Dd*?"
  - "Chant it while I give you hints: /d/–/d/–/d/–...."
  - "Raise your hand when you think you know the answer."
- Suggested target words

down	dinosaur	duck	door
dance	dog	dad	doctor

- Sample hints
  - *Down:* It's the opposite of *up*. This word rhymes with *frown, gown,* and *town.*
  - *Dinosaur:* It is a type of animal. It is extinct, which means that all of them died away. It lived millions of years ago. There were many different kinds—some of the kinds were called brachiosaurus, stegosaurus, triceratops, and tyrannosaurus rex. This word has three syllables (clap out three syllables).
  - *Duck:* It's a type of bird, but it's bigger than most birds. It swims. It says, "Quack, quack!" This word rhymes with *luck.*
  - *Door:* There is one of these in every room. It's something that opens and closes. Right now the one in our room is closed. If we want to leave the room, we will have to open it. This word rhymes with *four* and *more.*
  - *Dance:* This is a way of moving. It is something we do to music. Sometimes when we do it, we wiggle; sometimes we spin; sometimes we move our feet. This word rhymes with *pants.*
  - *Dog:* It is a type of animal. It has fur. It is a good pet. It says, "Woof, woof." This word rhymes with *hog* and *log.*
  - *Dad:* It is a man. It is a parent. It is the opposite of *mom.* This word rhymes with *mad* and *sad.*
  - *Doctor:* We see this person when we are sick. Sometimes this person gives us medicine. Sometimes this person gives us shots. This person's job is to keep us healthy.

4. Independent Thinking: Consonant Sound Game

> **NOTE TO TEACHER**
> The Consonant Sound Game for the small-group sessions in this chapter requires at least two game letters to be instructive. With that in mind, today's game involves the letter *Cc* plus the letter *Bb* from the last lesson. The letter *Dd* will be paired with the letter *Ff* in the next lesson.

- Gather the children into groups of three or four.
  - Give each child a copy of the Consonant Sound Game Activity Sheet: *Bb, Cc*, and explain what they will do.
    - At the very top of the page, in the blank provided, the children write their names the "grown-up" way (with the first letter in uppercase and the rest in lowercase).
    - Today's game letters are shown in both uppercase and lowercase.
      - Ask the children to name today's game letters (*Bb* and *Cc*).
      - Remind them that they learned the sound of the letter *Bb* in the last lesson, and ask for its sound.
      - Remind them that they learned the sound of the letter *Cc* in today's lesson, and ask them for its sound.
    - Tell the children how to complete the activity sheet.
      - Direct the children's attention to the top half of the page. Explain to the children that each of them will trace and then rewrite each pair of today's game letters in the space provided.
      - Direct the children's attention to the bottom half of the page. Explain that all of the things pictured begin with one of the game letters.
      - The group works together to decide what each picture represents (remembering that it must begin with a /b/ or a /k/ sound).
      - Each student then writes the corresponding pair of letters (both uppercase and lowercase) in the blank beneath the picture.
  - Tell the children that as they work on this task, you will call them out individually for a letter recognition activity.

> **LETTER RECOGNITION ASSESSMENT NOTE**
> Administer the Exit-Level Uppercase Letter Recognition and Exit-Level Lowercase Letter Recognition assessments individually. Ask the child to complete the assessments in the same sitting.
>
> Because there is no independent thinking activity in Lesson 10, there are eight lessons to complete these assessments. Plan accordingly so that all of the children have completed the assessments by the end of Lesson 9.
>
> Forms, instructions, and scoring guidance are provided in Appendix A.1.

LESSON 3 Introducing the Sounds of the Letters: *Ee, Ff*

Objectives
- To remind the children of the sounds of the letters *Aa, Bb, Cc,* and *Dd*
- To introduce the primary sounds of the letters *Ee* and *Ff*

Materials

1. **Warm-Up and Review**

    Alphabet Frieze

2. **Introducing *E, /ē/***

    Alphabet Frieze

    (*Optional*) Music for the "Vowel Name Song" (see online materials for links)

    (*Optional*) Music for "Apples and Bananas" (see online materials for links)

3. **Introducing *F, /f/***

    Alphabet Frieze

    Helicopter Game Picture Cards or objects for *Ff, /f/* (online)

4. **Independent Thinking: Consonant Sound Game (Small-Group Activity)**

    Consonant Sound Game Activity Sheet: *Dd, Ff* (one for each child; see Appendix B.7)

    Uppercase Letter Recognition assessment (one for each child; see Appendix A.1)

    Lowercase Letter Recognition assessment (one for each child; see Appendix A.1)

    Pencils (one for each child)

ACTIVITIES

1. Warm-Up and Review

    1.1. Remembering *Bb, /b/; Cc, /k/; Dd, /d/*

    - For each of the letters *Bb, Cc,* and *Dd*, point to the letter on the Alphabet Frieze and ask the children to
        - Name the letter
        - Tell you its sound
        - Repeat the sound of the letter with you (e.g., "/b/–/b/–/b/–/b/–/b/–...")
    - Remind the children how to play the I'm Thinking of Something game.
        - You are going to think of things that start with the sound of a letter.
        - You will give them hints.
        - While they are thinking, they will recite the sound of the letter.
        - When they know the answer, they will raise their hands.
    - For each word, continue repeating or adding clues until all of the children have raised their hands.

- Suggested target words

Band-Aid	cough	dessert
brain	cry	dirty

- Sample hints
  - *Band-Aid:* This is a sticky thing you put on a cut to stop it from bleeding. It sometimes has cartoon characters on it.
  - *Cough:* This is something you do when your throat tickles. It makes a loud sound. It rhymes with *off.*
  - *Dessert:* This is a sweet thing you have after a meal. It could be cake or ice cream.
  - *Brain:* This is what you use to think. It's in your head. It rhymes with *pain* and *train.*
  - *Cry:* This is what you do when you're sad. It makes tears. It rhymes with *why* and *try.*
  - *Dirty:* This is the opposite of *clean.* It rhymes with *thirty.*

1.2. Remembering *Aa,* /ā/

- Point to the *Aa* on the Alphabet Frieze, and ask the children to
  - Name the letter
  - Tell you its sound
  - Tell you what kind of a letter it is
- Challenge the children to name the five **vowels** of the alphabet.
- Have the children sing the "Vowel Names Song" to remember the five vowels.

Vowel Names Song

Five vowels in the alphabet,

I'll name them all for you:

A! E! I, O, U!

A! E! I, O, U!

A! E! I, O, U!

Now you can name them, too!

2. Introducing *Ee,* /ē/

- Point to the letter *Ee* in the Alphabet Frieze, asking the children to tell you
  - Its name
  - What kind of a letter it is

2.1. Listening for Vowels: /ē/

- Remind the children that one of the reasons that vowels are special is that they often say their own names in words.
- Ask them to play a quick round of the Listening for Vowels game with /ē/.
  - You will say a word, and they must listen carefully to decide whether it contains the /ē/ sound.
  - When they hear the sound /ē/ in a word, they should stand on their tiptoes, raise their arms to the sky, and repeat, "/ē/"!
  - If they do *not* hear the sound /ē/ in the word, they should stand flat footed and place their hands on their chests.

- Use the following list, left to right. Words that contain the /ē/ sound are bolded.

key	**me**	**she**	show	go
sow	bow	**bee**	**knee**	new
tee	too	true	**tree**	threw
three	**flea**	fly	fry	**free**
freeze	**sneeze**	snooze	ooze	**ease**
breeze	bruise	choose	**cheese**	**please**

2.2.   Extend the Song "Apples and Bananas" to *Ee*, /ē/

- Ask the children to sing "Apples and Bananas" with you.
  - Sing the basic version first:

Apples and Bananas

I like to eat, eat, eat apples and bananas!

I like to eat, eat, eat apples and bananas!

- Sing the song again, substituting the sound, /ā/, in each occurrence of the words, *eat*, *apples*, and *bananas*, as they did in Lesson 1:

I like to āt, āt, āt āpples and bānānās!

I like to āt, āt, āt āpples and bānānās!

- Sing the song again, substituting the sound, /ē/, in each occurrence of the words, *eat*, *apples*, and *bananas*:

I like to ēt, ēt, ēt ēpples and bēnēnēs!

I like to ēt, ēt, ēt ēpples and bēnēnēs!

3.   Introducing *Ff*, /f/

- Turn the children's attention to the next letter of the alphabet, *Ff*, asking them to
  - Name the letter
  - Tell you whether it is a *vowel* or a *consonant*
- Tell the children that the sound of the letter *Ff* is /f/.
- Ask the children to repeat the /f/ sound with you: "/f/–/f/–/f/–/f/–..."

3.1.   Helicopter Game: *Ff*, /f/

- Helicopter Game preparation
  - Direct the children's attention to the pictures for *Ff*, /f/:

    fan   flag   fox   fork

  - Explain that the words for everything shown start with the letter *Ff*.
  - Point to each of the pictures or objects in turn, and make sure all of the children
    - Know its intended name
    - Notice that the first sound of its name is /f/
- Helicopter Game play
  - Tell the students that it's time to play the Helicopter Game with the letter *Ff*.
  - Remind the students that when they announce each word, they will emphasize the initial sound as much as they can.

- Give the children practice saying the words while emphasizing the initial /f/ sound.
- Remind the students that as you move the helicopter pointer through the air, they will recite the target phoneme to make the helicopter sound: "/f/–/f/–/f/–/f/–/f/–/f/–/f/–/f/–…."

3.2. I'm Thinking of Something that Starts with: *Ff*

- Begin play by announcing, "I'm thinking of something that starts with the letter *Ff*."
- "What's the sound of the letter *Ff*?"
- "Chant it while I give you hints."
- "Raise your hand when you think you know the answer."

INSTRUCTIONAL NOTE
After providing each hint, pause to give the children ample time to think of, alter, or refine their hypotheses about what the word might be, based on the hints.

- Suggested target words

  | five | feet | feather | flower |
  | funny | frog | finger | fire |

- Sample hints
  - *Five:* This is a number. It's bigger than four. It's smaller than six. This word rhymes with *dive* and *hive*.
  - *Feet:* They are part of your body. They are on the ends of your legs. You stand on them. You wear shoes and socks on them. The word rhymes with *meet, seat,* and *beat.*
  - *Feather:* This is something soft and light. Birds have them. Birds use them to fly. The word rhymes with *leather* and *weather.*
  - *Flower:* This is part of a plant. It is the part of the plant that blooms. For many plants, it blooms in the spring and is often very pretty and smells good. It can be any of a number of colors—it can be pink, red, white, or yellow. This word rhymes with *shower, hour,* and *power.*
  - *Funny:* This word describes something that makes you laugh. It is the opposite of *sad.* This word rhymes with *honey, money,* and *sunny.*
  - *Frog:* This word names a little animal. It is an animal that often lives in the water. It is green. It jumps. It croaks. This word rhymes with *dog, log,* and *jog.*
  - *Finger:* This is part of your body. You use this part of your body to pick things up and to hold onto them. It's part of your hand. You have five of them on each hand. The littlest one is called your pinkie. This word rhymes with *linger.*
  - *Fire:* This is something very hot. It burns things. When it burns things, it makes smoke. This word rhymes with *tire* and *wire.*

4. Independent Thinking: Consonant Sound Game

NOTE TO TEACHER
The Consonant Sound Game requires at least two game letters to be instructive. With that in mind, today's game involves the letter *Ff* plus the letter *Dd* from the last lesson.

- Gather the children into groups of three or four.
  - Give each child a copy of the Consonant Sound Game Activity Sheet: *Dd, Ff*, and explain what they will do.
    - At the very top of the page, in the blank provided, the children write their names the "grown-up" way (with the first letter in uppercase and the rest in lowercase).
    - Today's game letters are shown next in both uppercase and lowercase.
      - Ask the children to name today's game letters (*Dd* and *Ff*).
      - Remind them that they learned the sound of the letter *Dd* in the last lesson, and ask for its sound.
      - Remind them that they learned the sound of the letter *Ff* in today's lesson, and ask them for its sound.
    - Tell the children how to complete the activity sheet.
      - Direct the children's attention to the top half of the page, and explain to the children that each of them will trace and then rewrite each pair of today's game letters in the space provided.
      - Direct the children's attention to the bottom half of the page. Explain that all of the things pictured begin with one of the game letters.
      - The group works together to decide what each picture represents (remembering that it must begin with a /d/ or an /f/ sound).
      - Each student then writes the corresponding pair of letters (both uppercase and lowercase) in the blank beneath the picture.
  - Tell the children that as they work on this task, you will call them out individually for a letter recognition activity.

LETTER RECOGNITION ASSESSMENT NOTE

Administer the Exit-Level Uppercase Letter Recognition and Exit-Level Lowercase Letter Recognition assessments individually. Ask the child to complete both the assessments in the same sitting. Plan so that all of the children have completed the assessments by the end of Lesson 9. Forms, instructions, and scoring guidance are provided in Appendix A.1.

Introducing the
Sounds of the Letters: *Gg, Hh*

| Objectives | • To remind children about the sounds of the consonants *Bb*, *Cc*, *Dd*, and *Ff* |
| | • To introduce the primary sounds of the letters *Gg* and *Hh* |

Materials
1. **Warm-Up and Review**
   Alphabet Frieze

2. **Introducing *G*, /g/**
   Alphabet Frieze
   Helicopter Game Picture Cards or objects for *Gg*, /g/ (online)

3. **Introducing *H*, /h/**
   Alphabet Frieze
   Helicopter Game Picture Cards or objects for *Hh*, /h/ (online)

4. **Independent Thinking: Consonant Sound Game (Small-Group Activity)**
   Consonant Sound Game Activity Sheet: *Gg, Hh* (one for each child; see Appendix B.7)
   Uppercase Letter Recognition assessment (one for each child; see Appendix A.1)
   Lowercase Letter Recognition assessment (one for each child; see Appendix A.1)
   Pencils (one for each child)

ACTIVITIES

1. Warm-Up and Review

   1.1. Remembering *Bb*, /b/; *Cc*, /k/; *Dd*, /d/; *Ff*, /f/

   • For each of the letters *Bb*, *Cc*, *Dd*, and *Ff*, in turn, point to the letter on the Alphabet Frieze and ask the children to

      • Name the letter

      • Tell you its sound

      • Repeat the sound of the letter with you (e.g., "/b/–/b/–/b/–/b/–...")

   • Remind the children how to play the I'm Thinking of Something game.

      • You are going to think of things that start with the sound of a letter.

      • You will give them hints.

      • While they are thinking, they will recite the sound of the letter.

      • When they know the answer, they will raise their hands.

   • For each word, continue repeating or adding clues until all of the children have raised their hands.

   • Suggested target words:

      four   dinner   full   comb   blanket

- Sample hints
  - *Four:* This is the number that comes after three and before five. It rhymes with *sore* and *door.*
  - *Dinner:* This is the last meal of the day. You usually eat it with your family. It rhymes with *thinner* and *winner.*
  - *Full:* This is the opposite of *empty.* It rhymes with *wool* and *bull.*
  - *Comb:* You use this to straighten your hair. It can be used instead of a brush. It rhymes with *foam* and *home.*
  - *Blanket:* This is something you use to stay warm. It goes on your bed, like a quilt. In the winter, you might have more than one on your bed to keep you extra warm.

2.   Introducing *Gg,* /g/

- Turn the children's attention to the next letter of the alphabet, *Gg,* asking them to
  - Name the letter
  - Tell you whether it is a *vowel* or a *consonant*
- Tell the children that the sound of the letter *Gg* is /g/.
- Ask the children to repeat the /g/ sound with you: "/g/–/g/–/g/–/g/–...."

2.1.   Helicopter Game: *Gg,* /g/

- Helicopter Game preparation
  - Direct the children's attention to the pictures for *Gg,* /g/:

    girl   goose   glove   goat

  - Explain that the words for everything shown start with the letter *Gg.*
  - Point to each of the pictures or objects in turn, and make sure all of the children
    - Know its intended name
    - Notice that the first sound of its name is /g/
- Helicopter Game play
  - Tell the students that it's time to play the Helicopter Game with the letter *Gg.*
  - Remind the students that when they announce each word, they will emphasize the initial sound as much as they can.
  - Give the children practice saying the words while emphasizing the initial /g/ sound.
  - Remind the students that as you move the helicopter pointer through the air, they will recite the target phoneme to make the helicopter sound: "/g/–/g/–/g/–/g/–/g/–/g/–/g/–...."

2.2.   I'm Thinking of Something that Starts with: *Gg*

- Remind the children how to play the I'm Thinking of Something game.
  - "What's the sound of the letter *Gg*?"
  - "Chant it while I give you hints."
  - "Raise your hand when you think you know the answer."

INSTRUCTIONAL NOTE
After providing each hint, pause to give the children ample time to think of, alter, or refine their hypotheses about what the word might be, based on the hints.

- Suggested target words

good	green	gas	garbage
glue	garden	grocery	gray

- Sample hints
  - *Good:* The opposite of *bad*. Rhymes with *wood*, *should*, and *hood*.
  - *Green:* It's a color. It's the color of grass. This word rhymes with *bean* and *mean*.
  - *Gas:* This is fuel for a car. The car won't run without it. A longer word for it is *gasoline*. This word rhymes with *pass*, *grass*, and *sass*.
  - *Garbage:* It is stuff that you need to throw away. It goes in a bag or a special can. I put mine out on the curb in front of my house every Monday, and a big truck comes and picks it up. It is another word for *trash*.
  - *Glue:* We use this to stick things together. Sometimes it comes in a bottle, sometimes in a tube, and sometimes in a stick, sort of like lipstick. It's like paste, but it's usually gooier than paste. This word rhymes with *shoe*, *flew*, and *blue*.
  - *Garden:* This is an outdoor place. It's a place where people grow plants. Sometimes people grow vegetables. Sometimes they grow flowers, like roses and tulips. This word rhymes with *pardon* and *harden*.
  - *Grocery:* This is a kind of store. It is the kind of store where people buy meat, fruit, salt, sugar, and other things that they need for cooking. Another word for this kind of store is *supermarket*. This word has three syllables (clap out three syllables).
  - *Gray:* This is a color. It is not black, and it is not white, but it is in between black and white. It is the color of the sky on a rainy day. This word rhymes with *lay*, *play*, and *tray*.

3. Introducing *Hh*, /h/
- Turn the children's attention to the next letter of the alphabet, *Hh*, asking them to
  - Name the letter
  - Tell you whether it is a *vowel* or a *consonant*
- Tell the children that the sound of the letter *Hh* is /h/.
- Ask the children to repeat the /h/ sound with you: "/h/–/h/–/h/–/h/–...."

3.1. Helicopter Game: *Hh*, /h/
- Helicopter Game preparation: *Hh*, /h/
  - Direct the children's attention to the pictures for *Hh*, /h/

    hat   heart   horse   house

  - Explain that the words for everything shown start with the letter *Hh*.
  - Point to each of the pictures or objects in turn, and make sure all of the children
    - Know its intended name
    - Notice that the first sound of its name is /h/

- Helicopter Game play: *Hh*, /h/
  - Tell the students that it's time to play the Helicopter Game with the letter *Hh*.
  - Remind the students that when they announce each word, they will emphasize the initial sound as much as they can.
  - Give the children practice saying the words while emphasizing the initial /h/ sound.
  - Remind the students that as you move the helicopter pointer through the air, they will recite the target phoneme to make the helicopter sound: "/h/–/h/–/h/–/h/–/h/–/h/– /h/–…."

3.2. I'm Thinking of Something that Starts with: *Hh*

- Remind the children how to play the I'm Thinking of Something game.
  - "What's the sound of the letter *Hh*?"
  - "Chant it while I give you hints."
  - "Raise your hand when you think you know the answer."
- Suggested target words

hot	heavy	hello	helicopter
helmet	hop	hammer	hiss

- Sample hints
  - *Hot:* This is another word that describes temperature. It describes the temperature of a steaming cup of coffee or a very, very warm day. It is the opposite of *cold*. This word rhymes with *not, lot,* and *rot*.
  - *Heavy:* We use this word to describe how much something weighs. It is the opposite of *light*. It does *not* describe how much a balloon weighs because a balloon is light. Bubbles and feathers are light, too; they weigh very little. It describes things that weigh a lot, like elephants and big rocks. This word rhymes with *bevy* and *levee*.
  - *Hello:* This is what I say when I answer the phone. This word is the opposite of *goodbye*. This word rhymes with *below*.
  - *Helicopter:* This is something that flies. It is not alive. It is a vehicle. It is different from an airplane: It can go straight up and down; it can hover or stay in a single spot in the air; it has propeller blades that spin to make it fly—on its roof. This word has four syllables (clap out four syllables).
  - *Helmet:* This is something that is like a hat, but it is very hard. The reason for wearing one is to keep your head safe. You should always wear one on your head when you are skating or riding a bicycle.
  - *Hop:* This is like jumping, except that you do it on only one foot. This word rhymes with *mop* and *top*.
  - *Hammer:* This is a tool. It is not a screwdriver. It is not a saw. People use it to bang nails into wood like this (mime hammering). This word rhymes with *stammer* and *glamour*.
  - *Hiss:* This is a noise that snakes make. The letter *Ss* also makes the sound named by this word. This word rhymes with *miss* and *kiss*.

4. Independent Thinking: Consonant Sound Game

- Gather the children into groups of three or four.

- Give each child a copy of the Consonant Sound Game Activity Sheet: *Gg, Hh*, and explain what they will do.
  - At the very top of the page, in the blank provided, the children write their names the "grown-up" way (with the first letter in uppercase and the rest in lowercase).
  - Today's game letters are shown next in both uppercase and lowercase.
    - Each child traces and then rewrites each pair of today's game letters in the space provided at the top of the page.
  - On the bottom half of the page, there are pictures of things that begin with one of the game letters.
    - The group then works together to decide what each picture represents (remembering that it must begin with a /g/ or a /h/ sound).
    - Each student writes the corresponding pair of letters (both uppercase and lowercase) in the blank beneath.
- Tell the children that as they work on this task, you will call them out individually for a letter recognition activity.

LETTER RECOGNITION ASSESSMENT NOTE
Administer the Exit-Level Uppercase Letter Recognition and Exit-Level Lowercase Letter Recognition assessments individually. Ask the child to complete both the assessments in the same sitting. Plan so that all of the children have completed the assessments by the end of Lesson 9. Forms, instructions, and scoring guidance are provided in Appendix A.1.

LESSON 5 Introducing the Sounds of the Letters: *Ii, Jj, Kk*

Objectives
- To review the sounds of the consonants, *Bb–Hh*
- To introduce the primary sounds of the letters *Ii, Jj,* and *Kk*

Materials

1. **Warm-Up and Review**

   Flashcards for the consonants *b, c, d, f, g,* and *h*

2. **Introducing *Ii, /ī/***

   Alphabet Frieze

   (*Optional*) Music for the "Vowel Name Song" (see online materials for links)

   (*Optional*) Music for "Apples and Bananas" (see online materials for links)

3. **Introducing *Jj, /j/***

   Alphabet Frieze

   Helicopter Game Picture Cards or objects for *Jj, /j/* (online)

4. **Introducing *Kk, /k/***

   Alphabet Frieze

   Helicopter Game Picture Cards or objects for *Kk, /k/* (online)

5. **Independent Thinking: Consonant Sound Game (Small-Group Activity)**

   Consonant Sound Game Activity Sheet: *Jj, Kk* (one for each child; see Appendix B.7)

   Uppercase Letter Recognition assessment (one for each child; see Appendix A.1)

   Lowercase Letter Recognition assessment (one for each child; see Appendix A.1)

   Pencils (one for each child)

ACTIVITIES

1. Warm-Up and Review

   1.1. Flashcard Review: The Sounds of the Consonants, *b, c, d, f, g, h*

   - Hold up the stack of Flashcards, and explain.
     - There is one lowercase letter on each card.
     - When you hold up a card, the children think of the sound that goes with the letter on that card.
     - When you give the signal, they say the sound of the letter on the card.
     - They do not say anything until you give the signal.
   - When the response sounds hesitant or confused, slip the letter back into the unused part of the pile so that it will quickly show up again.

TEACHER TIP

Once the children are comfortable with the game, use the Popsicle stick mug to switch unpredictably between requesting the response from the whole group and from individuals.

---

2. Introducing *Ii*, /ī/

- Point to the letter *Ii* in the Alphabet Frieze, asking the children to tell you
    - Its name
    - What kind of a letter it is (*vowel*)
- Have the children sing the "Vowel Name Song" to review the five vowels.

Vowel Name Song

Five vowels in the alphabet,

I'll name them all for you:

A! E! I, O, U!

A! E! I, O, U!

A! E! I, O, U!

Now you can name them, too!

2.1. Listening for Vowels: /ī/

- Remind the children that one of the reasons that vowels are special is that they often say their own names in words.
- Ask the children to play the Listening for Vowels game with /ī/.
    - You will say a word, and they must listen carefully to decide whether it contains the /ī/ sound.
        - When they hear the sound /ī/ in a word, they should stand on their tiptoes, raise their arms to the sky, and repeat, "/ī/"!
        - If they do *not* hear the sound /ī/ in the word, they should stand flat footed and place their hands on their chests.
- Use the following list, left to right. Words that contain the /ī/ sound are bolded.

my	**pie**	**why**	**tie**	too
who	**high**	**buy**	**bite**	boat
note	**night**	**sight**	suit	root
right	room	**rhyme**	**ripe**	**ride**
rice	race	space	**spice**	**mice**
moose	**nice**	noose	noon	**nine**
sign	**size**	sees	freeze	**fries**

2.2. Extend the Song "Apples and Bananas" to *Ii*, /ī/

- Ask the children to sing "Apples and Bananas" with you.
    - Sing the basic version first:

Apples and Bananas

I like to eat, eat, eat apples and bananas!

I like to eat, eat, eat apples and bananas!

- Sing the song again, substituting the sound, /ī/, in each occurrence of the words, *eat*, *apples*, and *bananas*, as they did in Lesson 1:

I like to īt, īt, īt īpples and bīnīnīs!

I like to īt, īt, īt īpples and bīnīnīs!

- Lead the children in singing the song again three more times: Once for each of the vowels, /ā/, /ē/, and /ī/.

3. Introducing *Jj*, /j/

- Turn the children's attention to the next letter of the alphabet, *Jj*, asking them to
  - Name the letter
  - Tell you whether it is a *vowel* or a *consonant*
- Tell the children that the sound of the letter *Jj* is /j/.
- Ask the children to repeat the /j/ sound with you: "/j–/j/–/j/–/j/–...."

3.1. Helicopter Game: *Jj*, /j/

- Helicopter Game preparation: *Jj*, /j/
  - Direct the children's attention to the pictures for *Jj*, /j/:

    juice   jeans   jet   jug

  - Explain that the words for everything shown start with the letter *Jj*.
  - Point to each of the pictures or objects in turn, and make sure all of the children
    - Know its intended name
    - Notice that the first sound of its name is /j/
- Helicopter Game play: *Jj*, /j/
  - Tell the students that it's time to play the Helicopter Game with the letter *Jj*.
  - Remind the students that when they announce each word, they will emphasize the initial sound as much as they can.
  - Give the children practice saying the words while emphasizing the initial /j/ sound.
  - Remind the students that as you move the helicopter pointer through the air, they will recite the target phoneme to make the helicopter sound: "/j/–/j/–/j/–/j/–/j/–/j/–/j/–...."

3.2. I'm Thinking of Something that Starts with: *Jj*

- Remind the children how to play the I'm Thinking of Something game.
  - "What's the sound of the letter *Jj*?"
  - "Chant it while I give you hints."
  - "Raise your hand when you think you know the answer."

> INSTRUCTIONAL NOTE
> After providing each hint, pause to give the children ample time to think of, alter, or refine their hypotheses about what the word might be, based on the hints.

- Suggested target words

    juice   jelly   jar   January   June

- Sample hints
  - *Juice:* This is something to drink. It is made from fruits. For example, it can be made from oranges, or it can be made from apples, or it can be made from grapes. This word rhymes with *loose, goose,* and *moose.*

- *Jelly:* This is something sweet. It comes in a jar. It is made from fruit like grapes or apples. You put it on sandwiches with peanut butter. This word rhymes with *smelly* and *belly.*

- *Jar:* This is like a glass but it has a top. The top usually screws on. Jelly comes in one. Mayonnaise comes in one. Peanut butter usually comes in one, too. This word rhymes with *bar* and *car.*

- *January:* This is the name of a month. It is in the middle of the winter. [Student] has a birthday during this month. It comes right before the month of February. This word has four syllables (clap out four syllables).

- *June:* This is also the name of a month. It is the last month of the school year. It is the month after May. [Student]'s birthday is during this month. This word rhymes with *moon* and *tune.*

4. Introducing *Kk,* /k/

- Turn the children's attention to the next letter of the alphabet, *Kk,* asking them to

  - Name the letter

  - Tell you whether it is a *vowel* or a *consonant*

- Tell the children that the sound of the letter *Kk* is /k/.

- Ask the children to repeat the /k/ sound with you: "/k/–/k/–/k/–/k/–...."

4.1. Helicopter Game: *Kk,* /k/

- Helicopter Game preparation: *Kk,* /k/

  - Direct the children's attention to the pictures for *Kk,* /k/:

    key   kite   kangaroo   king

  - Explain that the words for everything shown start with the letter *Kk.*

  - Point to each of the pictures or objects in turn, and make sure all of the children

    - Know its intended name

    - Notice that the first sound of its name is /k/

- Helicopter Game play: *Kk,* /k/

  - Tell the students that it's time to play the Helicopter Game with the letter *Kk.*

  - Remind the students that when they announce each word, they will emphasize the initial sound as much as they can.

  - Give the children practice saying the words while emphasizing the initial /k/ sound.

  - Remind the students that as you move the helicopter pointer through the air, they will recite the target phoneme to make the helicopter sound: "/k/–/k/–/k/–/k/–/k/–/k/–/k/–...."

4.2. I'm Thinking of Something that Starts with: *Kk*

- Remind the children how to play the I'm Thinking of Something game.

  - "What's the sound of the letter *Kk*?"

  - "Chant it while I give you hints."

  - "Raise your hand when you think you know the answer."

- Suggested target words

    king   ketchup   key   kiss   kindergarten

- Sample hints

    - *King:* This is a kind of person. It's a man. His son is a prince. His daughter is a princess. His wife is a queen. This word rhymes with *wing, ding,* and *thing.*

    - *Ketchup:* This is something that is good on hot dogs or hamburgers. It is not mustard. It is made from tomatoes. It is red. Some people like it on French fries, too.

    - *Key:* This is something small, and it's usually made out of metal. I have some in my coat pocket. People need them to start their cars and to unlock doors. To unlock a door, you stick one of these into the little hole in the door and turn it (mime the action). Then the door unlocks. This word rhymes with *see, me,* and *tea.*

    - *Kiss:* This is something we do to show how much we love somebody. It is not a hug. It is something we do with our mouths. This word rhymes with *miss, hiss,* and *this.*

    - *Kindergarten:* This is a very important grade in school. Students in this grade are usually 5 or 6 years old. It comes before first grade. It has four syllables (clap out four syllables).

5. Independent Thinking: Consonant Sound Game

- Gather the children into groups of three or four.

- Give each child a copy of the Consonant Sound Game Activity Sheet: *Jj, Kk,* and explain what they will do.

    - At the very top of the page, in the blank provided, the children write their names the "grown-up" way (with the first letter in uppercase and the rest in lowercase).

    - Today's game letters are shown next in both uppercase and lowercase.

        - Each child traces and then rewrites each pair of today's game letters in the space provided at the top of the page.

    - On the bottom half of the page, there are pictures of things that begin with one of the game letters.

        - The group then works together to decide what the picture represents (remembering that it must begin with a /j/ or a /k/ sound).

        - Each student writes the corresponding pair of letters (both uppercase and lowercase) in the blank beneath.

- Tell the children that as they work on this task, you will call them out individually for a letter recognition activity.

> LETTER RECOGNITION ASSESSMENT NOTE
> Administer the Exit-Level Uppercase Letter Recognition and Exit-Level Lowercase Letter Recognition assessments individually. Ask the child to complete both the assessments in the same sitting. Plan so that all of the children have completed the assessments by the end of Lesson 9. Forms, instructions, and scoring guidance are provided in Appendix A.1.

Introducing the Sounds of the Letters: *Ll, Mm, Nn*

Objectives	• To review the sounds of the consonants, *Bb–Kk*
	• To introduce the primary sounds of the letters *Ll, Mm,* and *Nn*

Materials

1. **Warm-Up and Review**

   Flashcards for each of the consonants covered so far: *b–k*

2. **Introducing *Ll*, /l/**

   Alphabet Frieze

   Helicopter Game Picture Cards or objects for *Ll*, /l/ (online)

3. **Introducing *Mm*, /m/**

   Alphabet Frieze

   Helicopter Game Picture Cards or objects for *Mm*, /m/ (online)

4. **Introducing *Nn*, /n/**

   Alphabet Frieze

   Helicopter Game Picture Cards or objects for *Nn*, /n/ (online)

5. **Independent Thinking: Consonant Sound Game (Small-Group Activity)**

   Consonant Sound Game Activity Sheet: *Ll, Mm, Nn* (one for each child; see Appendix B.7)

   Uppercase Letter Recognition assessment (one for each child; see Appendix A.1)

   Lowercase Letter Recognition assessment (one for each child; see Appendix A.1)

   Pencils (one for each child)

ACTIVITIES

1. Warm-Up and Review

   1.1. Flashcard Review: The Sounds of the Consonants, *b–k*

   - Hold up the stack of Flashcards, and explain.
     - There is one lowercase letter on each card.
     - When you hold up a card, the children think of the sound that goes with the letter on that card.
     - When you give the signal, they say the sound of the letter on the card.
     - They do not say anything until you give the signal.
   - When the response sounds hesitant or confused, slip the letter back into the unused part of the pile so that it will quickly show up again.

TEACHER TIP

Once the children are comfortable with the game, use the Popsicle stick mug to switch unpredictably between requesting the response from the whole group and from individuals.

2. Introducing *Ll, /l/*

-   Turn the children's attention to the next letter of the alphabet, *Ll*, asking them to
    -   Name the letter
    -   Tell you whether it is a *vowel* or a *consonant*
-   Tell the children that the sound of the letter *Ll* is /l/.
-   Ask the children to repeat the /l/ sound with you: "/l/–/l/–/l/–/l/–/l/–...."

2.1. Helicopter Game: *Ll, /l/*

VARIATION ON THE HELICOPTER GAME

As the children become better at this game, include a few objects or pictures that do not begin with the target letter, instructing the children to make an error sound (e.g., "oop-oop-oop!", raspberry sound) when the pointer lands on one of these items.

-   Helicopter Game preparation: *Ll, /l/*
    -   Direct the children's attention to the pictures for *Ll, /l/*:

        leaf   lamb   lips   lion
    -   Explain that the words for everything shown start with the letter *Ll*.
    -   Point to each of the pictures or objects in turn, and make sure all the children
        -   Know its intended name
        -   Notice that the first sound of its name is /l/
-   Helicopter Game play: *Ll, /l/*
    -   Tell the students that it's time to play the Helicopter Game with the letter *Ll*.
    -   Remind the students that when they announce each word, they will emphasize the initial sound as much as they can.
    -   Give the children practice saying the words while emphasizing the initial /l/ sound.
    -   Remind the students that as you move the helicopter pointer through the air, they will recite the target phoneme to make the helicopter sound: "/l/–/l/–/l/–/l/–/l/–/l/–/l/–/l/–...."

2.2. I'm Thinking of Something that Starts with: *Ll*

-   Remind the children how to play the I'm Thinking of Something game.
    -   "What's the sound of the letter *Ll*?"
    -   "Chant it while I give you hints."
    -   "Raise your hand when you think you know the answer."

INSTRUCTIONAL NOTE

After providing each hint, pause to give the children ample time to think of, alter, or refine their hypotheses about what the word might be, based on the hints.

-   Suggested target words

    | lunch | lemon | loud | laugh |
    | long | little | left | lollipop |

- Sample hints
  - *Lunch:* This is a word for a meal. It is not breakfast. It is not dinner. It is a meal we eat in the middle of the day. This word rhymes with *crunch, bunch,* and *hunch.*
  - *Lemon:* This is the name of a kind of fruit. It is a bright yellow fruit. It is related to an orange, but it is very sour.
  - *Loud:* This word describes sounds. It describes things that make a lot of noise. It is the opposite of *soft.* This word rhymes with *proud* and *cloud.*
  - *Laugh:* This is a noise that people make. It is a noise they make with their mouths and voices when they think something is funny. It is the opposite of *cry.* This word rhymes with *calf* and *half.*
  - *Long:* This word describes the length of something. It is the opposite of *short.* For example, if the length of a rope is not short, then it must be...? If a story is not short, then it must be...? This word rhymes with *strong* and *wrong.*
  - *Little:* This word describes the size of something. It is the opposite of *big.* It means almost the same thing as *small.* This word rhymes with *riddle* and *middle.*
  - *Left:* This word describes a direction. It is the opposite of *right.* Each of you has two hands: One of them is your right hand, the other is your...? Now I'm pointing to my right (point right), and now I'm pointing to my...?
  - *Lollipop:* This word names something to eat. It is a kind of candy. It comes on a stick. You hold the stick and lick or suck on it. This word has three syllables (clap out three syllables).

3. Introducing *Mm,* /m/
- Turn the children's attention to the next letter of the alphabet, *Mm,* asking them to
  - Name the letter
  - Tell you whether it is a *vowel* or a *consonant*
- Tell the children that the sound of the letter *Mm* is /m/.
- Ask the children to repeat the /m/ sound with you: "/m/–/m/–/m/–/m/–...."

3.1. Helicopter Game: *Mm,* /m/
- Helicopter Game preparation: *Mm,* /m/
  - Direct the children's attention to the pictures for *Mm,* /m/:

    man   moon   mouse   monkey

  - Explain that the words for everything shown start with the letter *Mm.*
  - Point to each of the pictures or objects in turn, and make sure all of the children
    - Know its intended name
    - Notice that the first sound of its name is /m/
- Helicopter Game play: *Mm,* /m/
  - Tell the students that it's time to play the Helicopter Game with the letter Mm.
  - Remind the students that when they announce each word, they will emphasize the initial sound as much as they can.
  - Give the children practice saying the words while emphasizing the initial /m/ sound.

- Remind the students that as you move the helicopter pointer through the air, they will recite the target phoneme to make the helicopter sound: "/m/–/m/–/m/–/m/–/m/–/m/– /m/–...."

3.2. I'm Thinking of Something that Starts with: *Mm*

- Remind the children how to play the I'm Thinking of Something game.
  - "What's the sound of the letter *Mm*?"
  - "Chant it while I give you hints."
  - "Raise your hand when you think you know the answer."
- Suggested target words

mom	mother	Monday	milk
morning	melt	money	mirror

- Sample hints
  - *Mom:* This is a word for a person. The person is a woman. She's grown-up. She is a parent. It is the opposite of *dad*. This word rhymes with *Tom*.
  - *Mother:* This is another word for a person. The person is a woman. She's grown-up. She is one of your parents. It is the opposite of *father*. This word rhymes with *other* and *brother*.
  - *Monday:* This is the name of one of the days of the week. It is the day after Sunday. It is the day before Tuesday.
  - *Milk:* This word describes something that we drink. It is white. It is very good for you. Babies drink it all the time. It comes from a cow. This word rhymes with *silk*.
  - *Morning:* This word names the time of day when the sun comes up. It is when we get out of bed and go to school. It is before lunch. It is the opposite of *evening*.
  - *Melt:* This word names what happens to solid things when they get warm and turn into liquids. For example, when you put a chocolate bar in your pocket, it will get all sticky and runny because it will...? When the sun gets warm, the ice will turn into water because it will...? This word rhymes with *felt* and *belt*.
  - *Money:* This is a word for something we use to buy and sell things. When people buy something, they use this to pay for it. Some of the different kinds are nickels, dimes, pennies, and dollars. This word rhymes with *honey* and *bunny*.
  - *Mirror:* This is the word for a special kind of glass. It is like a window, but you can't see through it. If you stand in front of one of these and look into it, what you will see is yourself looking back.

4. Introducing *Nn*, /n/

- Turn the children's attention to the next letter of the alphabet, *Nn*, asking them to
  - Name the letter
  - Tell you whether it is a *vowel* or a *consonant*
- Tell the children that the sound of the letter *Nn* is /n/.
- Ask the children to repeat the /n/ sound with you: "/n/–/n/–/n/–/n/–...."

4.1. Helicopter Game: *Nn*, /n/

- Helicopter Game preparation: *Nn*, /n/

- Direct the children's attention to the pictures for *Nn*, /n/:

    nail   nest   nine   nose

- Explain that the words for everything shown start with the letter *Nn*.
- Point to each of the pictures or objects in turn, and make sure all of the children
    - Know its intended name
    - Notice that the first sound of its name is /n/
- Helicopter Game play: *Nn*, /n/
    - Tell the students that it's time to play the Helicopter Game with the letter *Nn*.
    - Remind the students that when they announce each word, they will emphasize the initial sound as much as they can.
    - Give the children practice saying the words while emphasizing the initial /n/ sound.
    - Remind the students that as you move the helicopter pointer through the air, they will recite the target phoneme to make the helicopter sound: "/n/–/n/–/n/–/n/–/n/–/n/–/n/–...."

4.2.   I'm Thinking of Something that Starts with: *Nn*

- Remind the children how to play the I'm Thinking of Something game.
    - "What's the sound of the letter *Nn*?"
    - "Chant it while I give you hints."
    - "Raise your hand when you think you know the answer."
- Suggested target words

no	never	nobody	neat
night	new	noisy	nose

- Sample hints
    - *No:* This word is the opposite of *yes*. When you nod your head up and down (demonstrate), it means *yes*. When you shake your head back and forth (demonstrate), it means this word. This word rhymes with *go, so,* and *toe.*
    - *Never:* This word means not ever. It is the opposite of *always*. I *always* want you to do your best. How often do I want you to do your worst? This word rhymes with *ever* and *clever.*
    - *Nobody:* This word means not anybody. This word is the opposite of *everybody*. The word *everyone* means the same as the word *everybody. Someone* means the same as the word *somebody. Anyone* means the same as *anybody. No one* means the same as this word.
    - *Neat:* This word is the opposite of *messy*. When my desk gets messy, I clean it up so that it will look nice and...? This word rhymes with *eat, seat,* and *feet.*
    - *Night:* This word is the opposite of *day*. It is when the sun goes down and the stars come out. This word rhymes with *sight, fight,* and *white.*
    - *New:* This word is the opposite of *old*. If you just bought your shoes yesterday, then your shoes are...? This word rhymes with *you, two,* and *who.*
    - *Noisy:* This word means the same thing as *loud*. It is the opposite of *quiet*. When everybody starts talking and laughing in here, it gets very...?

- *Nose:* This word names a part of your body. It is part of your face. You use it to smell things. When you have a cold, it gets stuffed up. This word rhymes with *goes*, *chose*, and *rose*.

5. Independent Thinking: Consonant Sound Game
    - Gather the children into groups of three or four.
    - Give each child a Consonant Sound Game Activity Sheet: *Ll, Mm, Nn*, and explain what they will do.
        - At the very top of the page, in the blank provided, the children write their names the "grown-up" way (with the first letter in uppercase and the rest lowercase).
        - Today's game letters are shown next in both uppercase and lowercase.
            - Each child traces and then rewrites each pair of today's game letters in the space provided at the top of the page.
        - On the bottom half of the page, there are pictures of things that begin with one of the game letters.
            - The group then works together to decide what each picture represents (remembering that it must begin with a /l/, /m/, or /n/ sound).
            - Each student writes the corresponding pair (both uppercase and lowercase) of letters in the blank beneath it.
    - Tell the children that as they work on this task, you will call them out individually for a letter recognition activity.

LETTER RECOGNITION ASSESSMENT NOTE

Administer the Exit-Level Uppercase Letter Recognition and Exit-Level Lowercase Letter Recognition assessments individually. Ask the child to complete both the assessments in the same sitting. Plan so that all of the children have completed the assessments by the end of Lesson 9. Forms, instructions, and scoring guidance are provided in Appendix A.1.

LESSON 7 Introducing the Sounds
of the Letters: *Oo, Pp, Qq*

Objectives	• To review the sounds of the letters *Aa–Nn*
	• To introduce the primary sounds of the letters *Oo, Pp,* and *Qq*

Materials
1. **Warm-Up and Review**
   Flashcards for each of the consonants covered so far: *b–n*

2. **Introducing *Oo,* /ō/**
   Alphabet Frieze
   (*Optional*) Music for the "Vowel Name Song" (see online materials for links)
   (*Optional*) Music for "Apples and Bananas" (see online materials for links)

3. **Introducing *Pp,* /p/**
   Alphabet Frieze
   Helicopter Game Picture Cards or objects for *Pp,* /p/ (online)

4. **Introducing *Qq,* /kw/**
   Alphabet Frieze
   Helicopter Game Picture Cards or objects for *Qq,* /kw/ (online)

5. **Independent Thinking: Consonant Sound Game (Small-Group Activity)**
   Consonant Sound Game Activity Sheet: *Pp, Qq* (one for each child; see
   Appendix B.7)
   Uppercase Letter Recognition assessment (one for each child; see Appendix A.1)
   Lowercase Letter Recognition assessment (one for each child; see Appendix A.1)
   Pencils (one for each child)

ACTIVITIES

1. Warm-Up and Review

   1.1. Flashcard Review: The Sounds of the Consonants, *b–n*

   • Hold up the stack of Flashcards, and explain.
     • There is one lowercase letter on each card.
     • When you hold up a card, the children think of the sound that goes with the letter on that card.
     • When you give the signal, they say the sound of the letter on the card.
     • They do not say anything until you give the signal.
   • When the response sounds hesitant or confused, slip the letter back into the unused part of the pile so that it will quickly show up again.

TEACHER TIP
Once the children are comfortable with the game, use the Popsicle stick mug to switch unpredictably between requesting the response from the whole group and from individuals.

2. Introducing *Oo*, /ō/

    - Point to the letter *Oo* in the Alphabet Frieze, asking the children to tell you

        - Its name

        - What kind of a letter it is (*vowel*)

    - Have the children sing the "Vowel Name Song" to review the five vowels.

        Vowel Name Song

        Five vowels in the alphabet,

        I'll name them all for you:

        A! E! I, O, U!

        A! E! I, O, U!

        A! E! I, O, U!

        Now you can name them, too!

2.1. Listening for Vowels: /ō/

    - Remind the children that one of the reasons that vowels are special is that they often say their own names in words.

    - Ask the children to play the Listening for Vowels game with /ō/.

        - You will say a word, and they must listen carefully to decide whether it contains the /ō/ sound.

        - When they hear the sound /ō/ in a word, they should stand on their tiptoes, raise their arms to the sky, and repeat, "/ō/"!

            - If they do *not* hear the sound /ō/ in the word, they should stand flat footed and place their hands on their chests.

    - Use the following list, left to right. Words that contain the /ō/ sound are bolded.

go	**no**	**snow**	**grow**	gray
grain	**groan**	cone	cane	cake
coke	**joke**	**poke**	peek	**choke**
cheek	cheese	**chose**	**froze**	**nose**
knees	these	**those**	**rose**	rise
cries	wise	white	night	**note**
bite	**boat**	right	**wrote**	**roast**

2.2. Extend the Song "Apples and Bananas" to *Oo*, /ō/

    - Ask the children to sing "Apples and Bananas" with you.

        - Sing the basic version first:

            Apples and Bananas

            I like to eat, eat, eat apples and bananas!

            I like to eat, eat, eat apples and bananas!

    - Sing the song again, substituting the sound, /ō/, in each occurrence of the words, *eat*, *apples*, and *bananas*, as they did in Lesson 1:

            I like to ōt, ōt, ōt ōpples and bōnōnōs!

            I like to ōt, ōt, ōt ōpples and bōnōnōs!

    - Lead the children in singing the song again four more times: Once for each of the vowels, /ā/, /ē/, /ī/, and /ō/.

3. Introducing *Pp*, /p/

- Turn the children's attention to the next letter of the alphabet, *Pp,* asking them to
  - Name the letter
  - Tell you whether it is a *vowel* or a *consonant*
- Tell the children that the sound of the letter *Pp* is /p/.
- Ask the children to repeat the /p/ sound with you: "/p/–/p/–/p/–/p/–...."

3.1. Helicopter Game: *Pp*, /p/

VARIATION ON THE HELICOPTER GAME
As the children become better at this game, include a few objects or pictures that do not begin with the target letter, instructing the children to make an error sound (e.g., "oop-oop-oop!", raspberry sound) when the pointer lands on one of these items.

- Helicopter Game preparation: *Pp*, /p/
  - Direct the children's attention to the pictures for *Pp*, /p/:

      pig   pot   pie   plane

  - Explain that the words for everything shown start with the letter *Pp*.
  - Point to each of the pictures or objects in turn, and make sure all of the children
    - Know its intended name
    - Notice that the first sound of its name is /p/
- Helicopter Game play: *Pp*, /p/
  - Tell the students that it's time to play the Helicopter Game with the letter *Pp*.
  - Remind the students that when they announce each word, they will emphasize the initial sound as much as they can.
  - Give the children practice saying the words while emphasizing the initial /p/ sound.
  - Remind the students that as you move the helicopter pointer through the air, they will recite the target phoneme to make the helicopter sound: "/p/–/p/–/p/–/p/–/p/– /p/–...."

3.2. I'm Thinking of Something that Starts with: *Pp*

- Remind the children how to play the I'm Thinking of Something game.
  - "What's the sound of the letter *Pp*?"
  - "Chant it while I give you hints."
  - "Raise your hand when you think you know the answer."

INSTRUCTIONAL NOTE
After providing each hint, pause to give the children ample time to think of, alter, or refine their hypotheses about what the word might be, based on the hints.

- Suggested target words

      pencil   pen   paper   puppy
      potato   pull   pillow

- Sample hints
  - *Pencil:* This is something that we use to write and draw. It is not a crayon, and it is not a pen. Usually there is an eraser on one end so that we can fix our mistakes by erasing them.
  - *Pen:* This is something else that we can use to write or draw. This word rhymes with *ten* and *hen.*
  - *Paper:* This is something that we use a lot in our class. The pages of books are made of this. Our activity sheets are made of this. This is what we write on when we use our pencils.
  - *Puppy:* This is an animal. It is a baby animal. It is a baby dog. This word rhymes with *guppy* and *yuppie.*
  - *Potato:* This is a type of vegetable. It has brown skin and is white on the inside. It can be sliced or mashed or cooked in a soup. French fries are made from this. It rhymes with *tomato.*
  - *Pull:* This word is the opposite of *push.* It rhymes with *full* and *wool.*
  - *Pillow:* This word names something that is soft and fluffy. It's something that is in your bed. You put your head on it when you go to sleep.

4. Introducing *Qq,* /kw/
   - Turn the children's attention to the next letter of the alphabet, *Qq,* asking them to
     - Name the letter
     - Tell you whether it is a *vowel* or a *consonant*
   - Tell the children that the sound of the letter *Qq* is /kw/.
   - Ask the children to repeat the /kw/ sound with you: "/kw/–/kw/–/kw/–/kw/–...."

4.1. Helicopter Game: *Qq,* /kw/
   - Helicopter Game preparation: Qq, /kw/
     - Direct the children's attention to the pictures for *Qq,* /kw/:

       quail   queen   quilt   quarter

     - Explain that the words for everything shown start with the letter *Qq.*
     - Point to each of the pictures or objects in turn, and make sure all of the children
       - Know its intended name
       - Notice that the first sound of its name is /kw/
   - Helicopter Game play: Qq, /kw/
     - Tell the students that it's time to play the Helicopter Game with the letter *Qq.*
     - Remind the students that when they announce each word, they will emphasize the initial sound as much as they can.
     - Give the children practice saying the words while emphasizing the initial /kw/ sound.
     - Remind the students that as you move the helicopter pointer through the air, they will recite the target phoneme to make the helicopter sound: "/kw/–/kw/–/kw/–/kw/–/kw/–/ kw/–/kw/–...."

4.2. I'm Thinking of Something that Starts with: *Qq*
   - Remind the children how to play the I'm Thinking of Something game.

- "What's the sound of the letter Qq?"
- "Chant it while I give you hints."
- "Raise your hand when you think you know the answer."
- Suggested target words

quick	question	quiet
quack	queen	

- Sample hints
  - *Quick:* This word is about how fast something moves. It is the opposite of *slow.* It rhymes with *thick, pick,* and *lick.*
  - *Question:* This is a kind of sentence. It is the kind of sentence that we say or write when we want to know an answer. When we write one, we end it with a mark that looks like this (write a "?" on the board).
  - *Quiet:* This is the opposite of *noisy.* At night, when there is nobody here, this room is very, very...? Sometimes, when you are making too much noise, I ask you please to be...? This word rhymes with *riot* and *diet.*
  - *Quack:* This word names another animal sound. The animal that makes this sound is a bird. It is a big bird that swims in the water. This word rhymes with *sack, black,* and *whack.*
  - *Queen:* This is a special kind of person. This person is a woman. Her son is a prince. Her daughter is a princess. Her husband is a king. This word rhymes with *seen, mean,* and *teen.*

5. Independent Thinking: Consonant Sound Game

- Gather the children into groups of three or four.
  - Give each child a Consonant Sound Game Activity Sheet: *Pp, Qq,* and explain what they will do.
    - At the very top of the page, in the blank provided, the children write their names the "grown-up" way (with the first letter in uppercase and the rest in lowercase).
    - Today's game letters are shown next in both uppercase and lowercase.
      - Each child traces and then rewrites each pair of today's game letters in the space provided at the top of the page.
    - On the bottom half of the page, there are pictures of things that begin with one of the game letters.
      - The group then works together to decide what each picture represents (remembering that it must begin with a /p/ or a /kw/ sound).
      - Each student writes the corresponding pair of letters in the blank beneath it.
- Tell the children that as they work on this task, you will call them out individually for a letter recognition activity.

LETTER RECOGNITION ASSESSMENT NOTE

Administer the Exit-Level Uppercase Letter Recognition and Exit-Level Lowercase Letter Recognition assessments individually. Ask the child to complete both the assessments in the same sitting. Plan so that all of the children have completed the assessments by the end of Lesson 9. Forms, instructions, and scoring guidance are provided in Appendix A.1.

 **LESSON 8** Introducing the Sounds
of the Letters: *Rr, Ss, Tt*

Objectives
- To review the sounds of the consonants *Bb–Qq*.
- To introduce the primary sounds of the letters *Rr, Ss,* and *Tt*

Materials
1. **Warm-Up and Review**
   Flashcards for each of the consonants covered so far: *b–q*

2. **Introducing *Rr,* /r/**
   Alphabet Frieze
   Helicopter Game Picture Cards or objects for *Rr,* /r/ (online)

3. **Introducing *Ss,* /s/**
   Alphabet Frieze
   Helicopter Game Picture Cards or objects for *Ss,* /s/ (online)

4. **Introducing *Tt,* /t/**
   Alphabet Frieze
   Helicopter Game Picture Cards or objects for *Tt,* /t/ (online)

5. **Independent Thinking: Consonant Sound Game (Small-Group Activity)**
   Consonant Sound Game Activity Sheet: *Rr, Ss, Tt* (one for each child; see Appendix B.7)
   Uppercase Letter Recognition assessment (one for each child; see Appendix A.1)
   Lowercase Letter Recognition assessment (one for each child; see Appendix A.1)
   Pencils (one for each child)

ACTIVITIES

1. Warm-Up and Review

   1.1. Flashcard Review: The Sounds of the Consonants, *b–q*
   - Hold up the stack of Flashcards, and explain.
     - There is one lowercase letter on each card.
     - When you hold up a card, the children think of the sound that goes with the letter on that card.
     - When you give the signal, they say the sound of the letter on the card.
     - They do not say anything until you give the signal.
   - When the response sounds hesitant or confused, slip the letter back into the unused part of the pile so that it will quickly show up again.

TEACHER TIP
Once the children are comfortable with the game, use the Popsicle stick mug to switch unpredictably between requesting the response from the whole group and from individuals.

2.   Introducing *Rr*, /r/

- Turn the children's attention to the next letter of the alphabet, *Rr*, asking them to
  - Name the letter
  - Tell you whether it is a *vowel* or a *consonant*
- Tell the children that the sound of the letter *Rr* is /r/.
- Ask the children to repeat the /r/ sound with you: "/r/–/r/–/r/–/r/–...."

2.1.   Helicopter Game: *Rr*, /r/

VARIATION ON THE HELICOPTER GAME
As the children become better at this game, include a few objects or pictures that do not begin with the target letter, instructing the children to make an error sound (e.g., "oop-oop-oop!", raspberry sound) when the pointer lands on one of these items.

- Helicopter Game preparation: *Rr*, /r/
  - Direct the children's attention to the pictures for *Rr*, /r/:

    rake   ring   rose   rooster

  - Explain that the words for everything shown start with the letter *Rr*.
  - Point to each of the pictures or objects in turn, and make sure all of the children
    - Know its intended name
    - Notice that the first sound of its name is /r/
- Helicopter Game play: *Rr*, /r/
  - Tell the students that it's time to play the Helicopter Game with the letter *Rr*.
  - Remind the students that when they announce each word, they will emphasize the initial sound as much as they can.
  - Give the children practice saying the words while emphasizing the initial /r/ sound.
  - Remind the students that as you move the helicopter pointer through the air, they will recite the target phoneme to make the helicopter sound: "/r/–/r/–/r/–/r/–/r/–/r/–/r/–/r/–...."

2.2.   I'm Thinking of Something that Starts with: *Rr*

- Remind the children how to play the I'm Thinking of Something game.
  - "What's the sound of the letter *Rr*?"
  - "Chant it while I give you hints."
  - "Raise your hand when you think you know the answer."

INSTRUCTIONAL NOTE
After providing each hint, pause to give the children ample time to think of, alter, or refine their hypotheses about what the word might be, based on the hints.

- Suggested target words

    rooster   right   rich   round
    red   run   rabbit   refrigerator

- Sample hints
    - *Rooster:* This is a kind of bird. It lives on a farm. It's a kind of chicken. If it were a female, it would be called a *hen*. But this is the word for a male chicken. It says, "Cocka-doodle-doo." This word rhymes with *booster*.
    - *Right:* This word means the same thing as correct. It is the opposite of *wrong*. If you got nothing wrong, then you got everything.... This word rhymes with *sight, light,* and *white.*
    - *Rich:* This word is the opposite of *poor.* It describes somebody who has lots and lots of money. Somebody who has lots and lots of money is...? This word rhymes with *which, pitch,* and *itch.*
    - *Round:* This word describes a shape. It is the shape of a circle. It is the shape of a ball. It is the opposite of *square.* This word rhymes with *ground, found,* and *sound.*
    - *Red:* This word names a color. It is the color of strawberries, lipstick, nail polish, roses, and blood. This word rhymes with *said, bed,* and *dead.*
    - *Run:* This is a way of moving. It is something we do for exercise or when we want to go fast. This word rhymes with *bun* and *fun.*
    - *Rabbit:* This is an animal. It is a small animal that hops. It has long ears and a fluffy cottontail. This word rhymes with *habit.*
    - *Refrigerator:* This is the name of something in your kitchen. It is like a big cabinet or box, but it is cold inside. You put things in it that need to stay cold. This word has five syllables (clap out four syllables).

3. Introducing *Ss, */s/
    - Turn the children's attention to the next letter of the alphabet, *Ss,* asking them to
        - Name the letter
        - Tell you whether it is a *vowel* or a *consonant*
    - Tell the children that the sound of the letter *Ss* is /s/.
    - Ask the children to repeat the /s/ sound with you: "/s/–/s/–/s/–/s/–...."

3.1. Helicopter Game: *Ss, */s/
    - Helicopter Game preparation: *Ss,* /s/
        - Direct the children's attention to the pictures for *Ss,* /s/:
            snake   spoon   sun   socks
        - Explain that the words for everything shown start with the letter *Ss.*
        - Point to each of the pictures or objects in turn, and make sure all of the children
            - Know its intended name
            - Notice that the first sound of its name is /s/
    - Helicopter Game play: *Ss,* /s/
        - Tell the students that it's time to play the Helicopter Game with the letter *Ss.*
        - Remind the students that when they announce each word, they will emphasize the initial sound as much as they can.
        - Give the children practice saying the words while emphasizing the initial /s/ sound.

- Remind the students that as you move the helicopter pointer through the air, they will recite the target phoneme to make the helicopter sound: "/s/–/s/–/s/–/s/–/s/–/s/–/s/–...."

3.2. I'm Thinking of Something that Starts with: *Ss*

- Remind the children how to play the I'm Thinking of Something game.
  - "What's the sound of the letter *Ss*?"
  - "Chant it while I give you hints."
  - "Raise your hand when you think you know the answer."
- Suggested target words

slow	small	soft	sweet
stop	six	summer	sandwich

- Sample hints
  - *Slow:* This word describes the speed of something. It is the opposite of *fast*. Something that is not fast is...? This word rhymes with *go, show,* and *blow.*
  - *Small:* This word describes the size of something. It is the opposite of *large*. Something that is not large is...? This word rhymes with *tall, fall,* and *ball.*
  - *Soft:* This word describes sounds. It is the opposite of *loud*. Something that is not loud is...? This word rhymes with *coughed* and *loft.*
  - *Sweet:* This word describes the taste of sugar. It is the opposite of *sour*. This word rhymes with *seat, feet,* and *tweet.*
  - *Stop:* This word is the opposite of *go*. It rhymes with *shop, top,* and *mop.*
  - *Six:* This word names a number. It is a number that is bigger than five. It is a number that rhymes with *mix, fix,* and *tricks.*
  - *Summer:* This word describes a season. It is not fall or winter or spring. It is the warmest season of the year. It begins in the month of June, and it ends in the month of September. This word rhymes with *bummer, drummer,* and *plumber.*
  - *Sandwich:* This is a word for something we eat. On the outside, there are two pieces of bread. On the inside, there might be any of a variety of things—there might be turkey or cheese or ham or roast beef or tuna or peanut butter and jelly. Lots of us have one of these for lunch.

4. Introducing *Tt*, /t/

- Turn the children's attention to the next letter of the alphabet, *Tt*, asking them to
  - Name the letter
  - Tell you whether it is a *vowel* or a *consonant*
- Tell the children that the sound of the letter *Tt* is /t/.
- Ask the children to repeat the /t/ sound with you: "/t/–/t/–/t/–/t/–...."

4.1. Helicopter Game: *Tt*, /t/

- Helicopter Game preparation: *Tt*, /t/
  - Direct the children's attention to the pictures for *Tt*, /t/:

two	tent	train	tree

- Explain that the words for everything shown start with the letter *Tt.*
- Point to each of the pictures or objects in turn, and make sure all of the children
  - Know its intended name
  - Notice that the first sound of its name is /t/
- Helicopter Game play: *Tt, /t/*
  - Tell the students that it's time to play the Helicopter Game with the letter *Tt.*
  - Remind the students that when they announce each word, they will emphasize the initial sound as much as they can.
  - Give the children practice saying the words while emphasizing the initial /t/ sound.
  - Remind the students that as you move the helicopter pointer through the air, they will recite the target phoneme to make the helicopter sound: "/t/–/t/–/t/–/t/–/t/–/t/–/t/–…."

4.2.   I'm Thinking of Something that Starts with: *Tt*

- Remind the children how to play the I'm Thinking of Something game.
  - "What's the sound of the letter *Tt?*"
  - "Chant it while I give you hints."
  - "Raise your hand when you think you know the answer."
- Suggested target words

two	ten	top	take
tiny	tongue	teeth	toes

- Sample hints
  - *Two:* This is a number. It's the number of eyes we have. It's the number of ears we have. It's the number of feet we have. It's more than one. It's less than three. This word rhymes with *you, blue,* and *do.*
  - *Ten:* This is a number. It's the number of fingers we have. It's the number of toes we have. It's more than nine. It's less than eleven. This word rhymes with *men, hen,* and *pen.*
  - *Top:* This word is the opposite of *bottom.* This word rhymes with *hop, mop,* and *pop.*
  - *Take:* This word is the opposite of *give.* This word rhymes with *fake, bake,* and *make.*
  - *Tiny:* This is the opposite of *huge.* It is a word that describes something that is very, very small. This word rhymes with *spiny, shiny,* and *whiny.*
  - *Tongue:* This is a part of your body. It is inside your mouth. You depend on it when you talk. You can wiggle it back and forth. You can curl it up. You can even stick it out of your mouth. This word rhymes with *sung, hung,* and *young.*
  - *Teeth:* This is another part of our bodies. Kids your age usually have 20 of these, but from time to time, you may lose one or get a new one. Grown-ups should have 32 of them. Newborn babies don't have any at all. These are inside your mouth. We use them to bite and chew. We brush them to keep them clean and white.
  - *Toes:* This is another part of our body. Most people have 10 of these. They are like fingers, but they are part of our feet. This word rhymes with *nose, goes,* and *rose.*

5.   Independent Thinking: Consonant Sound Game

- Gather the children into groups of three or four.

- Give each child a copy of the Consonant Sound Game Activity Sheet: *Rr, Ss, Tt*, and explain what they will do.
  - At the very top of the page, in the blank provided, the children write their names the "grown-up" way (with the first letter in uppercase and the rest in lowercase).
  - Today's game letters are shown next in both uppercase and lowercase.
    - Each child traces and then rewrites each pair of today's game letters in the space provided at the top of the page.
    - On the bottom half of the page, there are pictures of things that begin with one of the game letters.
    - The group then works together to decide what each picture represents (remembering that it must begin with a /r/, /s/, or /t/ sound).
    - Each student writes the corresponding pair of letters (both uppercase and lowercase) in the blank beneath the picture.
  - Tell the children that as they work on this task, you will call them out individually for a letter recognition activity.

LETTER RECOGNITION ASSESSMENT NOTE
Administer the Exit-Level Uppercase Letter Recognition and Exit-Level Lowercase Letter Recognition assessments individually. Ask the child to complete both the assessments in the same sitting. Plan so that all of the children have completed the assessments by the end of Lesson 9. Forms, instructions, and scoring guidance are provided in Appendix A.1.

 **Introducing the Sounds of the Letters:** *Uu, Vv, Ww*

LESSON 9

<table>
<tr><td>Objectives</td><td>
• To review the sounds of the letters *Aa–Tt*
• To introduce the primary sounds of the letters *Uu, Vv,* and *Ww*
</td></tr>
<tr><td>Materials</td><td>

1. Warm-Up and Review

Flashcards for each of the consonants covered so far: *b–t*

2. Introducing *Uu, /ū/*

Alphabet Frieze

(*Optional*) Music for the "Vowel Name Song" (see online materials for links)

(*Optional*) Music for "Apples and Bananas" (see online materials for links)

3. Introducing *Vv, /v/*

Alphabet Frieze

Helicopter Game Picture Cards or objects for *Vv, /v/* (online)

4. Introducing *Ww, /w/*

Alphabet Frieze

Helicopter Game Picture Cards or objects for *Ww, /w/* (online)

5. Independent Thinking: Consonant Sound Game (Small-Group Activity)

Consonant Sound Game Activity Sheet: *Vv, Ww* (one for each child; see Appendix B.7)

Uppercase Letter Recognition assessment (one for each child; see Appendix A.1)

Lowercase Letter Recognition assessment (one for each child; see Appendix A.1)

Pencils (one for each child)
</td></tr>
</table>

ACTIVITIES

1. Warm-Up and Review

1.1. Flashcard Review: The Sounds of the Consonants, *b–t*

- Hold up the stack of Flashcards, and explain.

  - There is one lowercase letter on each card.

  - When you hold up a card, the children think of the sound that goes with the letter on that card.

  - When you give the signal, they say the sound of the letter on the card.

  - They do not say anything until you give the signal.

- When the response sounds hesitant or confused, slip the letter back into the unused part of the pile so that it will quickly show up again.

TEACHER TIP

Once the children are comfortable with the game, use the Popsicle stick mug to switch unpredictably between requesting the response from the whole group and from individuals.

---

2. Introducing *Uu*, /ū/

- Point to the letter *Uu* in the Alphabet Frieze, asking the children to tell you
  - Its name
  - What kind of a letter it is (*vowel*)
- Have the children sing the "Vowel Name Song" to review the five vowels.

Vowel Name Song

Five vowels in the alphabet,

I'll name them all for you:

A! E! I, O, U!

A! E! I, O, U!

A! E! I, O, U!

Now you can name them, too!

2.1. Listening for Vowels: *Uu*, /ū/

- Remind the children that one of the reasons that vowels are special is that they often say their own names in words.
- Ask the children to play the Listening for Vowels game with /ū/.
  - You will say a word, and they must listen carefully to decide whether it contains the /ū/ sound.
  - When they hear the sound /ū/ in a word, they should stand on their tiptoes, raise their arms to the sky, and repeat, "/ū/"!
  - If they do *not* hear the sound /ū/ in your word, they should stand flat footed and place their hands on their chests.
- Use the following list, left to right. Words that contain the /ū/ sound are bolded.

you	**view**	**blue**	**true**	tray
gray	**grew**	**glue**	**clue**	clay
due	day	neigh	**new**	**flew**
flea	see	cheese	**chews**	breeze
bruise	**cruise**	**use**	**news**	knees
neat	seat	**suit**	**cute**	**fruit**
fright	**flute**	flight	right	**route**
ride	**rude**	cried	**crude**	**dude**

2.2. Extend the Song "Apples and Bananas" to *Uu*, /ū/

- Ask the children to sing "Apples and Bananas" with you.
  - Sing the basic version first:

Apples and Bananas

I like to eat, eat, eat apples and bananas!

I like to eat, eat, eat apples and bananas!

  - Sing the song again, substituting the sound, /ū/, in each occurrence of the words, *eat*, *apples*, and *bananas*, as they did in Lesson 1:

I like to ūt, ūt, ūt ūpples and būnūnūs!

I like to ūt, ūt, ūt ūpples and būnūnūs!

- Ask the children to sing the song again using whichever of the five vowels you point to.
- Repeat at least once for each of the vowels, /ā/, /ē/, /ī/, /ō/, and /ū/.

3.   Introducing *Vv*, /v/

- Turn the children's attention to the next letter of the alphabet, *Vv*, asking them to
  - Name the letter
  - Tell you whether it is a *vowel* or a *consonant*
- Tell the children that the sound of the letter *Vv* is /v/.
- Ask the children to repeat the /v/ sound with you: "/v/–/v/–/v/–/v/–...."

3.1.   Helicopter Game: *Vv*, /v/

- Helicopter Game preparation: *Vv*, /v/
  - Direct the children's attention to the pictures for *Vv*, /v/:

    van   vase   vine   vulture

  - Explain that the words for everything shown start with the letter *Vv*.
  - Point to each of the pictures or objects in turn, and make sure all of the children
    - Know its intended name
    - Notice that the first sound of its name is /v/
- Helicopter Game play: *Vv*, /v/
  - Tell the students that it's time to play the Helicopter Game with the letter *Vv*.
  - Remind the students that when they announce each word, they will emphasize the initial sound as much as they can.
  - Give the children practice saying the words while emphasizing the initial /v/ sound.
  - Remind the students that as you move the helicopter pointer through the air, they will recite the target phoneme to make the helicopter sound: "/v/–/v/–/v/–/v/–/v/–/v/–...."

> **VARIATION ON THE HELICOPTER GAME**
> As the children become better at this game, you may include a few objects or pictures that do not begin with the target letter, instructing the children to make an error sound (e.g., "oop-oop-oop!", raspberry sound) when the pointer lands on one of these items.

3.2.   I'm Thinking of Something that Starts with: *Vv*

- Remind the children how to play the I'm Thinking of Something game.
  - "What's the sound of the letter *Vv*?"
  - "Chant it while I give you hints."
  - "Raise your hand when you think you know the answer."

> **INSTRUCTIONAL NOTE**
> After providing each hint, pause to give the children ample time to think of, alter, or refine their hypotheses about what the word might be, based on the hints.

- Suggested target words

  vowels   vegetables   vacuum (cleaner)

- Sample hints

  - *Vowels:* This is a word for a category of letters. There are five of these letters. The names of these five letters are *A, E, I, O,* and *U.* This word rhymes with *owl, howl,* and *towel.*

  - *Vegetables:* This is a category of things that we eat. Foods in this category are good for you, and you should eat some every day. Some of the foods in this category are beans, corn, potatoes, spinach, and peas.

  - *Vacuum (cleaner):* This is a kind of a machine. It's a machine that is used to clean. It is especially used to clean the floor. To use it, you have to plug it in and turn it on. It makes lots of noise. When you push it around the floor, it sucks up dirt.

4.   Introducing *Ww,* /w/

- Turn the children's attention to the next letter of the alphabet, *Ww,* asking them to

  - Name the letter

  - Tell you whether it is a *vowel* or a *consonant*

- Tell the children that the sound of the letter *Ww* is /w/.

- Ask the children to repeat the /w/ sound with you: "/w/–/w/–/w/–/w/–...."

4.1.   Helicopter Game: *Ww,* /w/

- Helicopter Game preparation: *Ww,* /w/

  - Direct the children's attention to the pictures for *Ww,* /w/:

    wand   web   whale   worm

  - Explain that the words for everything shown start with the letter *Ww.*

  - Point to each of the pictures or objects in turn, and make sure all of the children

    - Know its intended name

    - Notice that the first sound of its name is /w/

- Helicopter Game play: *Ww,* /w/

  - Tell the students that it's time to play the Helicopter Game with the letter *Ww.*

  - Remind the students that when they announce each word, they will emphasize the initial sound as much as they can.

  - Give the children practice saying the words while emphasizing the initial /w/ sound.

  - Remind the students that as you move the helicopter pointer through the air, they will recite the target phoneme to make the helicopter sound: "/w/–/w/–/w/–/w/–/w/–/w/–...."

4.2.   I'm Thinking of Something that Starts with: *Ww*

- Remind the children how to play the I'm Thinking of Something game.

  - "What's the sound of the letter *Ww*?"

  - "Chant it while I give you hints."

  - "Raise your hand when you think you know the answer."

- Suggested target words

wet	Wednesday	woman
white	winner	wash

- Sample hints
    - *Wet:* This word is the opposite of *dry*. When it rains, I wear a raincoat so I won't get...? This word rhymes with *get, set,* and *jet.*
    - *Wednesday:* This is the name of one of the days of the week. It comes after Tuesday. It comes before Thursday.
    - *Woman:* This is the word for a girl who is all grown up. This word is the opposite of *man.*
    - *White:* This is a color. Some things that can be this color are snow, teeth, milk, and older people's hair. This word is the opposite of *black.* This word rhymes with *sight, might,* and *right.*
    - *Winner:* In a race, this is the person who comes in first, who runs fastest. This word is the opposite of *loser.* This word rhymes with *spinner, inner,* and *dinner.*
    - *Wash:* This is when we use soap and water to make something clean. After dinner, we do this to the dishes. Before lunch, we do this to our hands. In the bathtub, we do this to our bodies. This word rhymes with *squash* and *gosh.*

5. Independent Thinking: Consonant Sound Game
    - Gather the children into groups of three or four.
    - Give each child a Consonant Sound Game Activity Sheet: *Vv, Ww,* and explain what they will do.
        - At the very top of the page, in the blank provided, the children write their names the "grown-up" way (with the first letter in uppercase and the rest in lowercase).
        - Today's game letters are shown next in both uppercase and lowercase.
            - Each child traces and then rewrites each pair of today's game letters in the space provided at the top of the page.
        - On the bottom half of the page, there are pictures of things that begin with one of the game letters.
            - The group then works together to decide what each picture represents (remembering that it must begin with a /v/ or /w/ sound).
            - Each student writes the pair of letters (upper and lower) in the blank beneath the picture.
    - Tell the children that as they work on this task, you will call them out individually for a letter recognition activity.

LETTER RECOGNITION ASSESSMENT NOTE
Administer the Exit-Level Uppercase Letter Recognition and Exit-Level Lowercase Letter Recognition assessments individually. Ask the child to complete both the assessments in the same sitting. Plan so that all of the children have completed the assessments by the end of Lesson 9. Forms, instructions, and scoring guidance are provided in Appendix A.1.

 **LESSON 10** Introducing the Sounds
of the Letters: *Xx, Yy, Zz*

Objectives	•	To review the sounds of the letters *Aa–Ww*
	•	To introduce the primary sounds of the letters *Xx, Yy,* and *Zz*
Materials	**1.**	**Warm-Up and Review**
		Flashcards for each of the consonants covered so far: *b–w*
	2.	**Introducing *Xx,* /ks/**
		Alphabet Frieze
	3.	**Introducing *Yy,* /y/**
		Alphabet Frieze
	4.	**Introducing *Zz,* /z/**
		Alphabet Frieze
		Helicopter Game Picture Cards or objects for *Zz,* /z/ (online)
	5.	**Letter-Sound Wrap-Up**
		(*Optional*) Music for the "Consonant Song" (see online materials for links)

ACTIVITIES

1. Warm-Up and Review

    1.1. Flashcard Review: The Sounds of the Consonants, *b–w*

    • Hold up the stack of Flashcards, and explain.

        • There is one lowercase letter on each card.

        • When you hold up a card, the children think of the sound that goes with the letter on that card.

        • When you give the signal, they say the sound of the letter on the card.

        • They do not say anything until you give the signal.

    • When the response sounds hesitant or confused, slip the letter back into the unused part of the pile so that it will quickly show up again.

> TEACHER TIP
> Once the children are comfortable with the game, use the Popsicle stick mug to switch unpredict-ably between requesting the response from the whole group and from individuals.

2. Introducing *Xx,* /ks/

    • Turn the children's attention to the next letter of the alphabet, *Xx,* asking them to

    • Name the letter

    • Tell you whether it is a *vowel* or a *consonant*

    • Tell the children that the sound of the letter *Xx* is /ks/.

    • Ask the children to repeat the /ks/ sound with you: "/ks/–/ks/–/ks/–/ks/–...."

    2.1. Hearing *Xx,* /ks/ in Words

    • Explain to the children that the letter *Xx* hardly ever shows up in the beginnings of words.

237

- That means they can't play the Helicopter Game with *Xx*.
- They can still listen for the sound of *Xx* in a few words.
- Tell the children that the letter *Xx* often shows up at the very end of words.
- For each of the words below,
  - Enunciate the word, and ask the children to repeat it
  - Ask the children to use the word in a sentence, showing what it means
- Ask the children to repeat the word five times, the first time normally but increasingly exaggerating the final /ks/ on each successive repetition.

Six: six!   si/kss/!   si /ksss/!   si–/kssss/!   si–/ksssss/!

six   fix   mix   box   fox   relax

3. Introducing *Yy*, /y/

- Turn the children's attention to the next letter of the alphabet, *Yy*, asking them to
  - Name the letter
  - Tell you whether it is a *vowel* or a *consonant*
  - *Note*: You may wish to let the children know that the letter *Yy* is sometimes a vowel, but that they will learn about that later.
- Tell the children that the sound of the consonant *Yy* is /y/.
- Ask the children to repeat the /y/ sound with you: "/y/–/y/–/y/–/y/–...."

3.1. Hearing *Yy*, /y/ in Words

- Tell the children that, although there aren't that many words that begin with the consonant *Yy*, the words that do begin with *Yy* are often very enthusiastic or "high-energy" words.
  - For each of the words below, ask the children to
    - Repeat the word
    - Name its first letter, *Yy*
    - Repeat the word five times, the first time normally but increasingly exaggerating the sound of the initial /y/ with each successive repetition

yes   yay   yum   yuck   yippee

NOTE TO TEACHER

Because the name of the letter *Yy* actually begins with a /w/ sound, wī, children are often cleverly, if mistakenly, inclined to use the letter *Yy* to represent words that begin with the phoneme, /w/, writing (e.g., ya for *way* and yi for *why*). Make opportunities to remind them that the sound of the consonant *Yy* is /y/, whereas the phoneme /w/ belongs to *Ww*.

3.2. I'm Thinking of Something that Starts with: *Yy*

- Remind the children how to play the I'm Thinking of Something game.
  - "What's the sound of the letter *Yy*?"
  - "Chant it while I give you hints."
  - "Raise your hand when you think you know the answer."

INSTRUCTIONAL NOTE
After providing each hint, pause to give the children ample time to think of, alter, or refine their hypotheses about what the word might be, based on the hints.

- Suggested target words

  yes   young   yell   yellow   yolk

- Sample hints
  - *Yes:* This word is the opposite of *no.* It rhymes with *dress, mess,* and *less.*
  - *Young:* This word is the opposite of *old.* It rhymes with *stung* and *hung.*
  - *Yell:* This word means the same thing as shout. It is the opposite of *whisper.* This word rhymes with *bell, sell,* and *well.*
  - *Yellow:* This is a color. It is the color of lemons, dandelions, and the middle of an egg. This word rhymes with *fellow, bellow,* and *Jello.*
  - *Yolk:* This is the word for the yellow part in the middle of an egg. This word rhymes with *poke, soak,* and *joke.*

4. Introducing *Zz, /z/*

- Turn the children's attention to the final letter of the alphabet, *Zz,* asking them to
  - Name the letter
  - Tell you whether it is a *vowel* or a *consonant*
- Tell the children that the sound of the letter *Zz* is /z/.
- Ask the children to repeat the /z/ sound with you: "/z/–/z/–/z/–/z/–...."

4.1. Helicopter Game: *Zz, /z/*

- Helicopter Game preparation: *Zz, /z/*
  - Direct the children's attention to the pictures for *Zz, /z/*:

    zero   zipper   zebra

  - Explain that the words for everything shown start with the letter *Zz.*
  - Point to each of the pictures or objects in turn, and make sure all of the children
    - Know its intended name
    - Notice that the first sound of its name is /z/
- Helicopter Game play: *Zz, /z/*
  - Tell the students that it's time to play the Helicopter Game with the letter *Zz.*
  - Remind the students that when they announce each word, they will emphasize the initial sound as much as they can.
  - Give the children practice saying the words while emphasizing the initial /z/ sound.
  - Remind the students that as you move the helicopter pointer through the air, they will recite the target phoneme to make the helicopter sound: "/z/–/z/–/z/–/z/–/z/–/z/–/z/–/z/–...."

5. Letter-Sound Wrap-Up

- Congratulate the children for having now learned the favorite sound of each of the letters in the alphabets—of all 5 vowels and all 21 consonants.

5.1. Review the Sounds of the Vowels

- Write the five vowels on the board, and ask the children to say the (long) sound of each as you point to it.
  - First point to the vowels in surprise order.
  - Finish by pointing to each vowel from left to right.

a   e   i   o   u

5.2. Review the Sounds of the Consonants.

- Write the first five consonants on the board, and ask the children to say the sound of each as you point to it.
  - First point to the letters in surprise order.
  - Finish by pointing to each letter from left to right, and repeat:

b   c   d   f   g

- Write the next five consonants beneath the first five, and repeat:

h   j   k   l   m

- Write the next seven of the consonants beneath, and repeat:

n   p   q   r   s   t   v

- Add the final four consonants beneath, and repeat:

w   x   y   z

- Tell the children that they need a song for the consonants.

5.3. Introducing the "Consonant Song"

- Sing the "Consonant Song" for the children (to the tune of "K-K-K-Katy").
- Lead the children to learn the song, line by line, as you point to the consonants written on the board:

The Consonant Song

b c d f g

h j k l m

n p q

r s t v

w x y z

- Remind the children to sing the **sound** of each letter (not its name). For example, the sound of *x* is /ks/.
- After practicing all of the lines, lead the children to sing the whole song from beginning to end.
  - Point to each letter on the board as you sing its sound.
  - Sing the song slowly and deliberately the first few times, emphasizing proper articulation of each successive phoneme as you point to its letter.
  - Sing it more quickly to make it fun.

Long and Short Vowels

LESSON 1 Long and Short Sounds of the Letter *Aa*

ASSESSMENT ALERTS

- *Initial Consonant Sounds assessment (individual administration):* conducted during independent thinking activity throughout Lessons 1–4
- *Exit-Level Uppercase Letter Writing (group administration):* completed by all children at the end of the last lesson (Lesson 5)
- *Exit-Level Lowercase Letter Writing (group administration):* completed by all children at the end of the last lesson (Lesson 5)
- *Vowel Identification and Sounds:* completed within 2 weeks of completion of the last lesson (Lesson 5)

Objectives
- To reinforce the understanding that every vowel has a long and short sound
- To give the children practice in discerning the long and short sounds of the letter *Aa*

Materials
1. **Remembering the "Consonant Song"**

   Display of the lines of the "Consonant Song" on the board or easel (print the lines in lowercase consonants; use for the entire chapter)

   (Optional) Music for the "Consonant Song" (see online materials for links)

2. **Introducing Long and Short Vowels: *Aa***

   Alphabet Frieze

   Display of the lines of the "Consonant Song" on the board or easel

   (Optional) Music for the "Consonant Song" (see online materials for links)

3. **Listening for Long and Short *Aa***

   No extra materials

4. **The "Long and Short Vowel Song" for *Aa***

   (Optional) Music for the "Long and Short Vowel Song" (see online materials for links)

5. **Independent Thinking: Long and Short *Aa* Picture Sort (Small-Group Activity)**

   Long and Short Vowel Picture Cards for *Aa*

Long *Aa* and Short *Aa* pile labels

Initial Consonant Sounds: Student Record Form (see Appendix A.4)

Initial Consonant Sounds: Picture Cards (see Appendix A.4)

ACTIVITIES

1. Remembering the "Consonant Song"
   - Engage the children in singing the "Consonant Song." (*Note:* Remind them to sing the **sounds** of each consonant, not the names. For example, the sound of *x* is /ks/.)

     Consonant Song

     (To the tune of "K-K-K-Katy")

     /b/ /c/ /d/ /f/ /g/

     /h/ /j/ /k/ /l/ /m/

     /n/ /p/ /q/

     /r/ /s/ /t/ /v/

     /w/ /x/ /y/ /z/
   - Ask the children what these letters are called. (*consonants*)

2. Introducing Long and Short Vowels: *Aa*
   - Pointing to the Alphabet Frieze, remind the children that the red letters are special. Ask them what they are called. (*vowels*)
   - Tell the children that they are now going to learn something else that is very special about the vowels.
   - Every vowel has *two* sounds. One is called its **long** sound, and the other is called its **short** sound.

   2.1. The Sound of Long *Aa*
      - Tell the children that they have already learned the **long** sounds of the vowels.
         - The *long* sound of each vowel is the same as its name.
         - Ask the children to recite the *long* sound of *Aa* with you. Stretch the sound out so that the children can hear and feel it:

           /ā/–/ā/–/ā/–/ā/–/ā/
      - Invite the children to sing the "Consonant Song" again with you, this time adding the *long* sound of *Aa* to each consonant sound:

        Consonant Song with Long Aa

On board	Pronunciation
b c d f g	/bā/ /kā/ /dā/ /fā/ /gā/
h j k l m	/hā/ /jā/ /kā/ /lā/ /mā/
n p q	/nā/ /pā/ /kwā/
r s t v	/rā/ /sā/ /tā/ /vā/
w x y z!	/wā/ /ksā/ /yā/ /zā/ /!

242

2.2. The Sound of Short *Aa*

- Tell the children that the **short** sound of the vowel *Aa* is /ă/

- Ask them to recite the *short* sound of *Aa* with you. Stretch the sound out so that the children can hear and feel it:

/ă/–/ă/–/ă/–/ă/–/ă/

- Ask the children to sing the "Consonant Song" again with you, this time adding the *short* sound of *Aa* to each consonant sound:

Consonant Song with Short *Aa*

On board	Pronunciation
b c d f g	/bă/ /kă/ /dă/ /fă/ /gă/
h j k l m	/hă/ /jă/ /kă/ /lă/ /mă/
n p q	/nă/ /pă/ /kwă/
r s t v	/ră/ /să/ /tă/ /vă/
w x y z!	/wă/ /ksă/ /yă/ /ză/!

- Sing the "Consonant Song" several times
  - At least once with long *Aa*
  - At least once with short *Aa*

3. Listening for Long and Short *Aa*

- Tell the children that it's time to play the Listening for Vowels game again, but today they will play it with the sounds of long and short *Aa*.

3.1. Discerning Long and Short *Aa*

- Explain to the children that you will say either the *long* sound of *Aa*, /ā/, or the *short* sound of *Aa* /ă/.
  - When they hear the *long* sound, /ā/, they should stand on their tiptoes, raise their arms to the sky, and repeat, "/ā/"!
  - When they hear the *short* sound, /ă/, they should repeat, "/ă/," while they bend their knees a little and sweep their arms down to their sides, hands out, like a curtsy.
  - In between each sound, they should stand flat footed and place their hands on their chests.
- Read the letters below, left to right, row by row. (*Note:* Long vowels are bold.)
  - For at least the first two or three rows, leave enough time between sounds so that the children have time to return their hands to their chests.
  - Once the children are comfortable and confident with the game, pick up the pace.

/ā/	/ă/	**/ā/**	/ă/	/ă/	**/ā/**
/ă/	/ă/	**/ā/**	**/ā/**	**/ā/**	/ă/
/ā/	/ă/	**/ā/**	/ă/	/ă/	/ă/
/ā/	/ă/	**/ā/**	/ă/	**/ā/**	/ă/
/ā/	/ă/	**/ā/**	/ă/	/ă/	**/ā/**

3.2. Listening for Long and Short *Aa* in Words

- Explain to the children that the difference between long and short *Aa* is very important: Depending on whether the vowel is long or short, the word can mean something very different!
  - "Listen to this word: *snake*."
    - "Do you hear the long /ā/ in *snake*? Listen: Sssnnn–ā–ke, /ā/, sn–ā–ke!"
  - "Listen to this word: *snack*."
    - "Do you hear the short /ă/ in *snack*? Listen: Sssnnn–ă–ck, /ă/, sn–ă–ck!"
  - "What's a *snake*?"
  - "What's a *snack*?"
  - "Which would you rather eat?"
- Ask the children to play the Listening for Vowels game again, but this time they will listen for the long and short sounds of *Aa* in real words.
- Read each line from left to right.
  - Take care that the children voice the long or short sound of *Aa* while responding.

snake	snack	**take**	tack	back
bake	**make**	**wake**	whack	pack
pat	cat	cap	**cape**	tap
tape	**shade**	**made**	mad	sad

4. The "Long and Short Vowel Song" for *Aa*

- Tell the children that they will learn a new song about the long and short sounds of *Aa*.
  - Teach the song, line by line.
  - Sing the whole song through several times.
- Ask the children to contrast the meanings of each long-short pair of words in the song.

Long and Short Vowel Song

(To the tune of "Rock My Soul in the Bosom of Abraham")

Change short to long and *shack* turns into *shake*

Long to short and *snake* turns into *snack*

Man–main, ran–rain, cap–cape, tap–tape

Long and short sounds of A, ă, ā!

INITIAL CONSONANT SOUNDS ASSESSMENT REMINDER

Remember to conduct the Initial Consonant Sounds assessments during the independent thinking activity in Lessons 1–4.

---

5. Independent Thinking: Long and Short *Aa* Picture Sort

Short Aa: bat, pan, man, hat, crab, fan, map, glass, rat, lamp, hand, ant

Long Aa: plane, rake, skate, tape, whale, bear, cane, snake, cage, cake, grapes, rain

- Gather the children into groups of two to four.
- Give each group a Long *Aa* and a Short *Aa* pile label.
- Ask them what the difference is between the two.

- Tell them that
  - The label with the tall or long *Aa* represents long *Aa*
  - The label with the short *Aa* represents short *Aa*
- Ask the children to place both cards on the floor, where everyone in their group can reach them.
- Give each group a shuffled stack of Long and Short Vowel Picture Cards for the letter *Aa*.
- Explain that the name of every picture in their stack contains the vowel *Aa*.
  - Sometimes the word contains the long *Aa* sound: /ā/.
  - Sometimes, it contains the short *Aa* sound: /ă/.
- Their job is to sort all of the pictures into two piles.
  - The names of all of the pictures in the first pile should contain a long *Aa*. All of these cards should be placed on or below the Long *Aa* label.
  - The names of all of the pictures in the second pile should contain a short *Aa*. All of these cards should be placed on or below the Short *Aa* label.

TEACHER NOTE

This is not an easy task. Again, it is difficult for children to gain awareness of vowels. In addition, the sounds of the vowels are colored by the consonants that surround them. The more salient examples of each vowel in these stacks should help the children begin to hear the more subtle examples, and their discussions and negotiations should help further. Most important, perhaps, all children should leave the activity with a solid awareness that every vowel has two major sounds, long and short.

- To clarify through demonstration, choose a card from one of the groups.
  - Hold it up for all to see.
  - Ask the children to agree on a name for the object depicted, reminding them that the name must contain one of the sounds of *Aa*, either /ā/ or /ă/.
  - Ask the children to discuss with their group whether the word contains a long *Aa* or a short *Aa*.
  - Call on several groups for their answer.
  - Then, ask for a show of hands for the long *Aa* and the short *Aa*.
- Agree with the correct answer, and explain that the card must therefore be sorted into the long or short *Aa* pile as marked by the appropriate label.
- Ask the children to work with their group until all of the picture cards have been sorted into one or the other pile.
- Explain that as they work together, you will
  - Visit their groups to answer questions and see how they are doing
  - Call out individuals for a special letter-sound activity

INITIAL CONSONANT SOUNDS ASSESSMENT NOTE

The Initial Consonant Sounds assessment is designed for individual administration. Plan so that all of the children complete the assessment by the end of Lesson 4. Materials, instructions, and scoring guidance are provided in Appendix A.4.

Long and Short Sounds of the Letter *Ee*

Objectives
- To reinforce the understanding that every vowel has a long and short sound
- To give the children practice in discerning the long and short sounds of the letter *Ee*

Materials
1. **Remembering Long and Short *Aa***
    Alphabet Frieze
    (*Optional*) Music for the "Long and Short Vowel Song" (see online materials for links)

2. **Introducing Long and Short Vowels: *Ee***
    Alphabet Frieze
    Display of the lines of the "Consonant Song" on board or easel
    (*Optional*) Music for the "Consonant Song" (see online materials for links)

3. **Listening for Long and Short *Ee***
    No extra materials

4. **The "Long and Short Vowel Song" for *Ee***
    (*Optional*) Music for the "Long and Short Vowel Song" (see online materials for links)

5. **Independent Thinking: Long and Short *Ee* Picture Sort (Small-Group Activity)**
    Long and Short Vowel Picture Cards for *Ee*
    Long *Ee* and Short *Ee* pile labels
    Initial Consonant Sounds: Student Record Form (see Appendix A.4)
    Initial Consonant Sounds: Picture Cards (see Appendix A.4)

ACTIVITIES

1. Remembering Long and Short *Aa*
    - Remind the children that one of the special things about vowels is that each of them has two sounds, a *long* sound and a *short* sound.
    - Point to the letter *Aa* in the Alphabet Frieze.
    - Ask the children to give *Aa's long* sound and then recite it together, stretching out the sound:

      /ā/–/ā/–/ā/–/ā/–/ā/

    - Ask the children to give *Aa's short* sound and then recite it together, stretching out the sound:

      /ă/–/ă/–/ă/–/ă/–/ă/

    - Lead the children in singing the "Long and Short Vowel Song" with the *Aa* verse.
    - Challenge the children to think of a short-*Aa* twin for each of the long-*Aa* words. (Answers are given in brackets.)
      - Shake [shack]
      - Snake [snack]
      - Bake [back]
      - Rain [ran]
      - Main [man]

- Cape [cap]
- Tape [tap]
- Scrape [scrap]

2. Introducing Long and Short Vowels: *Ee*

2.1. The Sound of Long *Ee*

- Pointing to the letter *Ee* in the Alphabet Frieze, ask the children
  - To name the letter
  - To raise their hands if they know its *long* sound
- Confirm for the children that the *long* sound of a vowel is the same as its name, so the *long* sound of the letter *Ee* is /ē/.
- Ask the children to recite the *long* sound of *Ee* with you. Stretch the sound out so that the children can hear and feel it:

/ē/–/ē/–/ē/–/ē/–/ē/

- Invite the children to sing the "Consonant Song" again with you, this time adding the *long* sound of *Ee* to each consonant sound:

Consonant Song with Long *Ee*

On board	Pronunciation
b c d f g	/bē/ /kē/ /dē/ /fē/ /gē/
h j k l m	/hē/ /jē/ /kē/ /lē/ /mē/
n p q	/nē/ /pē/ /kwē/
r s t v	/rē/ /sē/ /tē/ /vē/
w x y z!	/wē/ /ksē/ /yē/ /zē/!

2.2. The Sound of Short *Ee*

- Tell the children that the *short* sound of the vowel *Ee* is /ĕ/.
- Ask the children to recite the *short* sound of *Ee* with you. Stretch the sound out so that the children can hear and feel it:

/ĕ/–/ĕ/–/ĕ/–/ĕ/–/ĕ/

- Ask the children to sing the "Consonant Song" again with you, this time adding the *short* sound of *Ee* to each consonant sound:

Consonant Song with Short *Ee*

On board	Pronunciation
b c d f g	/bĕ/ /kĕ/ /dĕ/ /fĕ/ /gĕ/
h j k l m	/hĕ/ /jĕ/ /kĕ/ /lĕ/ /mĕ/
n p q	/nĕ/ /pĕ/ /kwĕ/
r s t v	/rĕ/ /sĕ/ /tĕ/ /vĕ/
w x y z!	/wĕ/ /ksĕ/ /yĕ/ /zĕ/!

- Sing the "Consonant Song" several times
  - At least once with long *Ee*
  - At least once with short *Ee*

3. Listening for Long and Short *Ee*

- Tell the children that it's time to play the Listening for Vowels game again, but today they will play it with the sounds of long and short *Ee*.

3.1. Discerning Long and Short *Ee*

- Explain to the children that you will say either the *long* sound of *Ee*, /ē/, or the *short* sound of *Ee*, /ĕ/.
  - When they hear the *long* sound, /ē/, they should stand on their tiptoes, raise their arms to the sky, and repeat, "/ē/"!
  - When they hear the *short* sound, /ĕ/, they should repeat, "/ĕ/," while they bend their knees a little and sweep their arms down to their sides, hands out, rather like a curtsy.
  - In between each sound, they should stand flat footed and place their hands on their chests.
  - Read the letters below, left to right, row by row. (*Note:* Long vowels are in bold.)
    - For at least the first two or three rows, leave enough time between sounds so that the children have time to return their hands to their chests.
    - Once the children are comfortable and confident with the game, pick up the pace.

/ē/	/ĕ/	**/ē/**	/ĕ/	/ĕ/	**/ē/**
/ĕ/	/ĕ/	**/ē/**	**/ē/**	**/ē/**	/ĕ/
/ē/	/ĕ/	**/ē/**	/ĕ/	/ĕ/	/ĕ/
/ē/	/ĕ/	**/ē/**	/ĕ/	**/ē/**	/ĕ/
/ē/	/ĕ/	**/ē/**	/ĕ/	/ĕ/	**/ē/**

3.2. Listening for Long and Short *Ee* in Words

- Explain to the children that the difference between long and short *Ee* is very important: Depending on whether the vowel is long or short, the word can mean something very different!
  - "Listen to this word: *beast.*"
    - "Do you hear the long *Ee* in beast? Listen for the /ē/ sound: b–ē–sst, /ē/, b–ē–st!"
  - "Listen to this word: *best.*"
    - "Do you hear the short *Ee* in best? Listen for the /ĕ/ sound: b–ĕ–st, /ĕ/, b–ĕ–st!"
  - "What is a *beast*?"
  - "What does *best* mean?"
  - "Which would you rather be? Would you rather be the *best*, or would you rather be a *beast*?"
- Lead the children in playing the Listening for Vowels game with long and short *Ee*.
  - Tell them that, this time, they will be listening for the long and short sounds of *Ee* in real words.
  - Read each line from left to right.
- Take care that the children voice the proper sound of *Ee* (long or short, depending on the word) while responding.

seed	bead	bed	wed	weed
week	peek	peck	pet	net
neat	bet	beat	set	seat
seem	steam	stem	step	steep

4. The "Long and Short Vowel Song" for *Ee*

- Tell the children that it's time to learn a new verse for the "Long and Short Vowel Song." They need a verse for the long and short sounds of *Ee*.

  - Teach the *Ee* verse, line by line.

  - Sing the *Ee* verse through several times.

- Ask the children to contrast the meanings of each long-short pair of words in the *Ee* verse.

- Add the *Aa* verse and sing both verses through.

    Long and Short Vowel Song

    (To the tune of "Rock My Soul in the Bosom of Abraham")

    Change short to long and *speck* turns into *speak*

    Long to short and *cheek* turns into *check*,

    Men–mean, ten–teen, fell–feel, well–wheel,

    Long and short sounds of *E, ĕ, ē*!

INITIAL CONSONANT SOUNDS ASSESSMENT REMINDER

Remember to conduct the Initial Consonant Sounds assessments during the independent thinking activity in Lessons 1–4.

---

5. Independent Thinking: Long and Short *Ee* Picture Sort

    Short Ee: dress, tent, nest, bread, bed, net, bench, shell, belt, bell, ten, men

    Long Ee: feet, wheel, tree, bee, cheese, three, key, T, deer, queen, meat, ear

- Gather the children into groups of two to four.

  - Give each group a Long *Ee* and a Short *Ee* pile label.

    - Ask them what the difference is between the two.

    - Tell them that

      - The label with the tall or long *Ee* represents long *Ee*

      - The label with the short *Ee* represents short *Ee*

  - Ask the children to place both cards on the floor, where everyone in their group can reach them.

- Give each group a shuffled stack of Long and Short Vowel Picture Cards for letter *Ee*.

  - Explain that the name of every picture in their stack contains the vowel *Ee*.

    - Sometimes the word contains the long *Ee* sound: /ē/.

    - Sometimes, it contains the short *Ee* sound: /ĕ/.

  - Their job is to sort all of the pictures into two piles.

- The names of all of the pictures in the first pile should contain a long *Ee*. All of these cards should be placed on or below the Long *Ee* label.
- The names of all of the pictures in the second pile should contain a short *Ee*. All of these cards should be placed on or below the Short *Ee* label.

> ### TEACHER NOTE
> This is not an easy task. Again, it is difficult for children to gain awareness of vowels. In addition, the sounds of the vowels are colored by the consonants that surround them. The more salient examples of each vowel in these stacks should help the children begin to hear the more subtle examples, and their discussions and negotiations should help further. Most important, perhaps, all children should leave this activity with a solid awareness that every vowel has two major sounds, long and short.

- To clarify through demonstration, choose a card from one of the groups.
  - Hold it up for all to see.
  - Ask the children to agree on a name for the object depicted, reminding them that the name must contain one of the sounds of *Ee*, either /ē/ or /ĕ/.
  - Ask the children to discuss with their group whether the word contains a long *Ee* or a short *Ee*.
  - Call on several groups for their answer.
  - Then ask for a show of hands for the long *Ee* and the short *Ee*.
- Agree with the correct answer and explain that the card must therefore be sorted into the long or short *Ee* pile as marked by the appropriate label.
- Ask the children to work with their group until all of the picture cards have been sorted into one or the other pile.
- Explain that as they work together, you will
  - Visit their groups to answer questions and see how they are doing
  - Call out individuals for a special letter-sound activity (Initial Consonant Sounds assessment)

> ### INITIAL CONSONANT SOUNDS ASSESSMENT NOTE
> The Initial Consonant Sounds assessment is designed for individual administration. Plan so that all of the children complete the assessment by the end of Lesson 4. Materials, instructions, and scoring guidance are provided in Appendix A.4.

Long and Short Sounds of the Letter *Ii*

Objectives	• To reinforce the understanding that every vowel has a long and short sound
	• To give the children practice in discerning the long and short sounds of the letter *Ii*
Materials	**1. Remembering Long and Short *Ee***
	Alphabet Frieze
	(*Optional*) Music for the "Long and Short Vowel Song" (see online materials for links)
	2. Introducing Long and Short Vowels: *Ii*
	Alphabet Frieze
	Display of the lines of the "Consonant Song" on board or easel
	(*Optional*) Music for the "Consonant Song" (see online materials for links)
	3. Listening for Long and Short *Ii*
	No extra materials
	4. The "Long and Short Vowel Song" for *Ii*
	(*Optional*) Music for the "Long and Short Vowel Song" (see online materials for links)
	5. Independent Thinking: Long and Short *Ii* Picture Sort (Small-Group Activity)
	Long and Short Vowel Picture Cards *Ii*
	Long *Ii* and Short *Ii* pile labels
	Initial Consonant Sounds: Student Record Form (see Appendix A.4)
	Initial Consonant Sounds: Picture Cards (see Appendix A.4)

ACTIVITIES

1. Remembering Long and Short *Ee*

   • Remind the children that one of the special things about vowels is that each of them has two sounds, a *long* sound and a *short* sound.

   • Point to the letter *Ee* in the Alphabet Frieze.

   • Ask the children to give *Ee*'s *long* sound and then recite it together, stretching out the sound:

     /ē/–/ē/–/ē/–/ē/–/ē/

   • Ask the children to give *Ee*'s short sound and then recite it together, stretching out the sound:

     /ĕ/–/ĕ/–/ĕ/–/ĕ/–/ĕ/

   • Lead the children in singing the "Long and Short Vowel Song" with the *Ee* verse.

   • Challenge the children to think of a short-*Ee* twin for each of the long-*Ee* words. (Answers are given in brackets.)

     • Speak [speck]

     • Cheek [check]

     • Mean [men]

     • Teen [ten]

     • Feel [fell]

- Wheel [well]
- Wheat [wet]
- Read [red]

2. Introducing Long and Short Vowels: *Ii*

- Remind the children that one of the special things about vowels is that each of them has two sounds, a *long* sound and a *short* sound.

2.1. The Sound of Long *Ii*

- Begin by reanchoring the *long* sound of *Ii*.
    - Pointing to the letter *Ii* in the Alphabet Frieze, ask the children
        - To name the letter
        - To raise their hands if they know its *long* sound
    - Confirm for the children that the *long* sound of a vowel is the same as its name, so the *long* sound of the letter *Ii* is /ī/.
- Ask the children to recite the *long* sound of *Ii* with you. Stretch the sound out so that the children can hear and feel it:

/ī/–/ī/–/ī/–/ī/–/ī/

- Invite the children to sing the "Consonant Sound" song again with you, this time adding the *long* sound of *Ii* to each consonant sound:

Consonant Song with Long *Ii*

On board	Pronunciation
b c d f g	/bī/ /kī/ /dī/ /fī/ /gī/
h j k l m	/hī/ /jī/ /kī/ /lī/ /mī/
n p q	/nī/ /pī/ /kwī/
r s t v	/rī/ /sī/ /tī/ /vī/
w x y z!	/wī/ /ksī/ /yī/ /zī/!

2.2. The Sound of Short *Ii*

- Tell the children that the *short* sound of the vowel *Ii* is /ĭ/.
    - Ask the children to recite the *short* sound of *Ii* with you. Stretch the sound out so that the children can hear and feel it:

/ĭ/–/ĭ/–/ĭ/–/ĭ/–/ĭ/

- Ask the children to sing the "Consonant Song" again with you, this time adding the *short* sound of *Ii* to each consonant sound:

Consonant Song with Short *Ii*

On board	Pronunciation
b c d f g	/bĭ/ /kĭ/ /dĭ/ /fĭ/ /gĭ/
h j k l m	/hĭ/ /jĭ/ /kĭ/ /lĭ/ /mĭ/
n p q	/nĭ/ /pĭ/ /kwĭ/
r s t v	/rĭ/ /sĭ/ /tĭ/ /vĭ/
w x y z!	/wĭ/ /ksĭ/ /yĭ/ /zĭ/!

- Sing the "Consonant Song" several times
  - At least once with long *Ii*
  - At least once with short *Ii*

3. Listening for Long and Short *Ii*

- Tell the children that it's time to play the Listening for Vowels game again, but today they will play it with the sounds of long and short *Ii*.

3.1. Discerning Long and Short *Ii*

- Explain to the children that you will say either the *long* sound of the letter *Ii*, /ī/, or the *short* sound of the letter *Ii*, /ĭ/.
  - When they hear the *long* sound, /ī/, they should stand on their tiptoes, raise their arms to the sky, and repeat, "/ī/"!
  - When they hear the *short* sound, /ĭ/, they should repeat, "/ĭ/," while they bend their knees a little and sweep their arms down to their sides, hands out, rather like a curtsy.
  - In between each sound, they should stand flat footed and place their hands on their chests.
- Read the letters below, left to right, row by row. (*Note:* Long vowels are in bold.)
  - For at least the first two or three rows, leave enough time between sounds so that the children have time to return their hands to their chests.
  - Once the children are comfortable and confident with the game, pick up the pace.

/ī/	/ĭ/	**/ī/**	/ĭ/	/ĭ/	**/ī/**
/ĭ/	/ĭ/	**/ī/**	/ĭ/	**/ī/**	/ĭ/
/ī/	/ĭ/	**/ī/**	/ĭ/	/ĭ/	/ĭ/
/ī/	/ĭ/	**/ī/**	/ĭ/	**/ī/**	/ĭ/
/ī/	/ĭ/	**/ī/**	/ĭ/	/ĭ/	**/ī/**

3.2. Listening for Long and Short *Ii* in Words

- Explain to the children that the difference between long and short *Ii* is very important: Depending on whether the vowel is long or short, the word can mean something very different!
  - "Listen to this word: *like*."
    - "Do you hear the long *Ii* in *like*? Listen for the /ī/ sound: lll–ī–ke, /ī/, l–/ī/–ke!"
  - "Listen to this word: *lick*."
    - "Do you hear the short *Ii* in lick? Listen for the /ĭ/ sound: llll–ĭ–ck, /ĭ/, l–ĭ–ck!"
  - "What does *lick* mean?"
  - "What does *like* mean?"
  - "Would you rather have somebody *lick* you or *like* you?"
- Ask the children to play the Listening for Vowels game again, this time listening for the long and short sounds of *Ii* in real words.
  - Read each line from left to right.
  - Take care that the children appropriately voice the long or short sound of *Ii* while responding.

like	lick	sick	**sight**	**tight**
bite	bit	fit	**fight**	**white**
wit	hit	hiss	miss	**mice**
nice	**dice**	dish	fish	wish

4. The "Long and Short Vowel Song" for *Ii*

- Tell the children that it's time to learn a new verse for the "Long and Short Vowel Song," this time for the long and short sounds of *Ii*.
  - Teach the *Ii* verse, line by line.
  - Sing the *Ii* verse through several times.
- Ask the children to contrast the meanings of each long-short pair of words in the *Ii* verse.
- If desired, add the *Aa* and *Ee* verses and sing all three verses through.

Long and Short Vowel Song

(To the tune of "Rock My Soul in the Bosom of Abraham")

Change short to long and *slim* turns into *slime*

Long to short and *dime* turns into *dim*,

Fit–fight, sit–sight, whip–wipe, strip–stripe,

Long and short sounds of *I*, *ĭ*, *ī*!

INITIAL CONSONANT SOUNDS ASSESSMENT REMINDER

Remember to conduct the Initial Consonant Sounds assessments during the independent thinking activity in Lessons 1–4.

---

5. Independent Thinking: Long and Short *Ii* Picture Sort

> **Short Ii:** mitt, pin, crib, bib, pig, lips, ship, chips, six, fish, chick, bridge
>
> **Long Ii:** fire, kite, slide, pipe, vine, bike, bride, five, hive, pie, knife, nine

- Gather the children into groups of two to four.
- Give each group a label for their long *Ii* and short *Ii* piles.
  - Ask them what the difference is between the two.
  - Tell them that
    - The label with the tall or long *Ii* represents long *Ii*
    - The label with the short *Ii* represents short *Ii*
  - Ask the children to place both cards on the floor, where everyone in their group can reach them.
- Give each group a shuffled stack of Long and Short Vowel Picture Cards for the letter *Ii*.
  - Explain that the name of every picture in their stack contains the vowel *Ii*.
    - Sometimes the word contains the long *Ii* sound: /ī/.
    - Sometimes, it contains the short *Ii* sound: /ĭ/.
  - The job, for each group, is to sort all of the pictures into two piles.

- The names of all of the pictures in the first pile should contain a long *Ii*. All of these cards should be placed on or below the Long *Ii* label.
- The names of all of the pictures in the second pile should contain a short *Ii*. All of these cards should be placed on or below the Short *Ii* label.

> **TEACHER NOTE**
> This is not an easy task. Again, it is difficult for children to gain awareness of vowels. In addition, the sounds of the vowels are colored by the consonants that surround them. The more salient examples of each vowel in these stacks should help the children begin to hear the more subtle examples, and their discussions and negotiations should help further. Most important, perhaps, all children should leave this activity with a solid awareness that every vowel has two major sounds, long and short.

- To clarify through demonstration, choose a card from one of the groups.
  - Hold it up for all to see.
  - Ask the children to agree on a name for the object depicted, reminding them that the name must contain one of the sounds of *Ii*, either /ī/ or /ĭ/.
  - Ask the children to discuss with their group whether the word contains a long *Ii* or a short *Ii*.
  - Call on several groups for their answer.
  - Then, ask for a show of hands for the long *Ii* and the short *Ii*.
- Agree with the correct answer and explain that the card must therefore be sorted into the (long or short) *Ii* pile as marked by the appropriate label.
- Ask the children to work with their group until all of the picture cards have been sorted into one or the other pile.
- Explain that as they work together, you will
  - Visit their groups to answer questions and see how they are doing
  - Call out individuals for a special letter-sound activity

> **INITIAL CONSONANT SOUNDS ASSESSMENT NOTE**
> The Initial Consonant Sounds Assessment is designed for individual administration. Plan so that all of the children complete the assessment by the end of Lesson 4. Materials, instructions, and scoring guidance are provided in Appendix A.4.

LESSON 4 — Long and Short Sounds of the Letter *Oo*

Objectives
- To reinforce the understanding that every vowel has a long and short sound
- To give the children practice in discerning the long and short sounds of the letter *Oo*

Materials
1. **Remembering Long and Short *Ii***
   Alphabet Frieze
   (*Optional*) Music for the "Long and Short Vowel Song" (see online materials for links)
2. **Introducing Long and Short Vowels: *Oo***
   Alphabet Frieze
   Display of the lines of the "Consonant Song" on board or easel
   (*Optional*) Music for the "Consonant Song" (see online materials for links)
3. **Listening for Long and Short *Oo***
   No extra materials
4. **The "Long and Short Vowel Song" for *Oo***
   (*Optional*) Music for the "Long and Short Vowel Song" (see online materials for links)
5. **Independent Thinking: Long and Short *Oo* Picture Sort (Small-Group Activity)**
   Long and Short Vowel Picture Cards for *Oo*
   Long *Oo* and Short *Oo* pile labels
   Initial Consonant Sounds: Student Record Form (see Appendix A.4)
   Initial Consonant Sounds: Picture Cards (see Appendix A.4)

ACTIVITIES

1. Remembering Long and Short *Ii*
   - Remind the children that one of the special things about vowels is that each of them has two sounds, a *long* sound and a *short* sound.
   - Point to the letter *Ii* in the Alphabet Frieze.
   - Ask the children to give *Ii*'s *long* sound and then recite it together, stretching the sound out:

     /ī/–/ī/–/ī/–/ī/–/ī/

   - Ask the children to give *Ii*'s short sound and then recite it together, stretching the sound out:

     /ĭ/–/ĭ/–/ĭ/–/ĭ/–/ĭ/

   - Lead the children in singing the "Long and Short Vowel Song" with the *Ii* verse.
   - Challenge the children to think of a short-*Ii* twin for each of the long-*Ii* words. (Answers are given in brackets.)
     - Slime [slim]
     - Rhyme [rim]
     - Wipe [whip]
     - Type [tip]
     - Ripe [rip]

256

- While [will]
- Pile [pill]
- Style [still]

2. Introducing Long and Short Vowels: *Oo*

- Remind the children that one of the special things about vowels is that each of them has two sounds, a *long* sound and a *short* sound.

2.1. The Sound of Long *Oo*

- Begin by reanchoring the *long* sound of *Oo*.
- Pointing to the letter *Oo* in the Alphabet Frieze, ask the children
  - To name the letter
  - To raise their hands if they know its *long* sound
- Confirm for the children that the *long* sound of a vowel is the same as its name, so the *long* sound of the letter *Oo* is /ō/.
- Ask the children to recite the *long* sound of *Oo* with you. Stretch the sound out so that the children can hear and feel it:

  /ō/–/ō/–/ō/–/ō/–/ō/

- Invite the children to sing the "Consonant Sound" song again with you, this time adding the *long* sound of *Oo* to each consonant sound:

Consonant Song with Long *Oo*

On board	Pronunciation
b c d f g	/bō/ /kō/ /dō/ /fō/ /gō/
h j k l m	/hō/ /jō/ /kō/ /lō/ /mō/
n p q	/nō/ /pō/ /kwō/
r s t v	/rō/ /sō/ /tō/ /vō/
w x y z!	/wō/ /ksō/ /yō/ /zō/!

2.2. The Sound of Short *Oo*

- Tell the children that the *short* sound of the vowel *Oo* is /ŏ/.
  - Ask the children to recite the *short* sound of *Oo* with you. Stretch the sound out so that the children can hear and feel it:

    /ŏ/–/ŏ/–/ŏ/–/ŏ/–/ŏ/

- Ask the children to sing the "Consonant Song" again with you, this time adding the *short* sound of *Oo* to each consonant sound:

Consonant Song with Short *Oo*

On board	Pronunciation
b c d f g	/bŏ/ /kŏ/ /dŏ/ /fŏ/ /gŏ/
h j k l m	/hŏ/ /jŏ/ /kŏ/ /lŏ/ /mŏ/
n p q	/nŏ/ /pŏ/ /kwŏ/
r s t v	/rŏ/ /sŏ/ /tŏ/ /vŏ/
w x y z!	/wŏ/ /ksŏ/ /yŏ/ /zŏ/!

- Sing the "Consonant Song" several times
  - At least once with long *Oo*
  - At least once with short *Oo*

3. Listening for Long and Short *Oo*

- Tell the children that it's time to play the Listening for Vowels game again, but today they will play it with the sounds of long and short *Oo*.

3.1. Discerning Long and Short *Oo*

- Explain to the children that you will say either the *long* sound of the letter *Oo*, /ō/, or the *short* sound of the letter *Oo*, /ŏ/.
  - When they hear the *long* sound, /ō/, they should stand on their tiptoes, raise their arms to the sky, and repeat, "/ō/"!
  - When they hear the *short* sound, /ŏ/, they should repeat, "/ŏ/," while they bend their knees a little and sweep their arms down to their sides, hands out, rather like a curtsy.
  - In between each sound, they should stand flat footed and place their hands on their chests.
- Read the letters below, left to right, row by row. (*Note:* Long vowels are in bold.)
  - For at least the first two or three rows, leave enough time between sounds so that the children have time to return their hands to their chests.
  - Once the children are comfortable and confident with the game, pick up the pace.

/ō/	/ŏ/	**/ō/**	/ŏ/	/ŏ/	**/ō/**
/ŏ/	/ŏ/	**/ō/**	**/ō/**	/ŏ/	/ŏ/
/ō/	/ŏ/	**/ō/**	/ŏ/	/ŏ/	/ŏ/
/ō/	/ŏ/	**/ō/**	/ŏ/	**/ō/**	/ŏ/
/ō/	/ŏ/	**/ō/**	/ŏ/	/ŏ/	**/ō/**

3.2. Listening for Long and Short *Oo* in Words

- Explain to the children that the difference between long and short *Oo* is very important: Depending on whether the vowel is long or short, the word can mean something very different!
  - "Listen to this word: *soak*."
    - "Do you hear the long *Oo* in *soak*? Listen for the /ō/ sound: ssss–ō–k, /ō/, s–ō–k!"
  - "Listen to this word: *sock*."
    - "Do you hear the short *Oo* in *sock*? Listen for the /ŏ/ sound: sss–ŏ–ck, /ŏ/, s–ŏ–ck!"
  - "What does *soak* mean?"
  - "What is a *sock*?"
  - "When something is very dirty, would you *soak* it or *sock* it?"
- Ask the children to play the Listening for Vowels game again, this time listening for the long and short sounds of *Oo* in real words.
  - Read each line from left to right.
  - Take care that the children voice the long or short sound of *Oo* while responding.

sock	soak	soap	hope	hop
hot	not	note	goat	got
rot	road	rope	mope	mop
pop	poke	woke	joke	job

4. The "Long and Short Vowel Song" with *Oo*

- Tell the children that it's time to learn a new verse for the "Long and Short Vowel Song," this time for the long and short sounds of *Oo*.
  - Teach the *Oo* verse, line by line.
  - Sing the *Oo* verse through several times.
  - Ask the children to contrast the meanings of each long-short pair of words in the *Oo* verse.
  - If desired, add the *Aa*, *Ee*, and *Ii* verses and sing all four verses through.

Long and Short Vowel Song

(To the tune of "Rock My Soul in the Bosom of Abraham")

Change short to long and *hop* turns into *hope,*

Long to short and *slope* turns into *slop*

Got–goat, knot–note, sock–soak, jock–joke,

Long and short sounds of O, ŏ, ō!

INITIAL CONSONANT SOUNDS ASSESSMENT REMINDER

Remember to conduct the Initial Consonant Sounds assessments during the independent thinking activity in Lessons 1–4.

---

5. Independent Thinking: Long and Short *Oo* Picture Sort

Short *Oo*: blocks, cop, clock, socks, knot, mop, dog, frog, log, fox, box, lock

Long *Oo*: snow, rope, nose, stove, bow, crow, toes, rose, phone, bone, hose, comb

- Gather the children into groups of two to four.
- Give each group labels for their piles of Long and Short Vowel Picture Cards for the letter *Oo*.
  - Ask them what the difference is between the two.
  - Tell them that
    - The label with the tall or long *Oo* represents long *Oo*
    - The label with the short *Oo* represents short *Oo*
- Ask the children to place both cards on the floor, where everyone in their group can reach them.
- Give each group a shuffled stack of Long and Short Vowel Picture Cards for *Oo*.
- Explain that the name of every picture in their stack contains the vowel *Oo*.
  - Sometimes the word contains the long *Oo* sound: /ō/.
  - Sometimes, it contains the short *Oo* sound: /ŏ/.
- Their job is to sort all of the pictures into two piles.
  - The names of all of the pictures in the first pile should contain a long *Oo*. All of these cards should be placed on or below the Long *Oo* label.

- The names of all of the pictures in the second pile should contain a short *Oo*. All of these cards should be placed on or below the Short *Oo* label.
- To clarify through demonstration, choose a card from one of the groups.
  - Hold it up for all to see.
  - Ask the children to agree on a name for the object depicted, reminding them that the name must contain one of the sounds of *Oo*, either /ō/ or /ŏ/.
  - Ask the children to discuss with their group whether the word contains a long *Oo* or a short *Oo*.
  - Call on several groups for their answer.
  - Then ask for a show of hands for the long *Oo* and the short *Oo*.
- Agree with the correct answer and explain that the card must therefore be sorted into the long or short *Oo* pile as marked by the appropriate label.
- Ask the children to work with their group until all of the picture cards have been sorted into one or the other pile.
- Explain that as they work together, you will
  - Visit their groups to answer questions and see how they are doing
  - Call out individuals for a special letter-sound activity

INITIAL CONSONANT SOUNDS ASSESSMENT NOTE

The Initial Consonant Sounds assessment is designed for individual administration. Plan so that all of the children complete the assessment by the end of Lesson 4. Materials, instructions, and scoring guidance are provided in Appendix A.4.

LESSON 5 Long and Short Sounds of the Letter *Uu*

Objectives
- To reinforce the understanding that every vowel has a long and short sound
- To give the children practice in discerning the long and short sounds of the letter *Uu*

Materials
1. **Remembering Long and Short *Oo***
   Alphabet Frieze
   (*Optional*) Music for the "Long and Short Vowel Song" (see online materials for links)

2. **Introducing Long and Short Vowels: *Uu***
   Alphabet Frieze
   Display of the lines of the "Consonant Song" on board or easel
   (*Optional*) Music for the "Consonant Song" (see online materials for links)

3. **Listening for Long and Short *Uu***
   No extra materials

4. **The "Long and Short Vowel Song" for *Uu***
   (*Optional*) Music for the "Long and Short Vowel Song" (see online materials for links)

5. **Independent Thinking: Uppercase and Lowercase Letter Writing Assessment (Small-Group Activity)**
   Lowercase Letter Writing assessment (one for each student; see Appendix A.3)
   Uppercase Letter Writing assessment (one for each student; see Appendix A.3)

ACTIVITIES

1. Remembering Long and Short *Oo*
    - Remind the children that one of the special things about vowels is that each of them has two sounds, a *long* sound and a *short* sound.
    - Point to the letter *Oo* in the Alphabet Frieze.
    - Ask the children to give *Oo*'s long sound and then recite it together, stretching the sound out:

      /ō/–/ō/–/ō/–/ō/–/ō/

    - Ask the children to give *Oo*'s short sound and then recite it together, stretching the sound out:

      /ŏ/–/ŏ/–/ŏ/–/ŏ/–/ŏ/

    - Lead the children in singing the "Long and Short Vowel Song" with the *Oo* verse.
    - Challenge the children to think of a short-*Oo* twin for each of the long-*Oo* words. (Answers are given in brackets.)
      - Hope [hop]
      - Cope [cop]
      - Mope [mop]
      - Slope [slop]
      - Soak [sock]
      - Cloak [clock]

- Robe [rob]
- Note [not/knot]

2. Introducing Long and Short Vowels: *Uu*

- Remind the children that one of the special things about vowels is that each of them has two sounds, a *long* sound and a *short* sound.

2.1. The Sound of Long *Uu*

- Begin by reanchoring the *long* sound of *Uu*.
  - Pointing to the letter *Uu* in Alphabet Frieze, ask the children
    - To name the letter
    - To raise their hands if they know its *long* sound
- Confirm for the children that the *long* sound of a vowel is the same as its name, so the *long* sound of the letter *Uu* is /ū/.
- Ask the children to recite the *long* sound of *Uu* with you. Stretch the sound out so that the children can hear and feel it:

/ū/–/ū/–/ū/–/ū/–/ū/

- Invite the children to sing the "Consonant Sound" song again with you, this time adding the *long* sound of *Uu* to each consonant sound:

Consonant Song with Long *Uu*

On board	Pronunciation
b c d f g	/bū/ /kū/ /dū/ /fū/ /gū/
h j k l m	/hū/ /jū/ /kū/ /lū/ /mū/
n p q	/nū/ /pū/ /kwū/
r s t v	/rū/ /sū/ /tū/ /vū/
w x y z!	/wū/ /ksū/ /yū/ /zū/!

2.2. The Sound of Short *Uu*

- Tell the children that the *short* sound of the vowel *Uu* is /ŭ/.
  - Ask the children to recite the *short* sound of *Uu* with you. Stretch the sound out so that the children can hear and feel it:

/ŭ/–/ŭ/–/ŭ/–/ŭ/–/ŭ/

- Ask the children to sing the "Consonant Song" again with you, this time adding the *short* sound of *Uu* to each consonant sound:

Consonant Song with Short *Uu*

On board	Pronunciation
b c d f g	/bŭ/ /kŭ/ /dŭ/ /fŭ/ /gŭ/
h j k l m	/hŭ/ /jŭ/ /kŭ/ /lŭ/ /mŭ/
n p q	/nŭ/ /pŭ/ /kwŭ/
r s t v	/rŭ/ /sŭ/ /tŭ/ /vŭ/
w x y z!	/wŭ/ /ksŭ/ /yŭ/ /zŭ/!

- Sing the "Consonant Song" several times.
  - At least once with long *Uu*
  - At least once with short *Uu*

3. Listening for Long and Short *Uu*

- Tell the children that it's time to play the Listening for Vowels game again, but today they will play it with the sounds of long and short *Uu*.

3.1. Discerning Long and Short *Uu*

- Explain to the children that you will say either the *long* sound of the letter *Uu*, /ū/, or the *short* sound of the letter *Uu*, /ŭ/.
  - When they hear the *long* sound, /ū/, they should stand on their tiptoes, raise their arms to the sky, and repeat, "/ū/"!
  - When they hear the *short* sound, /ŭ/, they should repeat, "/ŭ/," while they bend their knees a little and sweep their arms down to their sides, hands out, rather like a curtsy.
  - In between each sound, they should stand flat footed and place their hands on their chests.
- Read the letters below, left to right, row by row. (*Note:* Long vowels are in bold.)
  - For at least the first two or three rows, leave enough time between sounds so that the children have time to return their hands to their chests.
  - Once the children are comfortable and confident with the game, pick up the pace.

/ū/	/ŭ/	**/ū/**	/ŭ/	/ŭ/	**/ū/**
/ŭ/	/ŭ/	**/ū/**	**/ū/**	**/ū/**	/ŭ/
/ū/	/ŭ/	**/ū/**	/ŭ/	/ŭ/	/ŭ/
/ū/	/ŭ/	**/ū/**	/ŭ/	**/ū/**	/ŭ/
/ū/	/ŭ/	**/ū/**	/ŭ/	/ŭ/	**/ū/**

3.2. Listening for Long and Short *Uu* in Words

- Explain to the children that the difference between long and short *Uu* is very important: Depending on whether the vowel is long or short, the word can mean something very different!
  - "Listen to this word: *plume*."
    - "Do you hear the long *Uu* in *plume*? Listen for the /ū/ sound: plll–ū–me, /ū/, pl–ū–me!"
  - "Listen to this word: *plum*."
    - "Do you hear the short *Uu* in *plum*? Listen for the /ŭ/ sound: plll–ŭ–m, /ŭ/, /pl–ŭ–m!"
  - "What is a *plume*?"
  - "What is a *plum*?"
  - "Could birds fly if they grew *plums* on their tails?"
- Ask the children to play the Listening Vowels game again, this time listening for the long and short sounds of *Uu* in real words.
  - Read each line from left to right.

- Take care that the children appropriately voice the long or short sound of *Uu* while responding.

plume	plum	hum	dumb	**dude**
rude	luck	muck	duck	truck
true	**blue**	**new**	nut	rut
run	sun	**suit**	**fruit**	**cute**
cube	cub	rub	tub	**tube**

4. The "Long and Short Vowel Song" for *Uu*
   - Tell the children that its time to learn a new verse for the "Long and Short Vowel Song," this time for the long and short sounds of *Uu*.
   - Teach the *Uu* verse, line by line.
   - Sing the *Uu* verse through several times.
     - Ask the children to contrast the meanings of each long-short pair of words in the *Uu* verse.
     - Add the *Aa, Ee, Ii,* and *Oo* verses and sing all five verses through.

Long and Short Vowel Song

(To the tune of "Rock My Soul in the Bosom of Abraham")

Change short to long and *mud* turns into *mood*,

Long to short and *dude* turns into *dud*,

Rough–roof, puff–poof, cub–cube, tub–tube

Long and short sounds of *U*, ŭ, ū!

5. Independent Thinking: Uppercase and Lowercase Letter Writing Assessment
   5.1. Overview the Assessments
   - Hold up the Exit-Level Uppercase Letter Writing and Exit-Level Lowercase Letter Writing assessments, and introduce them to the children:
     - "Do these look familiar?" (Affirm that the assessments look like the Uppercase and Lowercase Letter Fill-Ins.)
     - "Today, I want each of you to fill in both of these sheets, all by yourselves."

   5.2. Uppercase Letter Writing Assessment
   - Hold up the Uppercase Letter Writing assessment.
     - Ask, "What's missing?"
     - Ask, "What do you need to do?"
     - Confirm that they need to fill in the uppercase letters.
   - Hold up the Lowercase Letter Writing assessment.
     - Ask, "What's missing on this sheet?"
     - Ask, "What do you need to do?"
     - Confirm that they need to fill in the uppercase letters.
   - Give every child a copy of the Exit-Level Uppercase Letter Writing assessment.
   - Explain that they will

- Write their *name* in the space provided at the top of the sheet
- Fill in as many of the uppercase letters as they can
- Raise their hands when they are done so that you can collect their work and give them the next activity sheet
- Remind them that this is an individual activity. The children will work by themselves.

5.3. Lowercase Letter Writing Assessment

- Give each child a copy of the Exit-Level Lowercase Letter Writing assessment as you collect his or her Exit-Level Uppercase Letter Writing assessment.
- Explain that they will
  - Write their *name* in the space provided at the top of the sheet
  - Fill in as many of the lowercase letters as they can
  - Raise their hands when they are done so that you can collect their work
- Remind them that this is not a group activity. The children will work by themselves.

ASSESSMENT NOTE

When collecting the children's Exit-Level Uppercase Letter Writing and Exit-Level Lowercase Letter Writing assessments, make sure the children have written their names on each. Also, add any notes, such as whether they finished quickly or took a long time. For details on scoring, see the instructions in Appendixes A.2 and A.3.

VOWEL IDENTIFICATION AND SOUNDS ASSESSMENT

Now that you have completed Lesson 5, remember to administer the Vowel Identification and Sounds Assessment (see Appendix A.5) within 2 weeks.

Assessments

 A.1 **Uppercase and Lowercase Letter Recognition**

Administration	Individual
Materials	<ul><li>Uppercase Letter Recognition: Student Page (choose version: Entry Level, Exit Level, Extra Check 1, Extra Check 2, Extra Check 3)</li><li>Lowercase Letter Recognition: Student Page (choose version: Entry Level, Exit Level, Extra Check 1, Extra Check 2, Extra Check 3)</li><li>Letter Recognition Individual Scoring Sheet (one for each child; choose version to match the Student Page)</li><li>Uppercase Letter Recognition: Class Record Form</li><li>Lowercase Letter Recognition: Class Record Form</li><li>Ledger card (to help the children attend to the correct line; e.g., a blank 5" × 8" index card or a folded piece of white paper)</li></ul>

SCHEDULE

- *Entry Level:* Prior to Chapter 1, Lesson 1
- *Exit Level:* During Unit IV, Chapter 12
- *Extra Check 1:* Interim/continued progress check
- *Extra Check 2:* Interim/continued progress check
- *Extra Check 3:* End of kindergarten school year check or interim/continued progress check

The Entry-Level and Exit-Level Uppercase and Lowercase Letter Recognition assessments can be administered in the same sitting to save time. Because phonemic awareness and phonics depend so critically on solid letter familiarity, you may wish to document interim or continued progress with children whose scores fell below benchmark on the entry or exit level assessments or who are otherwise receiving special help. Use the Extra-Check Letter Recognition Individual Scoring Sheet and Student Pages. If you are working with kindergartners, use Extra Check 3 to document end-of-year status.

PREPARATION

Create an Uppercase Letter Recognition: Class Record Form and a Lowercase Letter Recognition: Class Record Form. Both should have a row for each student in the class and five column headings for Entry Level, Extra Check 1, Extra Check 2, Exit Level, and Extra Check 3. Add the Total Correct column. Add the benchmark columns as indicated in the example.

UPPERCASE LETTER RECOGNITION: CLASS RECORD FORM

	Entry Level		Extra Check 1	Extra Check 2	Exit Level		Extra Check 3	
Date:								
Name	Total correct	Below 12	Total correct	Total correct	Total correct	Below 26	Total Correct	Below 26

INSTRUCTIONS

- Choose the proper Uppercase Letter Recognition: Student Page and Lowercase Letter Recognition: Student Page as well as the corresponding Letter Recognition Individual Scoring Sheet for the check point (Entry Level, Exit Level, Extra Check 1, Extra Check 2, or Extra Check 3).
- Make sure the student's name and the date are entered on the Letter Recognition Individual Scoring Sheet.
- Give the child the Uppercase Letter Recognition: Student Page as well as the ledger card.
- Begin with the first row:
  - Ask the child to place the ledger card just beneath the first row of uppercase letters on the Student Page.
  - Ask the child to name as many uppercase letters as possible in the first row, from left to right.
  - Circle all correctly identified uppercase letters on the child's Letter Recognition Individual Scoring Sheet. (Count immediate self-corrections as correct; e.g., "M...oops, I mean N" would be correct.)
- Repeat for the second through fifth rows.
- Enter the child's score on the Uppercase Letter Recognition: Class Record Sheet.
- Repeat the process for the lowercase letters using the Lowercase Letter Recognition: Student Page.
- Enter the child's score on the Lowercase Letter Recognition: Class Record Sheet.
- Save the child's Letter Recognition Individual Scoring Sheet.
- *Benchmarks*, or expected performance levels, for each checkpoint are provided on the Letter Recognition Individual Scoring Sheets. Plan to spend extra time working on the uppercase letters with all children whose scores fall below the benchmarks to help them catch up.

M R E J X

B Y L A P

O T K W F

S U D N C

Z H G Q I V

D O V C J

W B H U Y

Q T I R G

Z E M X S

L P F K A N

S N Z E R

I G B P X

K U C J M

T H Q F A

W V O Y L D

M X R V I

N W E J K

U D P S Y

F C L A Z

T A Q H G B

P D I B W

C J M O Q

X L Y N E

A K G H V

S U T Z F R

p　x　g　e　n

k　u　d　j　f

r　h　t　m　i

q　s　a　y　b

o　l　w　c　z　v

m l u j p

i f w z s

v y b c o

n a g h k

r d q e x t

o   c   t   s   p

y   e   d   w   r

j   b   g   i   v

m   q   u   h   z

f   l   k   x   a   n

p w x q u

i d b r t

y v e z n

l c g o k

f a s m h j

d   s   t   x   a

h   k   z   u   p

o   r   j   n   y

g   q   e   w   c

v   i   m   l   f   b

STUDENT NAME: _____

Uppercase Letters

Circle correctly identified
letters in the chart below:

M R E J X

B Y L A P

O T K W F

S U D N C

Z H G Q I V

Date: _____

Benchmark: 12 / 26

Number correct: _____ / 26

☐ Below benchmark

☐ At/above benchmark

Notes: _____

_____

_____

_____

Lowercase Letters

Circle correctly identified
letters in the chart below:

p x g e n

k u d j f

r h t m i

q s a y b

o l w c z v

Date: _____

Benchmark: 12 / 26

Number correct: _____ / 26

☐ Below benchmark

☐ At/above benchmark

Notes: _____

_____

_____

_____

STUDENT NAME: _____

Uppercase Letters

Circle correctly identified
letters in the chart below:

D O V C J

W B H U Y

Q T I R G

Z E M X S

L P F K A N

Date: _____

Benchmark: 26 / 26

Number correct: _____ / 26

☐   Below benchmark

☐   At/above benchmark

Notes: _____

_____

_____

_____

Lowercase Letters

Circle correctly identified
letters in the chart below:

m l u j p

i f w z s

v y b c o

n a g h k

r d q e x t

Date: _____

Benchmark: 26 / 26

Number correct: _____ / 26

☐   Below benchmark

☐   At/above benchmark

Notes: _____

_____

_____

_____

STUDENT NAME: _____

Uppercase Letters

Circle correctly identified
letters in the chart below:

S N Z E R

I G B P X

K U C J M

T H Q F A

W V O Y L D

Date: _____

Benchmark: _____ / 26

Number correct: _____ / 26

☐   Below benchmark

☐   At/above benchmark

Notes: _____

_____

_____

_____

Lowercase Letters

Circle correctly identified
letters in the chart below:

o c t s p

y e d w r

j b g i v

m q u h z

f l k x a n

Date: _____

Benchmark:_____ / 26

Number correct: _____ / 26

☐   Below benchmark

☐   At/above benchmark

Notes: _____

_____

_____

_____

STUDENT NAME: _____

Uppercase Letters

Circle correctly identified
letters in the chart below:

M X R V I

N W E J K

U D P S Y

F C L A Z

T A Q H G B

Date: _____

Benchmark: _____ / 26

Number correct: _____ / 26

☐   Below benchmark

☐   At/above benchmark

Notes: _____

_____

_____

_____

Lowercase Letters

Circle correctly identified
letters in the chart below:

p w x q u

i d b r t

y v e z n

l c g o k

f a s m h j

Date: _____

Benchmark: _____ / 26

Number correct: _____ / 26

☐   Below benchmark

☐   At/above benchmark

Notes: _____

_____

_____

_____

Uppercase Letters

Circle correctly identified
letters in the chart below:

P D I B W

C J M O Q

X L Y N E

A K G H V

S U T Z F R

Date: _____

Benchmark: 26 / 26

Number correct: _____ / 26

☐ Below benchmark

☐ At benchmark

Notes: _____

_____

_____

_____

Lowercase Letters

Circle correctly identified
letters in the chart below:

d s t x a

h k z u p

o r j n y

g q e w c

v i m l f b

Date: _____

Benchmark: 26 / 26

Number correct: _____ / 26

☐ Below benchmark

☐ At benchmark

Notes: _____

_____

_____

_____

A.2 Uppercase Letter Writing

	Administration	Whole Group

	Materials	• Form for the Uppercase Letter Writing assessment • Uppercase Letter Writing: Class Record Form

SCHEDULE

- *Entry Level:* End of Unit I, Chapter 3
- *Progress Check:* End of Unit II, Chapter 7
- *Exit Level:* During Unit IV, Chapter 13, Lesson 5
- *Extra Check:* End of kindergarten school year or for interim/continued progress

PREPARATION

Create an Uppercase Letter Writing: Class Record Form with a row for each student in your class and columns for Entry Level, Progress Check, Exit Level, and Extra Check. Add subcolumns for the total and benchmarks as shown in the example.

UPPERCASE LETTER WRITING: CLASS RECORD FORM

	Entry Level		Progress Check		Exit Level		Extra Check	
Date:								
Name	Total correct	Below 10	Total correct	Below 20	Total correct	Below 26	Total correct	Below 26

INSTRUCTIONS

- Give a copy of the form for the Uppercase Letter Writing assessment to each child.
- Ask the children to fill in the uppercase letter that goes with each of the lowercase letters on the sheet.
- When collecting the forms, make sure each child's name and the date are written on the sheet.

SCORING

- On the Uppercase Letter Writing: Class Record Form
  - Enter the date of the assessment
  - Enter the number of correctly entered uppercase letters
  - If the child's score is below the given benchmark, enter a check in the corresponding column
- *Benchmarks,* or expected performance levels, for each checkpoint are provided on the Uppercase Letter Writing: Class Record Form sample above. Plan to spend extra time working on the uppercase letters with all children whose scores fall below the benchmarks, doing your best to help them catch up.

APPENDIX A.2 UPPERCASE LETTER WRITING

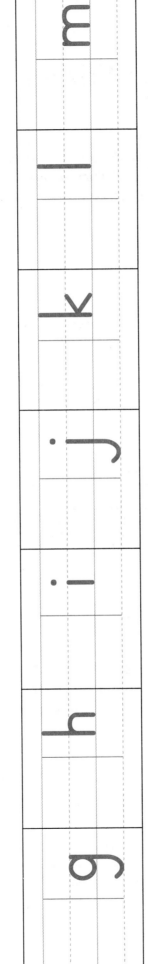

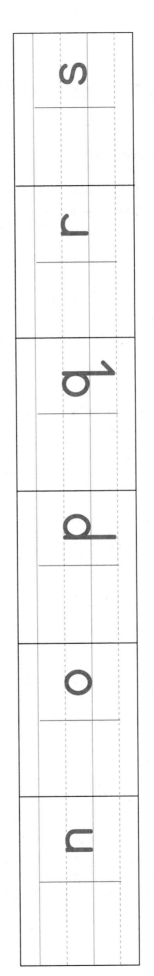

| a | b | c | d | e | f |

| g | h | i | j | k | l | m |

| n | o | p | q | r | s |

| t | u | v | w | x | y | z |

A.3 Lowercase Letter Writing

....

Administration	Whole Group
Materials	• Form for the Lowercase Letter Writing assessment • Lowercase Letter Writing: Class Record Form

SCHEDULE

- *Entry Level:* End of Unit III, Chapter 8, Lesson 1
- *Progress Check:* During Unit III, Chapter 11, Lesson 2
- *Exit Level:* During Unit IV, Chapter 13, Lesson 5
- *Extra Check:* End of kindergarten school year or for interim/continued progress

PREPARATION

Create a Lowercase Letter Writing: Class Record Form with a row for each student in your class and columns for Entry Level, Progress Check, Exit Level, and Extra Check. Add subcolumns for the total and benchmarks as shown in the example.

LOWERCASE LETTER WRITING: CLASS RECORD FORM

Date: Name	Entry Level		Progress Check		Exit Level		Extra Check	
	Total correct	Below 10	Total correct	Below 20	Total correct	Below 26	Total correct	Below 26

INSTRUCTIONS

- Give a copy of the form for the Lowercase Letter Writing assessment to each child.
- Ask the children to fill in the lowercase letter that goes with each of the uppercase letters on the sheet.
- When collecting the forms, make sure each child's name and the date are written on the sheet.

SCORING

- On the Lowercase Letter Writing: Class Record Form
  - Enter the date of the assessment
  - Enter the number of correctly entered lowercase letters on the Class Record Form
  - If the child's score is below the given benchmark, enter a check in the corresponding column
- *Benchmarks,* or expected performance levels, for each checkpoint are provided on the Lowercase Letter Writing: Class Record Form sample above. Plan to spend extra time working on the uppercase letters with all children whose scores fall below the benchmarks, doing your best to help them catch up.

STUDENT NAME: _____

DATE: _____

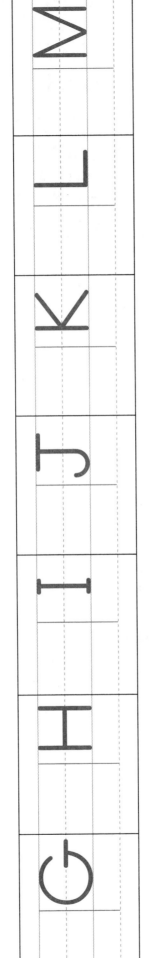
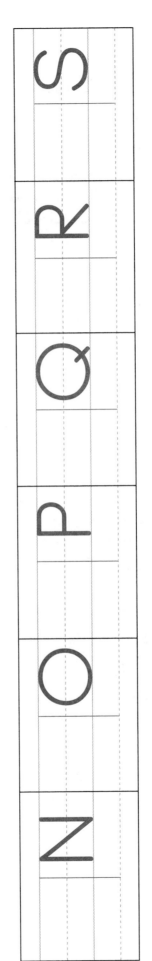
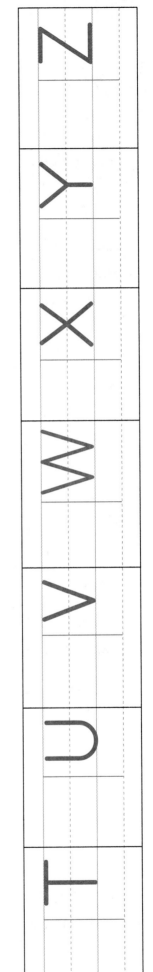

A B C D E F

G H I J K L M

N O P Q R S

T U V W X Y Z

ABC Foundations for Young Children: A Classroom Curriculum by Marilyn Jager Adams. Copyright © 2013 Paul H. Brookes Publishing Co., Inc. All rights reserved.

287

Initial Consonant Sounds

Administration	Individual
Materials	• Initial Consonant Sounds: Picture Cards (Set A and Set B)
	• Initial Consonant Sounds: Student Record Form (one for each student)
	• Initial Consonant Sounds: Class Record Form

SCHEDULE

This assessment is individually administered after students have completed Unit IV, Chapter 12. It is scheduled to be completed over the course of Unit IV, Chapter 13. *Note:* For kindergartners, you may wish to readminister this assessment at the end of the school year. Space is provided on the Initial Consonant Sounds: Class Record Form.

PREPARATION

1. **Initial Consonant Sounds: Picture Cards**

   • Set A and Set B of the Initial Consonant Sounds: Picture Cards are found in this appendix.
   • Both sets of Initial Consonant Sounds: Picture Cards should be backed for stiffness, and lamination is also recommended.
   • Cut each sheet along the dotted lines, making 12 separate picture squares for each set.
   • The squares in each set should be stacked in order of the numbers in their upper right corners and as listed in the chart on page 289.
   • Take care not to mix Set A and Set B.

2. **Initial Consonant Sounds: Student Record Form**

   A copy of the Initial Consonant Sounds: Student Record Form is provided following the Initial Consonant Sounds: Picture Cards. A separate copy is needed for each student.

3. **Initial Consonant Sounds: Class Record Form**

   Create an Initial Consonant Sounds: Class Record Form with a row for each student in the class and three columns for Set A, Set B, and Total. If desired, add a section for an extra/end of year readministration of the assessment versus the exit-level administration.

INITIAL CONSONANT SOUNDS: CLASS RECORD FORM

Name	Exit Level			Extra/End of year		
	Set A	Set B	Total	Set A	Set B	Total

INSTRUCTIONS

• Write the student's name and the date of the session at the top of the Initial Consonant Sounds: Student Record Form.

- Begin the assessment with Set A.
    - Lay out the first three Initial Consonant Sounds: Picture Cards from Set A, three in a row.
    - Pointing to each of the three cards in turn, tell the child the name of the depicted object, as given in the corresponding row of the Initial Consonant Sounds: Student Record Form.
    - Ask the student to point to the picture whose name begins with the letter specified in the corresponding row of the record form.
        - "Point to the picture that begins with the letter L."
    - Mark whether the student chooses correctly or incorrectly in the corresponding row on the record form.
        - If the student chooses correctly, remove that picture card from the row on the table and replace it with the next picture card in the set.
        - If the student chooses incorrectly,
            - Point to the correct picture card, providing feedback, "No, this one begins with the letter L. Listen: The sound of Ll is /l/. Lion begins with Ll, lllion."
            - Then, remove the picture card from the row on the table and replace it with the next picture card in the set.
- When you have finished every row for Set A, repeat the procedure for Set B.
- When you have finished both Set A and Set B,
    - Enter the child's total score from both sets at the bottom of her or his Initial Consonant Sounds: Student Record Form
    - Enter the child's Set A, Set B, and Total scores on the Initial Consonant Sounds: Class Record Form
    - Restack the Initial Consonant Sounds: Picture Cards in Set A and Set B, making sure each set is complete and properly ordered
    - Ask the student to get the next student for you

Ordered List of Set A
Initial Consonant Sounds: Picture Cards

Card number	Letter	Picture
1A	Ll	Lion
2A	Pp	Pig
3A	Tt	Toothbrush
4A	Ww	Whale
5A	Ss	Spoon
6A	Kk	Key
7A	Nn	Nine
8A	Jj	Jet
9A	Rr	Rabbit
10A	Extra	Feather
11A	Qq	Queen
12A	Extra	Broom

Ordered List of Set B
Initial Consonant Sounds: Picture Cards

Card number	Letter	Picture
1B	Bb	Bus
2B	Hh	Horse
3B	Cc	Cat
4B	Zz	Zipper
5B	Ff	Fork
6B	Gg	Grapes
7B	Mm	Mittens
8B	Yy	Yo-yo
9B	Dd	Dog
10B	Extra	Knife
11B	Vv	Volcano
12B	Extra	Shoes

ABC Foundations for Young Children: A Classroom Curriculum by Marilyn Jager Adams.
Copyright © 2013 Paul H. Brookes Publishing Co., Inc. All rights reserved.

1B

2B

3B

4B

5B

6B

7B

8B

9B

10B

11B

12B

INITIAL CONSONANT SOUNDS:
STUDENT RECORD FORM
DURING UNIT IV, CHAPTER 13

STUDENT NAME: _____

DATE: _____

Set A Student Record Form

	Displayed Initial Consonant Picture Cards			Which one starts with?	Student choice	
					Correct	Incorrect
1	**lion**	pig	toothbrush	Ll		
2	whale	pig	**toothbrush**	Tt		
3	**whale**	pig	spoon	Ww		
4	key	pig	**spoon**	Ss		
5	key	**pig**	nine	Pp		
6	key	**jet**	nine	Jj		
7	**key**	rabbit	nine	Kk		
8	feather	**rabbit**	nine	Rr		
9	feather	queen	**nine**	Nn		
10	feather	**queen**	broom	Qq		
		Subtotal, Set A:			____ /10	____ /10

Set B Student Record Form

	Displayed Initial Consonant Picture Cards			Which one starts with?	Student choice	
					Correct	Incorrect
1	bus	horse	**cat**	Cc		
2	bus	**horse**	zipper	Hh		
3	**bus**	fork	zipper	Bb		
4	**grapes**	fork	zipper	Gg		
5	mittens	**fork**	zipper	Ff		
6	mittens	yo-yo	**zipper**	Zz		
7	mittens	**yo-yo**	dog	Yy		
8	mittens	knife	**dog**	Dd		
9	**mittens**	knife	volcano	Mm		
10	shoes	knife	**volcano**	Vv		
		Subtotal, Set B:			____ /10	____ /10
		Total, Sets A and B			____ / 20	____ /20

A.5 Vowel Identification and Sounds

Administration	Individual
Materials	• Lowercase Letter Cards: *a, e, i, o, u, c, m, r, s, t* • Vowel Identification and Sounds: Class Record Form

SCHEDULE

The Vowel Identification and Sounds assessment is administered within 2 weeks of finishing Unit IV, Chapter 13. For children who err or struggle, the assessment should be administered again after they have received additional instruction and practice with the vowels.

INSTRUCTIONS

- Make sure the student's name and the date are entered on the Vowel Identification and Sounds: Class Record Form.

1. Vowel Identification
    - Scramble the 10 Lowercase Letter Cards (*a, e, i, o, u, c, m, r, s, t*) and lay them out, face up, on the table.
    - Ask the child to select and name the five letters that are vowels from the scrambled letters.
    - In the Vowel Identification column of the scoring sheet, enter a 1 for each vowel that is correctly selected and named.
    - Give the child feedback by correctly naming each vowel as you arrange the Letter Cards in order before the child:

        a   e   i   o   u

2. Vowel Sounds
    - For each of the five vowels, in order,
        - Point to its card, and ask the child to
            - Tell you its long sound
            - Tell you its short sound
        - Indicate whether each response is correct on the Class Record Form by entering a 1 in the corresponding column.
        - Enter a 1 in the column labeled Confidence if the child's overall performance sounded quick and confident.
            - Regardless of accuracy, children whose responses show signs of difficulty or uncertainty (e.g., long deliberation, dithering) should also receive extra practice and retesting, lest they forget.
    - Sum the child's score, left to right, and enter it in the column labeled Score.
    - If the child's score is a perfect 16, enter a check in the column labeled Mastery.
    - *Benchmarks:* In accordance with the Common Core State Standards, all children are expected to attain a perfect score (16) on this assessment by the end of kindergarten.

Student	Date	Vowel identification						Long sound						Short sound						Confidence	Score	Mastery
		a	e	i	o	u		a	e	i	o	u		a	e	i	o	u			/16	
																					/16	
																					/16	
																					/16	
																					/16	
		a	e	i	o	u		a	e	i	o	u		a	e	i	o	u			/16	
																					/16	
																					/16	
																					/16	
																					/16	
		a	e	i	o	u		a	e	i	o	u		a	e	i	o	u			/16	
																					/16	
																					/16	
																					/16	
																					/16	

Materials

APPENDIX
B

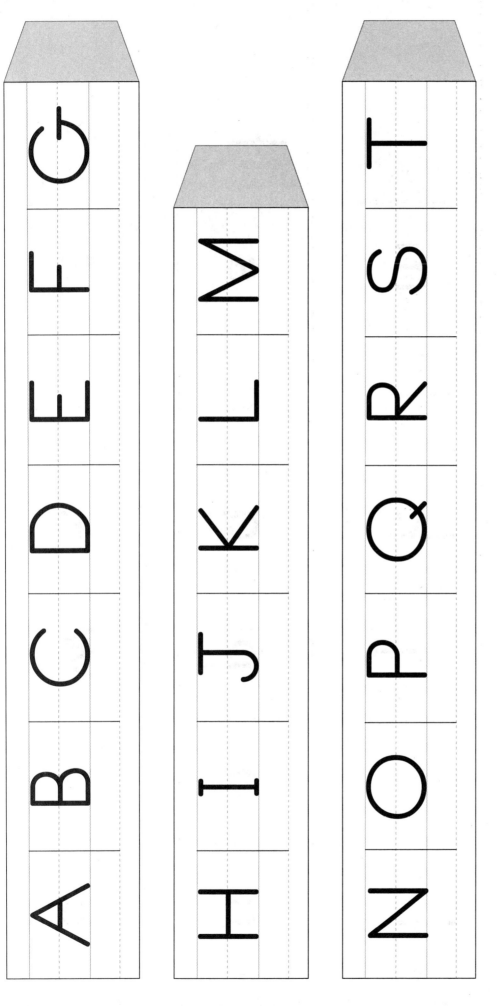

A B C D E F G

H I J K L M

N O P Q R S T

U V W X Y Z

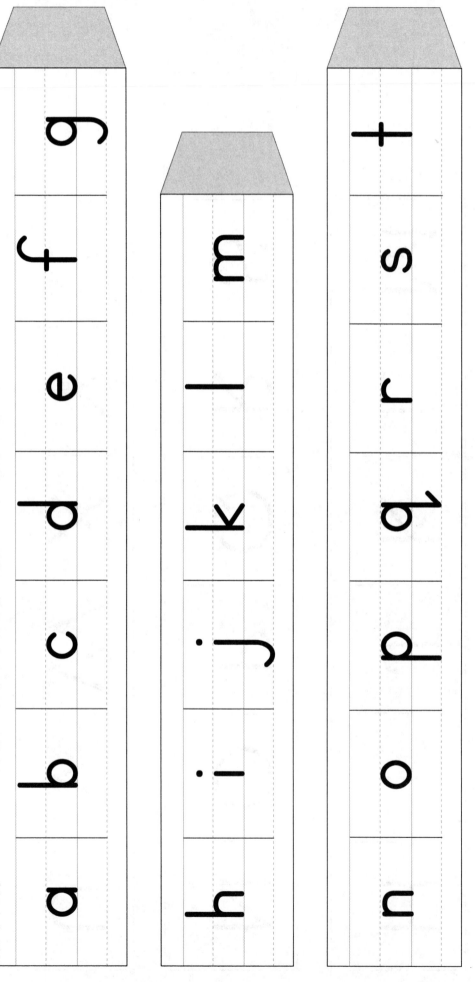

a   b   c   d   e   f   g

h   i   j   k   l   m

n   o   p   q   r   s   t

u   v   w   x   y   z

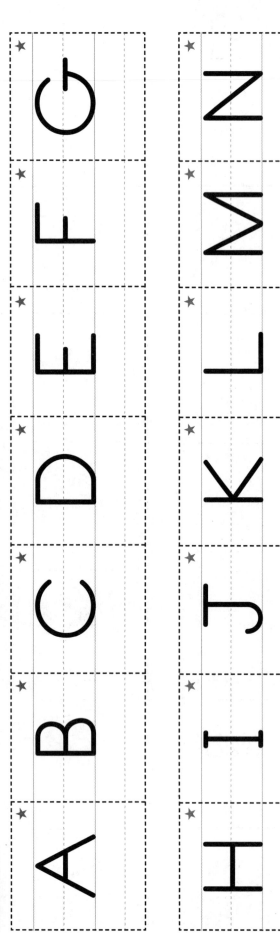

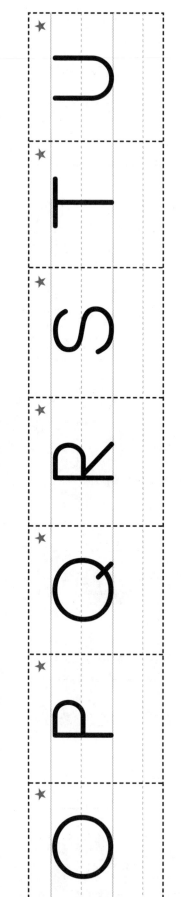

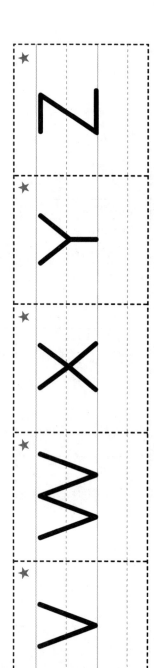

A B C D E F G

H I J K L M N

O P Q R S T U

V W X Y Z

ABC Foundations for Young Children: A Classroom Curriculum by Marilyn Jager Adams. Copyright © 2013 Paul H. Brookes Publishing Co., Inc. All rights reserved.

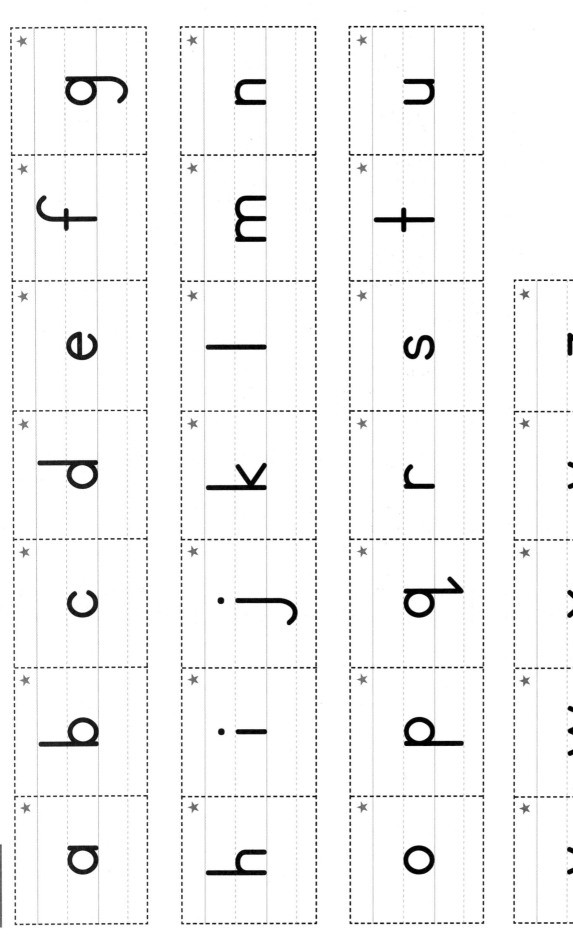

a   b   c   d   e   f   g

h   i   j   k   l   m   n

o   p   q   r   s   t   u

v   w   x   y   z

APPENDIX B.3   UPPERCASE ALPHABET FILL-IN   UNIT II, CHAPTERS 4–7

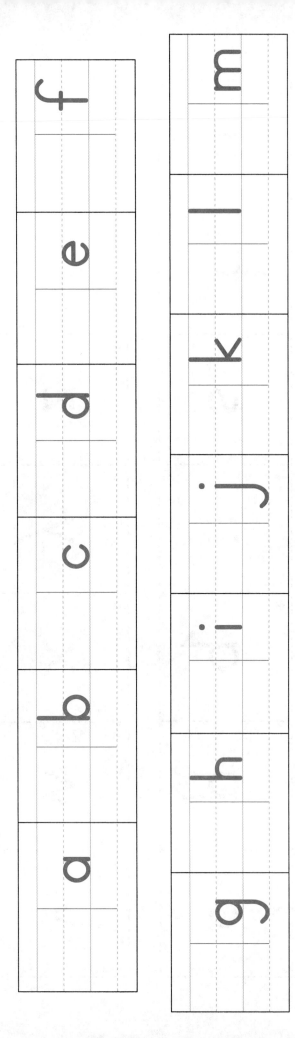

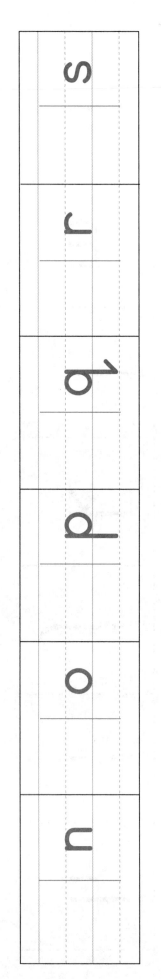

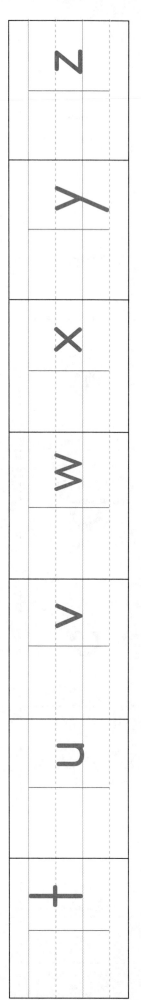

UPPERCASE LETTER WRITING PRACTICE SHEET: *L, T*   UNIT II, CHAPTER 4, LESSON 1

STUDENT NAME: _____

STUDENT NAME: _____

UPPERCASE LETTER WRITING PRACTICE SHEET: *F, E*   UNIT II, CHAPTER 4, LESSON 3

STUDENT NAME: _____

UPPERCASE LETTER WRITING PRACTICE SHEET: A, Z   UNIT II, CHAPTER 5, LESSON 1

STUDENT NAME: _____

ABC Foundations for Young Children: A Classroom Curriculum by Marilyn Jager Adams. Copyright © 2013 Paul H. Brookes Publishing Co., Inc. All rights reserved.

STUDENT NAME: _____

N M

UPPERCASE LETTER WRITING PRACTICE SHEET: V, W, X UNIT II, CHAPTER 5, LESSON 3

STUDENT NAME: _____

UPPERCASE LETTER WRITING PRACTICE SHEET: *Y, K*   UNIT II, CHAPTER 5, LESSON 4

STUDENT NAME: _____

STUDENT NAME: _____

APPENDIX B.3 UPPERCASE LETTER WRITING PRACTICE SHEET: *D, B* **UNIT II, CHAPTER 6, LESSON 1**

STUDENT NAME: _____

APPENDIX B.3 UPPERCASE LETTER WRITING PRACTICE SHEET: Q, G   UNIT II, CHAPTER 7, LESSON 2

314

UPPERCASE LETTER WRITING PRACTICE SHEET: S   UNIT II, CHAPTER 7, LESSON 3

APPENDIX B.3

APPENDIX B.4 LOWERCASE ALPHABET FILL-IN UNIT III, CHAPTERS 8–11

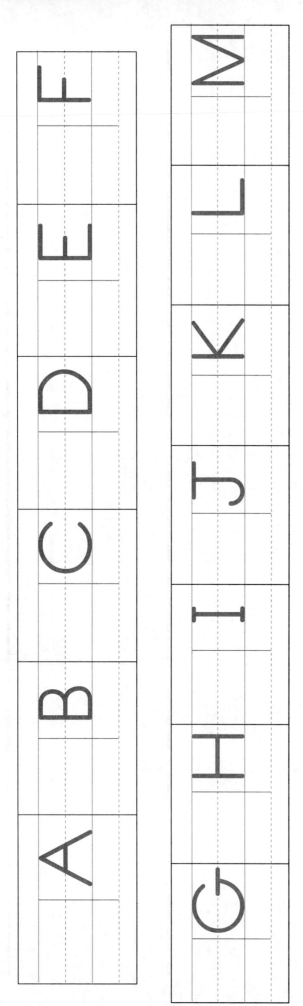

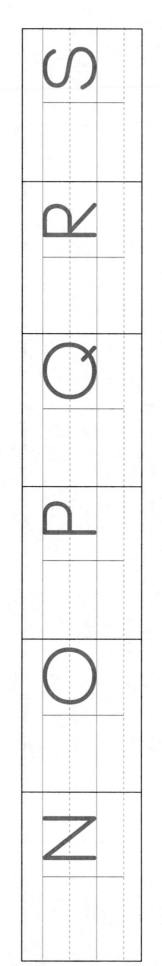

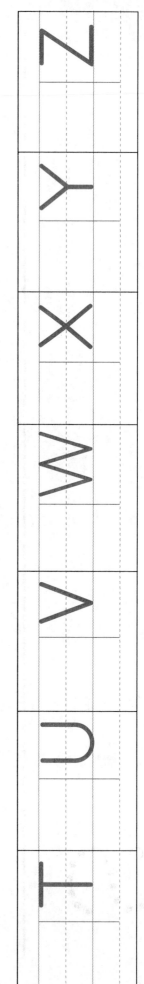

316

APPENDIX B.4   LOWERCASE LETTER WRITING PRACTICE SHEET: *o, c*   UNIT III, CHAPTER 8, LESSON 2

ABC Foundations for Young Children: A Classroom Curriculum by Marilyn Jager Adams. Copyright © 2013 Paul H. Brookes Publishing Co., Inc. All rights reserved.

STUDENT NAME: _____

LOWERCASE LETTER WRITING PRACTICE SHEET: *g, q*   UNIT III, CHAPTER 8, LESSON 4

STUDENT NAME: _____

APPENDIX B.4 LOWERCASE LETTER WRITING PRACTICE SHEET: *s, f*   UNIT III, CHAPTER 8, LESSON 5

STUDENT NAME: _____

LOWERCASE LETTER WRITING PRACTICE SHEET: *b, p*   UNIT III, CHAPTER 9, LESSON 1

STUDENT NAME: _____

LOWERCASE LETTER WRITING PRACTICE SHEET: *n, m*   UNIT III, CHAPTER 9, LESSON 2

STUDENT NAME: _____

LOWERCASE LETTER WRITING PRACTICE SHEET: *r, h*   UNIT III, CHAPTER 9, LESSON 3

STUDENT NAME: _____

LOWERCASE LETTER WRITING PRACTICE SHEET: *u, j, e* UNIT III, CHAPTER 9, LESSON 4

STUDENT NAME: _____

LOWERCASE LETTER WRITING PRACTICE SHEET: v, w UNIT III, CHAPTER 10, LESSON 1

STUDENT NAME: _____

x

z

LOWERCASE LETTER WRITING PRACTICE SHEET: *k, y*   UNIT III, CHAPTER 10, LESSON 3

STUDENT NAME: _____

LOWERCASE LETTER WRITING PRACTICE SHEET: *l, t, i* **UNIT III, CHAPTER 11, LESSON 1**   STUDENT NAME: _____

APPENDIX B.5 WRITE YOUR OWN NAME (UPPERCASE)   UNIT II, CHAPTER 7, LESSON 4

WRITE YOUR OWN NAME (LOWERCASE)   **UNIT III, CHAPTER 11, LESSON 2**

STUDENT NAME: _____

CONSONANT SOUND GAME
ACTIVITY SHEET: *Bb, Cc*
UNIT IV, CHAPTER 12, LESSON 2

STUDENT NAME: _____

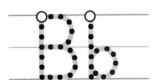

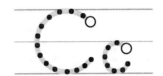

CONSONANT SOUND GAME
ACTIVITY SHEET: *Dd, Ff*
UNIT IV, CHAPTER 12, LESSON 3

STUDENT NAME: _____

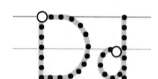   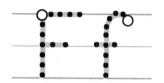

_____   _____   _____   _____

_____   _____   _____   _____

_____   _____   _____   _____

_____   _____   _____   _____

_____   _____   _____   _____

_____   _____   _____   _____

_____   _____   _____   _____

_____   _____   _____   _____

_____   _____   _____   _____

CONSONANT SOUND GAME
ACTIVITY SHEET: *Gg, Hh*
UNIT IV, CHAPTER 12, LESSON 4

STUDENT NAME: _____

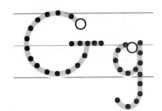
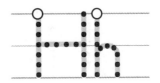

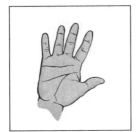

STUDENT NAME: _____

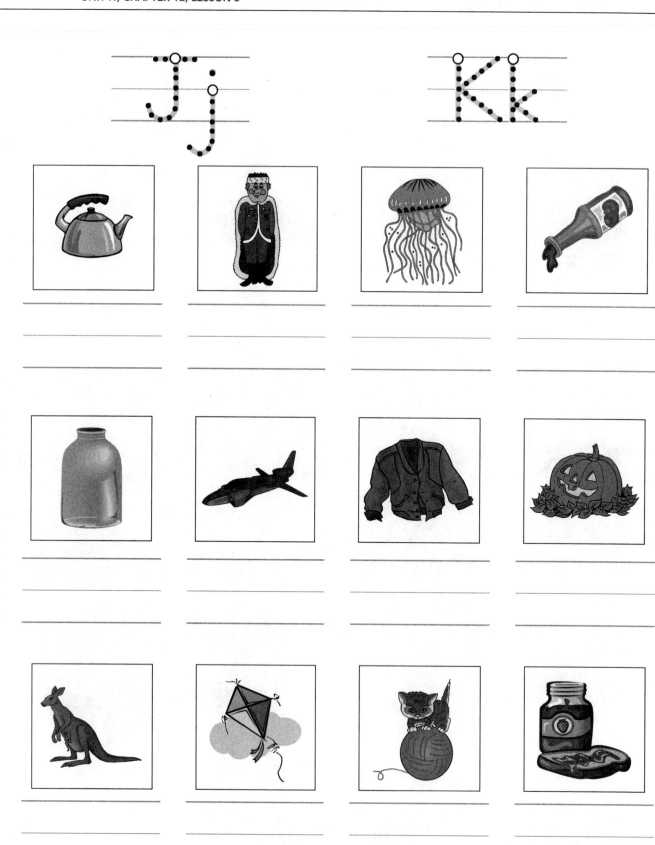

CONSONANT SOUND GAME
ACTIVITY SHEET: *Ll, Mm, Nn*
UNIT IV, CHAPTER 12, LESSON 6

STUDENT NAME: _____

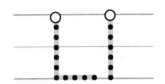 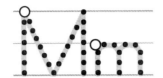 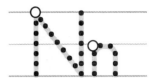

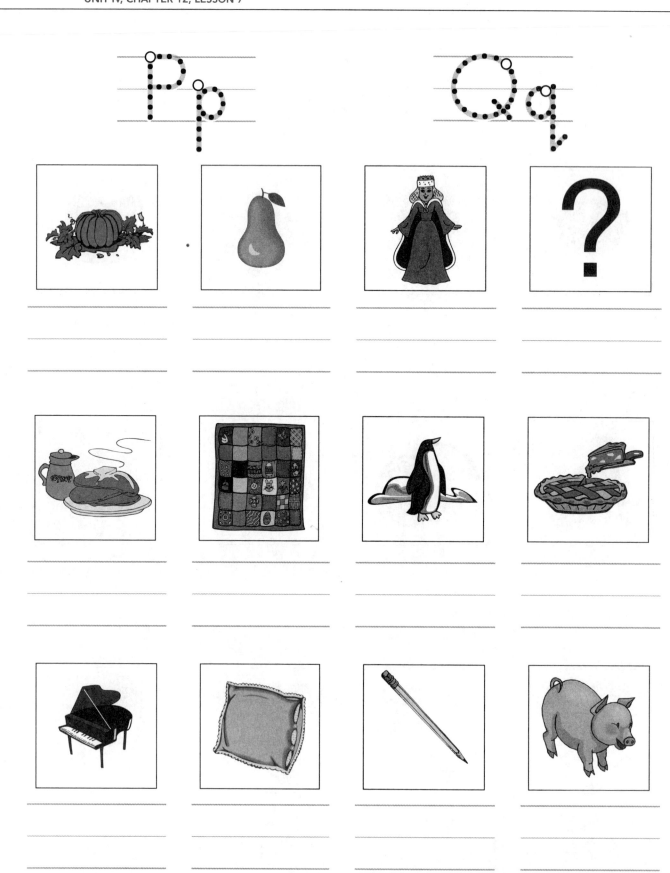

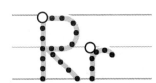 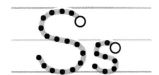 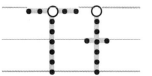

   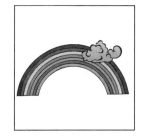

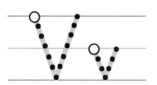

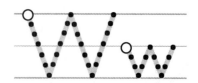

ABC Foundations for Young Children: A Classroom Curriculum by Marilyn Jager Adams.

Index

··